TEACHING WRITING:

THEORIES AND

PRACTICES

JOSEPHINE KOSTER TARVERS
Rutgers University

TO ACCOMPANY
**THE SCOTT, FORESMAN
HANDBOOK FOR WRITERS**
HAIRSTON/RUSZKIEWICZ

SCOTT, FORESMAN AND COMPANY

Glenview, Illinois
Boston
London

ISBN: 0-673-48641-9

12345678 – EBI – 90898887

PREFACE

> Freshman writing is a barrage of intellectual and social challenges masquerading as prose.
>
> —Robert Pattison

This is the hardest writing assignment I've ever faced: "In about 200 pages, write down everything someone might need to know about the theories and practices of teaching writing. Your audience will be people who are trained in literary criticism but may not be familiar with rhetorical and composition scholarship. Be comprehensive but succinct."

The more I prepared to complete this assignment, the more I talked to friends and colleagues about it, the less able I've felt to write it. Rhetorical and composition scholarship has bloomed in the last twenty-five years, and it has proven impossible for me to read everything produced on the subject, let alone digest it all here. So my first compromise with this assignment has been to focus it very sharply: I'll discuss, sometimes not in very great detail, what I think someone with a literary criticism background should know to start teaching writing. The bibliography has had to be focused in the same way; I've outlined some key works, picked a few comprehensive articles to be included here, and included from the rest some of the works I've found most useful and have recommended to others. (By the way, Scott, Foresman and I would be delighted to have your suggestions about works or topics you'd like to see included in later editions of this manual. Send them to me care of Constance Rajala, English Editor, Scott, Foresman and Company, 1900 East Lake Avenue, Glenview IL, 60025.) There's a great deal more material out there, which I can only begin to hint at. Where I could, I've included practical tips, examples, and strategies for you to use. I hope that what's helped me can in some ways help you.

The first four chapters of this book review some of the most important theoretical bases for the teaching of writing. They include a brief discussion of the nature of literacy, a survey of major critical approaches to language from the New Critics to the poststructuralists, a description of some of the most important theories of discourse, and an overview of the writing process, as we best understand it. The emphasis is on the relationship between scrutiny of language already produced (literary criticism) and scrutiny of the way in which language is produced (writing process theory); where possible, I've attempted to show how the two theoretical schools have made parallel discoveries. The last chapter of Part I poses important questions about the amount of theory you will bring to your own classroom.

Part II covers the more practical aspects of writing instruction, from course inception to conclusion. Writing programs vary widely: some schools emphasize self-discovery; some the mastery of various modes and genres; some writing about the writings of others, nonfictional and fictional; and some emphasize writing in a variety of disciplines. The information in Part II is designed to be applied in any of these situations; it does not endorse any particular kind of curriculum. This section begins with basic information about the design of courses and the selection of course materials. It moves on to conducting classes, designing writing assignments, and helping students understand and improve their abilities in all stages of the writing process. Two chapters are devoted to evaluation; the first deals with the evaluation of students' writing, and the second with the evaluation of whole courses and the performances of students and teachers in them. A final chapter discusses external concerns affecting the writing classroom, such as copyright and plagiarism.

Part III provides a small reference section for your information. It begins with four position statements on students' language, the nature of the discipline "English," the essential requirements for teaching writing, and the training, professional development, and responsibilities of writing teachers. These may help you not only improve your teaching, but also improve the writing program at your school. The position statements are followed by nine articles on the teaching of writing. Three articles review our understanding of the writing process. Maxine Hairston attempts to reclassify kinds of writing by the kinds of processes needed to produce it; John Hayes and Linda Flower discuss it in terms of cognitive research; and James Reither discusses writing in contexts outside the English classroom. Next, four articles move theory into practice. Erika Lindemann examines the rhetoric of being a teacher; Douglas Park analyzes the notion of audience; Richard Haswell suggests a practical technique for minimizing the pain of marking papers; and Nancy Sommers deconstructs teachers' usual comments on papers. Finally, two articles discuss the context of writing instruction. Maxine Hairston discusses why we teach writing as process, not product, and Jay L. Robinson discusses the (uneasy at best) relations between teachers of writing and teachers of English. The nine authors represented are all participating classroom teachers, and their articles are characterized by a keen sense of translating theory into practice and by the provision of useful bibliographic references for follow-up. Part III concludes with a small core collection of books and articles all writing teachers should know and a longer bibliography of secondary references.

Although I take the responsibility for what's included in this book, I have to offer thanks to many people for getting me to a point where I could write it. George Kane, Erika Lindemann, and Robert Bain have taught me more about writing, teaching, and professionalism than I can ever acknowledge. My good friends Lynn Quitman Troyka, Susan Betts Landstrom, and Emily Seelbinder over the years have made me digest what I know about writing and express it in clear, effective language. My colleagues at Rutgers, particularly Robert Parker and Janet Emig, have provided ideas, encouragement, and sympathy; among other visitors to the Rutgers Colloquium on Issues in Teaching Writing, David Bartholmae, Patricia Bizzell, Toby Fulwiler, and Donald McQuade have offered valuable insights. Maxine Hairston and John Ruszkiewicz in their own work have provided me not only models to emulate, but challenges to match. My students have been the most help of all, by not only exploring theories but their practical classroom applications with me. Constance Rajala, Anne Smith, and Marisa L. L'Heureux have emphatically proven Harriet Vane wrong about editors. To all of these fine people I am immensely grateful. Needless to say, any weaknesses in this book are not their fault.

My husband, Rich, has been a pillar of support, even in the weeks when the study floor disappeared under a layer of photocopies and my temper had gone far beyond sour. If this book is any good, he's the reason.

J.K.T.

CONTENTS

PART I
WRITING AND THEORY

CHAPTER 1
INTRODUCTION: THE BATTLE OF THE BOOKS

> what we have loved,
> Others will love, and we will teach them how.
> *The Prelude* XIV. 446–47

Why *are* you going to teach writing? Because you want to? Because you believe in it? Because your department makes you do it? Because you need the money? Just because?

All of us who are in this business have at least one thing in common: we love well-chosen words. Most of us love—and have been trained to love—the words selected and arranged by "great" writers, the professional authors of past and present. Chaucer, Austen, Milton, Nabokov, Morrison, Naipul, Didion—the list can go on and on. A growing number of us, too, have learned to prize words *about* well-chosen words; Derrida, Eagleton, Kristeva, Culler, Fish, Kolodny, and Vygotsky are among the names we value. It's safe to love these words; they're printed in anthologies, shelved in libraries, and discussed in scholarly journals. They pose no threat to us; they're literature, that highly valued kind of writing that keeps English departments in business. But whose values define literature? Who decides what works are "literate"? Jay L. Robinson argues that English departments have a particularly narrow view:

> English departments mean by the term literacy one particular and quite specialized thing: an easy familiarity with a certain body of texts, a particular attitude toward them, and special practices for reading texts so that they will yield the appropriate attitudes. . . . It is with help from this system of discourse that

1

we in the English departments find means to ignore the needs of our students, especially those of our most needy students, and yet feel good about it. Except when we are talking about our "introductions to literature," we characterize our students' difficulties with reading and writing as "deficiencies" needful of "remediation"; we characterize what students do in composition classes as practice in basic skills. (484)

Such a view of texts and literacy, almost Luddite (the term is Richard Lanham's) in its parochialism, excludes a great deal of reading and writing, isolating it as the less-privileged Other. Ghettoized, the other survives in "service courses," "basic skills instruction," by whatever name—composition courses. This polarity is a product of the late-nineteenth and twentieth centuries, conditioned by political, sociological, and economic changes affecting universities. Wayne Booth laments that

Of all our current fake polarities, perhaps the one that would surprise our ancestors most is that between "composition" and "literature." It would have surprised them because they could never have dreamed that one might try to teach scholars to write well without at the same time trying to teach them to read and enjoy what is well-written. (1)

Yet this "fake" polarity exists and continues to have a serious effect on the teaching of writing. In most schools (the term that I will use to embrace universities, four-year colleges, and two-year colleges), the facaulty is clearly divided into the elite, which teaches "interpretation," and the underclass, which teaches "composition." Since we like to believe that manners still count for *something,* the Mandarin wars between the post-Derrideans and the cognitivists have so far been confined to traditional academic battlefields: the journal article, the conference panel, and the tenure committee. The truce that holds, however, is uneasy at best. Indeed, some composition theorists have gone so far as to insist that writing teachers no longer try to fit into departments of interpretation, to try to squeeze into paradigms and definitions set by a profession that is no longer our own. They want to cut the umbilical cord (to use Maxine Hairston's metaphor).

This book doesn't advocate that stance. It's about composition and rhetoric in their own right as a discipline. But it maintains that many developments in literary criticism can inform the teaching of writing and give us insights to use in understanding the evolution of texts. Literary critics—and teachers who are trained primarily in the literary critical tradition—can participate in Robinson's fuller definition of literacy:

Literacy that is worth the name . . . develops only through the productive exercise of available and developing competencies with language—through the use of such competencies in composing and comprehending texts, through the use of language to make meanings that count for something in contexts where learning and sharing what is learned count for something. Literacy is an outcome, not a skill, and not (even) a competency. It is something that is achieved when competencies are enabled through exercise of the human capacity to make meaning. (485)

This book is about that wider kind of literacy—and about what we can do to help students achieve it.

CHAPTER 2
THE PROBLEM OF LANGUAGE

Derrida opens *Of Grammatology* with an observation that has the ring of truth: "However the topic is considered, the *problem of language* has never been simply one problem among others." Because language is our chief way of making and expressing meaning, the complex difficulties it poses must occupy the chief part of our attention. Derrida's "problem of language," of course, is the province of literary criticism. What follows is an attempt to sketch briefly some major critical responses to language as problem and to suggest their relations to composition theory. This discussion, of necessity, can't delve into the deepest complexities of the subject; it's intended rather to suggest affinities between literary and composition theory.

The New Critics and Formalists have had a tremendous impact on the older, product-oriented schools of composition, with their emphasis on the essential identity of form and content and the consequent privileging of the study of form as inviolable and unassailable. Context and historical questions became irrelevancies; Terry Eagleton sarcastically describes the New Critics' procedures in this way:

> The New Critics . . . [insisted] that the author's intentions in writing, even if they could be recovered, were of no relevance to the interpretation of his or her text. Neither were the emotional responses of particular readers to be confused with poem's meaning . . . . Rescuing the text from author and reader went hand in hand with disentangling it from any social or historical context . . . . Literature was a solution to social problems, not part of them; the poem must be plucked free of the wreckage of history and hoisted into a sublime space above it. (48)

The text, not its effects, then, lies at the heart of New Criticism. Coherence, shapeliness, and appropriate language (especially metaphor) are the proper objects of scrutiny. Such theories are still reflected in composition textbooks. Traditionally these will include descriptions of various modes or forms of discourse (narration, description, exposition, argumentation, poetry); the shapes such forms take ("keyhole" introductions, the five-paragraph theme, the sentence outline, the research paper); and the language for coherent, appropriate discourse (figurative language, logical fallacies, transitions). Likewise, because form was so effectively linked with content, texts influenced by the New Critics tend to omit exercises that encourage students to imitate models or to experiment with different ways of treating a particular subject. They are also (historically) weak on invention or prewriting exercises; idea and shape are expected to come into existence together, embodying Eliot's famous criteria of "wholeness, harmony, and brilliance." In student writing, these criteria are manifested as correctness.

Cleanth Brooks and Robert Penn Warren's *Modern Rhetoric* (1949) was the first textbook adaptation of New Critical principles to the teaching of writing; it is still in print, testimony to the generations of scholars believing in its approach. Other New Critics who have influenced modern composition theory and practice are Kenneth Burke, whose "dramatistic" theory of discourse between a sender and receiver and "pentad" of questions for invention (discussed below, p. 55), are incorporated in many texts, and I.A. Richards, whose emphasis on "coherence" and the text's ability to confound our expectations is still reflected in grading standards.

In response to the New Critics, the so-called "Chicago School" argued for the restoration of a classical rhetoric with a neo-Aristotelian emphasis on invention, classification, and imitation. The work of the Chicago critics led to the reintroductions of heuristics *topoi* (described below, p. 55), to the use of literary examples to teach style, and, through ways too complex to describe here, to the development of sentence-combining strategies (again, see below, p. 64). Wayne Booth's essay "The Rhetorical Stance" (summarized by Lindemann in the article included below) introduced the study of audience and voice. Francis Christensen's generative rhetoric of the sentence and paragraph (both described below, p. 62) came from a reapplication of Aristotle's principles. And the impulse to classify forms of discourse (summarized below) led to the work of Kinneavy, Britton, and Moffett, among others.

Both speech-act and reader-response theories have also played an important role in our understanding of writing. Speech-art theory has at its core the assumption that discourse is a form of action; we use language to obtain some tangible or intangible result. Textbooks incorporating this assumption focus on both the writer's purpose (the result she is trying to obtain) and very pragmatic forms of transactional discourse (hence the ubiquitous sections on business writing, résumés, report writing, and documentation). Reader-response theory currently plays an important role in composition theory; as G. Douglas Atkins has wryly noted, "as reading as an activity has declined, the Age of the Reader has arrived . . . . In what amounts to a virtual paradigm shift, emphasis on the reader seems to have replaced focus on 'the text itself'." (49) One of the earliest versions of reader-response criticism was Louise Rosenblatt's *Literature as Explora-*

tion (1938), which challenged the New Critics by emphasizing the reader's affective response to the text, especially as that response was conditioned by the reader's past experiences. Although obscured for many years by the New Critics, Rosenblatt's work has been resurrected in recent years, and her 1978 book *The Reader, the Text, the Poem* is now required reading in many graduate seminars on rhetoric. Stanley Fish's earlier essays (many collected in *Is There a Text in This Class* (1980)) discuss how students construct hypotheses (which are either confirmed or refuted by the text) as they read and have led to his theory of interpretative communities, the notion that readers construct texts from the cues provided by the author based on communally-held assumptions. Wolfgang Iser, especially in *The Implied Reader* (1974), also focuses on this concept of cues the readers interpret.

Reading and writing as ways of knowing, both for the writer and reader, are currently very popular subjects in composition theory. Ann Berthoff's work on reading and writing as ways of making meaning are rooted in reader-response; so are the discourse systems of Moffett and Britton, which believe that all writing must start from what the writer knows and move toward what he needs to discover. Cue-recognition is at the heart of David Bartholmae, Anthony Petrosky, Patricia Bizzell, and James Reither's expansion of the writing process into academic and institutional discourse situations. (These are described in section IV, below.)

Semiotics has also been allied to reader-response criticism. Semiotic theorists argue that the writer must be aware of the reader as she creates her text and that the reader may choose—or not choose—to enter into dialogue with the author by attending to or ignoring the cues the author provides. Umberto Eco, in *The Role of the Reader,* sums up the semiotic position with regard to author-reader transactions thus:

> An "open" text cannot be described as a communicative strategy if the role of its addressee (the reader, in the case of verbal texts) has not been envisaged at the moment of its generation *qua* text. . . . The reader as an active principal [sic] of interpretation is a part of the picture of the generative process of the text. . . . At the minimal level, every type of text explicitly selects a very general model of possible reader through the choice (i) of a specific linguistic code, (ii) of a certain literary style, and (iii) of specific specialization-indices [i.e., jargon]. . . . The reader finds his freedom (i) in deciding how to activate one or another of the textual levels and (ii) in choosing which codes to apply. (3, 4, 7, 39)

Such semiotic structures distinguish between two kinds of readings. The first, which Barthes calls "reading," is simply reproducing the text; the second, "interpretation" or "critical reading," means deciphering one of the many possible meanings of the text. These two semiotic varieties of reading reflect on composition in many ways: in group workshops to respond to texts, in discussing the varieties of American English, especially with respect to "standard" English, and in assessments of audience knowledge, background, and likely hypotheses (see the article by Park, below).

Barthes, who in his early work bridges the gap between semiotics and structuralism, also points us to the structuralist influence on composition theory. A key assumption of structuralism is the mulitplicity of meanings inherent in any text; connotation provides the possibility for a number of reader responses, all of which may be substantiated in the text. Composition theorists have incorporated this theory into a number of studies of audience (see the included article by Park). The work of Saussure gave structuralism three key concepts that have broad applications for writing: *langue*, the system and convention of language; *parole*, an individual communicative act conditioned by *langue*; and *écriture*, the combination of personal and cultural codes as writing. There is an obvious connection between *langue/parole* and both the *competence/performance* opposition of transformational-generative grammar and modern theories of error analysis. Likewise Young, Becker, and Pike's theory of tagmemic invention (described below, p. 56) is based on the structural concept of the sign and how it differs from other signs in its particular discourse system. The study of institutional-based discourse communities also draws on the concept of écriture in its requirement for differing, and sometimes conflicting, implicit and explicit "codes" in writing.

Two forms of post-structuralist literary theory, deconstruction and intertexuality, have recently begun to appear in composition theory and texts. Deconstruction, the critical exploitation of ambiguities and illogic often inherent in a text, as practiced by some looks like the tradtional teacher's method of marking student papers. Vincent B. Leitch describes this kind of deconstructive criticism thus:

> The deconstructer does not simply enter a work with a attentive eye for the loose thread or the alogical element that will decanter the text; he or she intends *beforehand* to reverse the tradtional hierarchies that constitute the grounds of the text. (81)

In other words, the deconstructer is confident that the text can be decentered, that gaps can be found. Yet deconstruction, in its multiple possibilities for dialogue between reader and author, in it conflict between ideal structure and actual construct, between competing hierarchies of meaning (if such are possible) seems to offer great resources for the teacher of writing. Teaching students the sense of linguistic "play"—perhaps loosely paraphrased as "flexiblity"—might open them up to other choices, other structures, other strategies, and other ways of communicating. While deconstruction has seeped into the thoretical journals in composition, it hasn't appeared noticeably in classroom texts. When it does make its appearance, we may all be in for a surprise.

The theory of intertextuality, like deconstruction, is another attempt to move beyond the binary oppositions of structuralism. Its chief proponent, Robert Scholes, sees reading and writing not just as parts of discourse communities, but also as crucial ways in which we create those communities:

> . . . reading and writing are important because we read and write our world as well as our texts, and are read and written by them in turn. Texts are places where

power and weakness become visible and discussable, where learning and ignorance manifest themselves, where the structures that enable and constrain our
thoughts become palpable.

In teaching students to question texts, to question the authority of texts, we teach them
to question the codes underlying authority. This practice currently enjoys widespread
support under the labels "critical thinking" and "critical inquiry," though it is doubtful
if many who so complacently endorse it as such would do so if they thought it through
to its revolutionary conclusion. In a sense, Scholes' intertextuality is the logical conclusion to theories of discourse that emphasize the contexts and historical circumstances
that produce certain linguistic codes. Manifested as feminist criticism and new
historicism, it has penetrated the footnotes of composition studies. Its integration into
texts is yet to come.

CHAPTER 3
THEORIES AND FORMS OF DISCOURSE

One of the greatest difficulties facing scholars in rhetoric and composition has been the description of the kinds of writing that can be produced. In the classical world, one form received the majority of rhetoricians' attention—persuasion. This mode was studied as it applied to three separate audiences: the Forum, the laws courts, and ceremonial gatherings. These three kinds of rhetoric, called respectively deliberative, forensic, and epideictic, had individual functions, styles, and structural characteristics. This distinction of kinds by audience, that is to say by the roles they played in shaping the opinions of various segments of society, has had an enduring influence in discourse theory.

Over the centuries, other modes of composing came to be valued as rhetoric became firmly allied with education and the inculcation of morals and mores (this sweeping change is best explained by George Kennedy; it's too involved to retail here). The Scots in the eighteenth and nineteenth centuries were particularly important in forging this alliance, arguing that those who spoke and wrote correctly achieved a moral excellence. One of the last great Scots rhetoricians, Alexander Bain, in his 1866 textbook *English Composition and Rhetoric: A Manual,* divided the products, or forms, rhetoric took into the five modes many of us still recognize as standard: narration, description, exposition, argumentation, and poetry (what we would now call "creative writing"). Bain's division shows how the social function of rhetoric had dimished over time; the emphasis was on the correctness of form rather than on the use of particular forms to move audiences to correct actions. This "product-oriented" approach to writing, with its Formalistic focus on shape and correctness, became institutionalized as the "proper" method for writing instruction in the late nineteenth century; its influence remains strong today.

But as twentieth century theorists looked at the kinds and purposes of rhetoric and their effects on audiences, they came to realize that neither the classical triad nor Bain's rigid taxonomy yielded a satisfactory description of the varieties of writing now produced in Western culture. Thus, in the late 1960s and early 1970s, a number of discourse theorists proposed hypotheses "to identify the most significant principles and concepts in the field which make intelligible everything [rhetoricians] do" (D'Angelo 1976, 143). Of these proposals, four have gained considerable status among composition researchers: James Moffett's in *Teaching the Universe of Discourse* (1968); James Britton's in *The Development of Writing Abilities (11-18)* (1975); James Kinneavy's in *A Theory of Discourse* (1971); and Frank D'Angelo's in *A Conceptual Theory of Rhetoric* (1975). While vastly different, all four theories have many points in common; for instance, they all work with full pieces of discourse (as opposed to isolated paragraphs or passages, as in Bain); they all attempt to be comprehensive; they all locate the origin of composing in thinking skills; and they all view the relationship between writer, reader, and subject (the "communications triangle" in Roman Jakobson's terms) as a social one, constrained by overt and implicit codes. Schematically represented, that relationship looks like this:

Modern literary criticism, particularly semiotics, deconstruction, and reader-response theory, has focused on the reader/subject relationship in this scheme. Most rhetorical theorists, however, have concentrated on the other two possibilities. James Moffett locates his hypotheses in the relationships of writer and reader and writer and subject. His writer/reader relationship is based largely on Jean Piaget's theory of developmental decentering, suggesting that this conversation can move from egocentrism (inner dialogue) to increasingly wider audiences (dialogue, correspondence, public narrative, inference). Likewise, his writer/subject relationship is shaped by Piaget's notion of abstaction. Moffett separates fictive from nonfictive discourse; fictive moves from the personal expression of poetry and plays through fiction to the abstract level of the essay. Nonfictive begins with the writer's perception of what is happening (description or drama) and gradually becomes less personal. Next come narration (what happened), exposition (what happens), and finally argumentation (what might happen). In *Student-Centered Language Arts and Reading K-13* (3rd ed. 1983), Moffett and his colleague Betty Jane

Wagner created an entire curriculum that ties these kinds of writer-reader and writer-subject relationships to the appropriate stages of their cognitive development. This theory is widely respected in schools of education and has had considerable influence on elementary and secondary education.

James Britton and his colleagues at the University of London began in 1966 one of the most ambitious studies of writing ever; over nine years they collected and analyzed over 2000 "scripts," pieces of writing done by British schoolchildren between the ages of 11 and 18. Britton, like Moffett, concentrates on the writer/reader and writer/subject sides of the triangle. The writer/reader relationship begins with the self as audience, moves to teachers, then a "wider" audience, and finally an unknown audience (what our students like to call "the general public"). The writer/subject relationship is defined by the writer's purposes in tackling a particular subject: those that use language to express the self ("expressive"); those that use language in recognized patterns for artistic purposes ("poetic"); those that use language to influence actions and behavior ("persuasive"); and finally those that use language to get or impart knowledge ("informative"). Britton's conclusions were critical of the product-oriented approach used to teach writing; students were largely forced to compose transactional (informative or persuasive) writing for an audience of teachers, even if they were cognitively before or past the stage at which such writing was appropriate. The results were decreased abilities to write and think speculatively. Britton's criticisms have influenced many secondary and college curricula.

James Kinneavy's *Theory of Discourse* does not include a cognitive element as do Moffett's and Britton's; he has admitted this as a weakness. But his is perhaps the most elaborate theory of discourse yet. He expands the communications triangle into a pyramid, adding a fourth point, language; and he argues that theorists must consider not two-dimensional but three-dimensional relationships. Since language must be a dimension in each consideration, his theory is pragmatic and essentially semiotic; it involves the use of meaningful signals or codes. (Kinneavy's theory in this respect appears to be heavily influenced by Kenneth Burke's notion of language as symbolic action.) His subdivisions of the parts of discourse are the kinds of signals (the language arts of speaking, writing, listening, and reading); the media through which these signals are transmitted (from monologues to mass media); the modes or "hows" of discourse (narration, description, evaluation, and classification); and the aims or purposes of discourse (reference, persuasion, literature, and self-expression). (Kinneavy argues that Bain's five "modes" mix modes and purposes.) Most of his book discusses aims, the reasons why writers create discourse. In this respect, his theory harks back to the notion of rhetoric as social function as derived from the classical world. Kinneavy's work has been very influential in graduate training in rhetoric and composition; teachers with this training have begun the exert a noticeable influence on college composition curricula.

Finally Frank D'Angelo has developed a discourse theory based on the classical *topoi* or sources for arguments. He identifies two large categories of discourse, dividing them by what kind of product the writer produces, and applies to them the classical labels of logical and nonlogical. However, his groupings of products are not very like the classical proofs. His nonlogical topics are drawn from cognitive research into creativity (condensation, displacement, transformation). His logical topics, those which can be rationally perceived, are distinguished by the changes they describe over time or space. Static topics (which include most of the traditional expository modes) do not change over time or space. Dynamic topics (which change over time or space) either show progression (narration, process analysis, cause/effect, syllogisms) or repetition (iteration, negation, alternation). D'Angelo provides elaborate heuristics for readers and writers that attempt to describe the cognitive structures that underly each category. Like Kinneavy's theory, however, his model fails to provide a developmental component and has had more influence on teachers than on curricula so far.

Each of these theories has its enthusiastic proponents and each its perceptive critics. Kinneavy's has probably received the most attention in published scholarship; the other three have been very influential in the classroom. All emphasize a notion that product-oriented rhetoric had lost sight of: as the relationships between writer, reader, subject, and audience vary, so does rhetoric. Each relationship requires a different kind of attention; there is no universal "right" way to write. So situational or purposive theories of discourse have come to dominate our thinking about written products. The journal, the literary critical essay, the résumé, and the lab report each require a different application of rhetorical strategies. *The Scott, Foresman Handbook for Writers* is based in part on Maxine Hairston's theory of different processes for different products; her article describing this hypothesis is included below.

CHAPTER 4
UNDERSTANDING THE WRITING PROCESS

The shift from a theory of rhetoric based on the products of a writer's work to one based on the ways writers produce products represents a virtual paradigm shift in the study of writing. Maxine Hairston in her article "The Winds of Change" (included below) has described how, gradually, this new governing perspective has gained respectability and is seeping into the classrooms of even untrained writing teachers. We have gradually evolved models of the writing process that approximate what goes on when a writer sits down to compose a work. But we have only begun to scratch the surface of this immensely complex activity. Most theorists agree that there are at least three components to the writing process: prewriting, the finding and exploration of ideas (in classical terminology, *invention*); drafting, getting the ideas on paper; and revision, reconsidering the ideas, the treatment they receive, and the way they are expressed (in classical terminology, *arrangement, style,* and, to some extent, *delivery*). The theories discussed below accept these divisions of the writing process, but emphasize the three components differently.

Early theories of the writing process focused on its expressive content, the attempts of writers to use language to mold and tell truth as they perceive it. D. Gordon Rohman and Albert O. Wlecke argue that techniques such as meditative exercises (drawn from seventeeth-century religious practice), journal keeping, and the composition of analogies (called "existential sentences") help writers find truth in even the most abstract of subjects. Rohman and Wlecke argue that such prewriting techniques would lead in a smooth and linear fashion to drafting and revision as writers refined the expression of the truth they told. This privileging of self-discovery, what is sometimes called the romantic view of composing, is also held by Peter Elbow, Ken Macrorie, William Coles, and Donald Murray, to name a few of its most influential proponents. Elbow argues for the primacy of prewriting in helping writers explore ideas; Macrorie prizes it because it forces students to go beyond the obvious clichés, which he calls "Engfish" (because they stink of insincerity). Coles values prewriting because it allows students to explore their many possible relationships to writers and subjects (what he calls "plural I's"); Murray likes it because it cultivates surprise, new ideas, and combinations of ideas that lead to personal growth. The romantic theory supposes that discovery is the most important part of the writing process, drafting simply happens, and revision, when it is discussed at all, is seen as further invention. Romantic theories also see the writer as somewhat isolated from social questions and codes; they in fact encourage students to break rules, to flaunt or exploit conventions and expectations. These beliefs have thus attracted a great deal of criticism. However, the romantics also made an important advance in our understanding of revision by clearly separating it from editing. Revision means getting the ideas right; editing means adjusting the etiquette of presentation (spelling, punctuation, and the like).

A second theory of the writing process roots it deeply in psychology, particularly in studies of cognition. For such theorists, "protocols" (detailed descriptions of how a work is composed) and draft analysis play a key role. One of the earliest such theories is Janet Emig's. In *The Composing Process of Twelfth Graders* (1971), she studied writing behaviors: how student writers found and developed their ideas. She found that these processes varied with audience: if students wrote for themselves (expressively), they were concerned (even obsessed) with mechanical correctness. Emig concluded that writers develop some kinds of implicit knowledge about adjusting their writing for its readers. Nancy Sommer's comparisons of student and experienced adult writers show that experienced writers come to value development of ideas far more than mechanical correctness, whereas to students correctness remains all.

Richard Young, Alton Becker, and Kenneth Pike also developed a cognitive theory of the writing process; however theirs depends not on the writer's knowledge of the audience but of the subject. Their "tagmemics" theory models cognitive efforts to know a subject; it focuses on how writers perceive a subject's individuality, variability, and place in a larger system. (This tagmemic heuristic will be discussed further below, p. 56.) These cognitive efforts should help writers find and develop new combinations of ideas. Like the romantic theories, tagmemics emphasizes prewriting and only thinly discusses drafting or revision.

The cognitivist position has been most fully expanded by Linda Flower, John Hayes, and their graduate students and colleagues at Carnegie-Mellon University. Their theory is complex; it is summarized in the included article by Flower and Hayes. Basically they view the composing process as a series of decision-making strategies: planning texts, translating those plans into sentences, and revising the texts produced to bring them in line with the original (or reshaped) plans. Although Emig first suggested it, Flower and Hayes have done most to demonstrate the recursive and heirarchial levels of the writing process. Cognitivists find Rohman and Wlecke's linear model too simplistic; they argue that writers continually move back and forth between stages to adjust their plans. Like the romantics, cognitivists value personal expression highly, claiming it reflects true ways of thinking. Cognitivists have spent very little time discussing the forms writing produces; for them, it is the brain work that is important. Again, this position has been strongly challenged.

Most recently, as theorists have come clearly to see the social function of writing, studies of the writing process have broadened to include the contexts in which writing occurs, to define the discourse community in which any particular writing process exists. This broadening has also been influenced by the changing demographics of college students. As more and more nontraditional—which is to say nonyoung, white, middle-class—students have entered the academy, teachers have been forced to change their expectations about the kinds of knowledge students bring with them. No longer can a teacher take for granted that her students know what an essay looks like, or what thesis and support are, or how academics think. One response to this situation has been to teach these students the kinds of discourse that we—trained in literary criticism—know; thus the romantics' emphasis on journals, poetry, writing fiction, and the Formalists' emphasis on analyzing other authors' writings. Implicitly we are trying to get students to recognize what constitutes discourse in English departments. Many theorists now argue that we should be doing more: "Rather than teaching them how to write in only one institutional role for only one type of institutional audience, we should help our students discover the basic strategies by which they can determine and fulfill the requirements of various types of discourse" (Perelman 476).

Such community-centered theories of the writing process have two current focuses. The political focus, represented by David Bartholmae, Patricia Bizzell, Ann Berthoff, and others influenced by Paolo Freire, sees awareness of the constraints of a discourse community as politically liberating, as potentially enabling and revolutionary. For such theorists, identifying the contexts in which students write comes before any other part of the writing process. The context is as important, if not more so, than finding and developing ideas and presenting them in a form that the discourse community approves. The pedagogical focus sees writing as a fundamental tool for learning in all communities and attempts to foster the teaching of writing in departments beside English. These "writing across the curriculum" and "writing in the disciplines" movements have achieved mixed success at various schools; the theory is neater than the practice. Development of both focuses is proceeding rapidly and undoubtedly will come to influence classroom practice as well as theory more and more.

In summary, then, the writing process is complex. It has a great deal to do with how the writer is able to perceive and explore herself and her world. It has a great deal to do with how the writer thinks about her subject and audience and adjusts her hypotheses accordingly. It has a great deal to do with how the writer understands her writing situation, and how she uses or circumvents the constraints her purpose and situation impose. It has a great deal to do with how the writer understands, and to some degree invents, her audiences; the interested teacher might also want to read Karl Wallace's "*Topoi* and the Problem of Invention," which suggests heuristics for helping writers determine their audience and situation. The strategies for teaching elements of the writing process (below) focus on the mechanics of the process. For now, we must content ourselves with James Reither's summation (from the article, included below): "Writing is clearly a more multidimensioned process than current theory and practice would have us believe, and one that begins long before it is appropriate to commence working with strategies for invention" (623).

CHAPTER 5
THEORY IN THE CLASSROOM

In such a Babel of theories, you may wonder (and rightly so), can any of them be carried into the classroom? If so, which ones? The answers vary. Charlyce and Arn Tibbetts, arguing from their experience in writing textbooks, say no; teachers want mechanics and correctness, not innovation. Flower and Hayes, on the other hand, arguing from their successful projects at Carnegie-Mellon University, say "writing instruction is one area in which research has actually had a large and visible impact on teaching" (1106). The disparity in answers shouldn't surprise you.

Actually, you can incorporate as much theory into your course as you like and are comfortable with; theory, as D'Angelo reminds us, helps us "see our field of inquiry and . . . see it whole" (1976, 143). In particular, theory will help you answer five of the most perplexing questions you'll face in determining your classroom practice:

> What community's notion of discourse will I teach?
> Who are my students?
> What models for good writing will I use?
> What will my role be in the classroom?
> What kinds of competencies will I try to teach?

Each question requires a separate kind of consideration.

What community's notion of discourse will you teach? If your theory of writing accords it a social function, you will have to identify the society or societies your students need to know about and in which they must write. Certainly, since you are teaching writing in college, the academic community will be one of the societies you select.

But which segment of it? Just the English department? Or the humanities? Or will you include both arts and sciences? If so, what kinds of writing occasions will you construct to help students learn about and write for these varying communities? Will you also ask students to write for more personal communities—themselves, their classmates, friends? Or less personal communities—the world of work, other forms of professional discourse? Again, what occasions will students have to learn about and write for these communities? And in all cases, how will you judge that writing? Students implicity know a great deal about the constraints of communities. Asked to describe a campus party that got a bit overenthusiastic, they'll choose one strategy for writing to a friend at home, another for writing to grandma, and a third for writing an excuse for the Dean, and yet another for writing an account for the local newspaper or *Newsweek on Campus*. How can you help them tap that implicit knowledge? Your decisions about the authority of discourse communities and the role of that community in the writing process will help you decide.

Who are your students? Typically, textbooks address a narrow range of students: middle-class, mainstream, implicitly white. But when you look at the faces in your classroom, you are likely to see a very different group: some minority, some older, some very inexperienced, some professional. How do you mold this group into a coherent class? Again, theory can help you decide. Since many will be at different developmental stages, you'll want to include a variety of kinds of and purposes for writing and a variety of audiences, to stretch all your students. At times, you may have to arrange students in groups according to their backgrounds, so that each group can work on particular problems; on the other hand, you'll often want to mix students within groups so that they experience many perspectives. Differing student populations make it possible for you to talk with students about different discourse communities and their expectations (writing, for instance, looks different to students who never write at all outside school than it does to students who write forty or fifty sales letters a week). I've occasionally reminded new teachers and my students that students aren't milk; they can't be homogenized. I use the analogy of blended Scotch whiskey: many individual malts are carefully blended to provide a new, full flavor that retains distinct traces of the individual elements. (The analogy works for me; it may not be appropriate in your teaching situation. If not, try spaghetti sauce or musical counterpoint or something else that represents a delicate balance of disparate elements.)

What models for good writing will you use? Again, your notion of what kinds of discourse "count" will give you your answer. Because most of us are trained in the analysis of *belles lettres,* that's where many composition teachers turn. The anthologies we use in expository writing classes include fiction, poetry, and belletristic essays from *Harper's, The New Yorker, Atlantic* and *New Republic.* We're comfortable with these models; they represent the kinds of writing prized in our discourse community, English departments. As Edward P.J. Corbett sympathetically remarks,

I always understood why the young, eager instructors succumbed to the temptation to sneak literature into that writing class. Literature was what those instructors loved most and what their formal training had best qualified them to talk about. They yearned for an opportunity to introduce their students to the delights of literature. They were not deliberately ignoring the directives . . . for the course; they just could not resist the siren call of literature. (1983, 181).

Such models work, then, if we believe the only discourse that counts is that of the English department. If we believe that other communities have valid discourses that students should learn, then we introduce other examples as well: scientific articles (especially if written by belletristic scientists such as Lewis Thomas or Carl Sagan), political speeches (especially those filled with belletristic references by John F. Kennedy and Martin Luther King, Jr.) and the like. If we believe that students should know that not all writers are white males, we include (token) women writers and minority writers. Sometimes we even include writers from non-Western cultures.

This theory of models, though, conveys a pernicious message to students: professionals write well; students don't. After all, professionals get published; their work is typeset; people pay to buy it. Somebody put it in a textbook, so of course it's good. The only other kind of writing most students see is their own, and that is rarely praised. It's covered with corrections and comments. It's rarely typeset. If it's included in textbooks, it's always a weak example—see what this student did wrong. Students draw the inevitable conclusion: all professional writing is good and strong; all student writing is bad and weak. Yet we ask them to produce good, strong student writing. Is this a contradiction? There are ways to show students this isn't the case. Teachers can use student examples in class, including drafts; this helps students see that they, too, can learn to revise and produce good work. Student writing can be circulated; more and more anthologies include some sample student essays, and a few are devoted almost wholly to student writing. We can encourage students to bring pieces of their writing that have been successful: an essay exam from political science that got full credit, a physics lab report that received an A, a sales letter that won a big contract, or a letter home that got money from Mom. We can encourage students to talk about these successes, to analyze what they did well, and to consider how those strategies might transfer to other writing situations. We can even publish our students' writing; the advent of "desktop publishing" and fancy printers makes it possible for nearly anyone with a word processor and access to a photocopier to put student writing in print. If you decide that student writing is important, you can do a lot to implement that theory in your class.

What will your role be in the classroom? This is one of the hardest decisions for new teachers to make; inexperience leads them to believe that their lack of years or title or practice somehow disqualifies them as teachers. The compensating disguises they adapt could be amusing, if they weren't so potentially dangerous for teacher and student alike. Robert Bain, my first mentor in teaching, told me "Just put on your best teacher like a jacket. Wear that teacher's style—how he talked, how he moved, what he did, how he worked—until you find your own under it. Then you can take that jacket off." I've always found this good advice; even now, I wear a bit of Bob Bain's "jacket" in the classroom. Most of us can remember specific likes and dislikes about our teachers: this one really listened, that one popped her knuckles, this one made lectures lively, that one droned on and on. These memories can help you decide what to do and what not to do as a teacher. Experience, then, can be your first determiner.

But theory can also help. If you don't believe in what Freire calls "banking education"—the notion that a teacher deposits information in a passive student and gets it back with interest on exams and papers—then you can design your classes so that students take a more active role in their own learning, through topic selection and group work, for example. If you believe that writing should help students learn, then you can design activities that help them explore new subjects and ideas and let them write about their discoveries. If you agree with Robert Scholes that "in an age of manipulation, when our students are in dire need of critical strength to resist the continuing assaults of all the media, the worst thing we can do is to foster in them an attitude of reverence before texts" (16), then you can employ strategies to help them question the authority of texts, the constraints of code, their own work, and the work of "great authors." (This is one productive use of deconstruction in the classroom.)

Likewise, the small decisions you make about theory can greatly affect your role in the classroom. As Erika Lindemann observes in the article included below, teaching is a rhetorical act, conditioned by constraints of writer, reader, subject, and language. For instance, will you use lots of exotic terminology? Or will you use a commmon language? Will you help students find out about the work they're reading and doing, or will you set yourself up as the Great Answer-giver? Will there only be two ways in your class—your way and the wrong way? Will you exert your authority by your own example—showing them your work as a writer and the ways you've solved writing problems you've faced? Or will you exert authority by the power of the gradebook and red pen? Will you, or textbooks, do the teaching? Where will the center of the class lie, with students and their writing or with you and your brilliant *explications de texte*? Scholes again has the appropriate remark:

> The more culturally at home in a text our students become, the less dependent they will be on guidance from the instructor. I hate to say it, but I must observe that one of the reasons we teachers favor the big anthology is that it keeps our students dependent on us, justifying our existence. We must get beyond this. There are better ways to make ourselves seem useful. One of them is to *be* useful. (27)

What competencies will you try to teach? Here I've found useful four terms used by John Passmore in his *The Philosophy of Teaching*. He defines the competencies involved in any learning act as closed, narrow, open, and broad. Closed competencies are those that can be mastered with practice by nearly everyone of normal intelligence; in composition, these would include spelling, punctuation, grammar, construction of a topic sentence, and the like. They are the building blocks: essential, but not complete in themselves. They are the kinds of competencies that can be tested by standardized exams. Test scores in almost all cases represent students' mastery of closed competencies and nothing else. Narrow competencies are those that apply only to select situations: writing a goal statement for a résumé, for instance, or writing the materials and methods section for a scientific paper, or explicating a poem. Their focus is restricted. Again, they are essential skills, stepping stones to master on the way to bigger and better things. Given time and guided practice, most people can master them.

Open competencies—and writing and teaching are two of the best examples of these—require that persons apply closed competencies in ways they never have before, in ways they've never been taught to apply them. In other words, an open competency is the surprise discovery acheived through the application of closed skills. A student may know all the rules for an introductory paragraph, for instance (a closed skill), but only rarely achieve an introduction that is lively and interesting—that, in fact, *introduces* the subject. When the student writes that surprising introduction, she's shown an open competency. Teachers can provide guidance, constructive criticism, and feedback, but they can't "teach" open competencies. They have to be achieved; and not all students can achieve them with the same degrees of success. Some won't achieve them at all. (Donald Murray is one the leading proponents of the cultivation of surprise or open competencies in composition, though he does not use the "competency" terminology.) A broad competency is the ability to generalize, to apply what one has learned from narrow competencies to different or more generalized situations. When students realize, for instance, that the skills required to explicate a poem (for instance the closed capacities of identifying metaphors and connotations) may be used to analyze advertisements or political speeches, or that the strategies used to write a persuasive essay may be employed in conducting successful fund-raising drives, they are learning to transfer the narrow competencies they've learned into broader fields. Teachers can suggest how those competencies are achieved, but they can't make the students transfer the knowledge.

As a teacher, then, you'll have to decide what competencies you feel it's important for your students to master. You want them to acquire the open competency of writing, so you'll need to let them write (in guided practice) to do so. This means that while you may spend some of your class time reviewing punctuation or paragraph development as isolated skills, most of your time will be better spent in having students write— and commenting on problems with closed skills in the context of student writing, usually through comments on student papers. You want them too to acquire the broad competencies of generalization, so you'll need to provide opportunities for them to generalize. If students write only five-paragraph themes, for instance, how can they learn which strategies transfer to writing larger and different structures? If they examine only belletristic discourse, how can they determine which skills would work in other forms of discourse? Sometimes your school may require you to focus on narrow, closed competencies, perhaps by requiring that students pass a minimum competency test on spelling, vocabulary, reading comprehension, paragraph development and the like. In such cases, you will need to teach these capacities; however there's no law that says you can't teach them in the context of acquiring broader, open competencies. Forster's maxim—"Only connect"—applies as much to deciding which competencies you will emphasize as it does to literary criticism.

But this, of course, is all theory. What follows is a discussion of how you can put theory into practice as a writing teacher. Good luck! And keep in mind Herman Melville's prayer for writers: "O Time, Strength, Cash, and Patience!"

PART II
PRACTICING THEORY

CHAPTER 6
ORGANIZING A WRITING COURSE

Understanding the theories that underlie the teaching of writing is one thing. *Doing* something with those theories, in a structured and purposeful way, is quite another. This is the challenge we face in designing a writing course. How do the elements go together? Can the theory somehow transfer into the classroom on some cloudy Tuesday in October? The answer, of course, is yes; but as in any other structure, the success will depend more on the architect than on architecture. Experienced teachers have learned, usually the hard way, how to organize and pace a course and how to fit the material into the eight or ten or thirteen or fifteen weeks available. It doesn't just happen in a semester, either; after nearly ten years of teaching writing, I still find myself tinkering with my syllabi in midsemester. What follows, then, is not a foolproof recipe for constructing a writing course. It's commonsense advice that should save you from making some of the more painful mistakes in putting your course together.

Even if you've never taught writing—or any other suject—before, you can construct a course that is clear and coherent. First, you need to consider the three chief elements in course design: goals, time management, and flexibility.

GOALS, TIME MANAGEMENT, AND FLEXIBILITY
Goals

Goals for any class are set by asking three questions. At what level are my students beginning? By the end of the course, what level should they have attained? Along the way, what subordinated goals should they achieve? These three questions define the territory you must cover. Once you have these answers, you can begin to consider strategy.

Many departments will answer the first two questions for you. You'll be told that your class contains students whose test scores, for example, fell between 400 and

600 on the SAT, or students who got B's in high school English. (Remember that these scores mark mastery of closed and usually narrow competencies.) More and more schools gather writing samples from students, either through the application process or during the school's orientation period. These samples are far better indicators of the actual level of your students' writing abilities and will give you a far clearer indication of their competence than mere numbers will. Usually, you will find that a large majority of students show similar levels of skill in focusing, developing, and supporting topics, although their closed skills (including punctuation, grammar, and spelling) may vary widely, especially on timed writing samples. If a few students seem markedly advanced or behind in their skills, see if your department has a procedure for changing their class placement to one commensurate with their level. (If your school does not collect writing samples for you, you'll have time on the first day to elicit them. Don't neglect this important diagnostic tool.)

Likewise, most departments have clear requirements established for passing writing courses. These requirements take a number of forms: a minimum grade, submission of an acceptable writing portfolio, a passing score on a competency examination, or the like. The ideal situation, of course, is to have all students pass the writing course. But in reality, some won't. Resolve now to be firm; students who have not met the minimum requirements should not be sent on to other coursework. If you pass a student who is not able to write according to your school's standards, you help no one — not yourself, your colleagues or school (who will have to cope with an unprepared student), and especially not the student. It's unpleasant to make a student repeat a course, but it's far less unpleasant than sending that student into a discourse community without adequate communications skills.

The goals you will most frequently set are the subordinate ones, the milestones along the way. Sometimes you'll be given guidelines for these: students must write in six or seven modes, or master five set forms, or submit 10 papers or 7000 words, and so on. You may set conceptual goals for the whole class: everyone should be able to support an assertion with evidence and analysis, or incorporate sources without plagiarism, or create an inductive argument. There will also be individual goals, drawn from the diagnositc essays and the students' own work: Jerry will solve his dialect interference problems, Casey will conquer the comma splice, Lynn will learn to write complex sentences. Some goals will be teacher-specific: I'm fighting a losing battle, but I still expect my students to learn when and where to use an apostrophe, despite the road signs on my campus for the "Farmers Market" and newspaper articles on "Rutgers basketball team." Many of these goals will be set in your writing assignments and in comments on student papers: they'll be discussed below.

Time Management

Life is short, we know, and semesters are far shorter (quarters barely start before they're over). So a ruthless sense of realism must go into planning your course schedule. Start by laying out on a calendar or class planner the actual boundaries of your class: how many class meetings will you have? Be sure to figure in both academic and personal events; legal or religious holidays may reduce the number of class meetings, as may a professional meeting or your own academic and personal commitments. (Your department will probably require you to find a substitute for personal absences; if so, try to make the arrangements well in advance.) If in-class midterm and/or final examinations are required at your school, reserve those class meetings as well.

Next, schedule in the due dates for graded assignments. Assignments in the beginning of the semester usually take longer to complete than those later in the term; space out the due dates accordingly. You may need a fourth class period for more discussion or draft work, for example, early in the semester; later on, this may be dispensed with. If you plan to hold conferences during the semester, you may have to cancel a class meeting for these as well. Some creative scheduling may be needed to prevent assignments from backing up on desks. The last thing you want is a stack of papers due the weekend the job list arrives or the week of your doctoral examinations. Some papers, particularly the longer ones, take longer to grade; they'll need to be in several weeks before the end of the term if you're to report class grades promptly. Likewise, students will need longer to complete some papers than others. To use time efficiently, you may have students complete several shorter papers, for instance, while work on the research paper is in progress. And despite good intentions, very few students will work on an assignment over a break period. It's best to schedule an assignment to come in the last class before a vacation; then at least the students can go on holiday with a clear desk.

Flexibility

The best laid plans, of course, still go awry. No course schedule is carved in granite. Sometimes students will master material more rapidly than you'd anticipated; at other times, they may need extra time to complete an assignment. Be ready to give a little, in the interests of the sanity of all concerned. (Some experienced teachers try to leave a few open days in their schedules for catching up; if by some miracle the class is on schedule, this leaves time for conferences, editing practice, and public sharing of students' work. If your schedule permits, one such day in each month's schedule can be invaluable.)

And, too, there'll be events outside your control that disrupt even the most careful planning. Flu epidemics, a candidate's visit to campus, the basketball team's unexpected success in the NCAA tournament—all of these may require class cancellations or reschedulings. Last year our spring semester began with a strike by the secretarial and maintenance staffs, accompanied by three major snowstorms in seven class days. With no clerical help to conduct registration and course changes, uncleared sidewalks and parking lots, and picket lines around unheated buildings, it took us until Spring Break to really get things back to normal. While you should still have a clear idea of pace for your class, leave yourself space to react to changing circumstances.

By establishing major and subordinate goals for yourself, working out a reasonable time schedule, and allowing for flexibility, you can establish a clear and effective skeleton for your course. Now it's time to put some flesh on that structure.

CHOOSING COURSE MATERIALS

Most departments simplify matters for both themselves and their new instructors by prescribing which texts will be used in each writing course offered. These texts could include a complete rhetoric, a reader, a handbook, a departmental policy guide, a research paper guide, a dictionary, software, or combinations thereof. Obviously the *real* "texts" in any writing course are those produced by the students; the other materials are supplementary. It's up to you to decide what kind of materials you'll use and when and how you'll use them.

There are over thousands of composition texts on the market today. How do you choose from this bewildering variety? In some departments, the director of composition chooses the texts from the many examination copies that are sent to her or him each year. Some departments have a committee that makes these decisions. Sometimes the staff participates in such decisions through an election or book fair. Textbook company sales "reps" are always willing to swamp teachers with information and sample copies. But if you're starting cold, what do you do?

First, you need to decide what sort of theory you want in your textbook. If you like the traditional "product-oriented" approach, there are a number of old chestnuts in the field. But many textbooks now are partially or wholly process-oriented. A few include cognitive research, and many recent ones are beginning to address the problem of discourse communities. The book(s) you pick should reflect your view of writing; you don't want to contradict the text for the entire semester. The journal *Writing Program Administration* each year publishes an annotated guide to texts published in that year; this can help you choose a group of texts to examine more carefully. Ask your book reps for texts that use your approach; ask like-minded colleagues at your school (and others) what texts they're examining. And don't neglect the book exhibits at professional meetings; there's a great deal more available there than coffee.

Next, you have to decide what sorts of texts you want to use. Most instructors want their students to have some kind of handbook for reference, and students find it reassuring to have that book to hang on to. (The publishers of this monograph certainly have a good handbook to recommend.) A good college-level dictionary with some information on usage, such as the *American Heritage* or *Webster's New Collegiate,* is absolutely essential. (Remember that most high school students rent or borrow their books from the school; they don't have these books to fall back on.) If your course is going to focus intensively on student writing, you may choose to use a rhetoric or reader with examples (readers now exist that include only student writing). You may wish to find your own models for students or to have them bring in models to discuss; if so, remember the restrictions of the new copyright law (discussed below, p. 92). If you will need to demonstrate a number of rhetorical modes or forms to students, a full rhetoric text may be useful. If there is to be a great deal of documented writing, a research paper guide may come in handy. If your school requires or encourages computer use, a certain kind of software may be prescribed.

Once you have decided what categories of books to examine and have narrowed down the field to a handful of choices, you need to examine the books themselves closely. You want a text that supports you, of course: it should cover the topics you want to cover, with examples, exercises, discussion questions, and activities that will help you present material to your students. But remember that you know this material; students don't. So look at the texts from their point of view as well. Do the examples and exercises really help students master these competencies? Are the explanations clear and to the point? (I still remember one student comment on an evaluation; he complained that the text took twelve pages to say "Be concise.") Is the book designed and produced well, with a good index, readable type, wide margins for notes, and a strong spine to avoid lost pages? Is the author's tone condescending? Does the preface intimidate or invite students? If a question arises at 2 a.m., can the student find the answer in the text? And how much does the text cost? (Teachers get free desk copies, but students in a course with rhetoric, reader, handbook, research guide, and dictionary may spend more than $60. Add software and writing tools and the cost becomes prohibitive.) Spend the time to pick a book both you and the students can live with. Good texts are invaluable; unsuitable ones waste time, money, paper, and goodwill.

THE SYLLABUS

Once you have created a skeleton for your course and chosen the materials you'll use to teach it, you are ready to put a syllabus on paper. The syllabus establishes a contract between you and your students; it explains what both parties can expect from the course. Some teachers prefer to hand out only the simplest of syllabi and modify from week to week; others (and I fall into this group) like to lay out matters clearly at the beginning of the term to avoid the protest of "You never told us" later on. The following checklist, adopted from Erika Lindemann's *A Rhetoric for Writing Teachers,* 2nd ed. (1987), includes eight key points for syllabus information:

1. *Descriptive Information.* The name and number of the course, its prerequisites and other requirements, and the instructor's name, office location and hours, and phone number(s).

2. *Specifications of Course Goals and Content.* The goals—short- and long-term—of the course and of the individual course parts.
3. *Reading Materials.* Names of texts, where to acquire them, a list of reading assignments, and the dates by which these should be completed.
4. *Writing Assignments.* The number and description of writing assignments, with due dates, policies on late and revised papers, group work, and presentation requirements.
5. *Description of Instructional Procedures.* Time devoted to lectures, group work, writing workshops, etc.
6. *Course Requirements.* When and how work is due, how it will be evaluated, attendance and participation, missing and late assignment policies.
7. *Course Schedule.* A meeting-by-meeting calendar of events.
8. *Evaluation and Grading of Students.* Required assignments, how they will be graded, and how final grade will be assessed.

Below is the syllabus for a freshman writing course. It's not as detailed as some, because I allow students a considerable voice in choosing reading assignments from the texts the department requires they buy. However, you can see from the annotations how the eight elements are included and how easy it would be to include reading assignments in the course schedule.

ENGLISH 101: K3 FALL 198X

TTh5   Dr. Tarvers
Scott 103   Murray 207
X-6842 (office; x-7633 (messages); 555-1212 (home)TTh 10–12 and appts.

Texts (all at R.U. Books, Ferren Dock):
    Scott, Foresman Handbook [SF]
    Writing at Rutgers [WR]

Other materials:
    A folder to keep all your papers and drafts
    Writing materials (bring these to class)
    A good, college-level dictionary (if you don't own one, invest!)

English 101 is a course in critical reading, writing, and thinking. Rutgers believes it is important that you be able not only to read material, but also to understand it: its assumptions, biases, hidden agendas, messages. This course, we hope, will help you develop your critical skills. The course will be conducted partially in lecture/discussion form, and partly in workshop form, to give you maximum practice in developing these skills.

Be prepared to write frequently—often for every class, and to prepare about 30–40 pages of reading material for each class.

Attendance for this course is mandatory; please be familiar with the material in the Appendix to *WR*, since this explains the policy I will follow. Certainly, if you miss 5 or more classes, you can expect your grade to be lowered—significantly. Education is not like banking; I can't simply "deposit" information in your brains and expect to get it back with interest. If you want to learn to write well, you have to work at it, to make it important to you. This means you have responsibilities to yourself, to your classmates, and to me. Be on time; do your preparation; bring your materials to class; be awake! On days when we hold writing group sessions, you are expected to bring a readable draft to class (and copies, if it is your turn to read a draft aloud); if you aren't prepared for these sessions, I will count you absent. You can take one 24-hour extension on a due date this semester, provided you notify me a class in advance. Otherwise I don't accept late papers.

Grades for the class will be based on your 10 graded papers, with consideration given to your attendance and the quality of your participation in class discusssion and writing group sessions. Obviously, later papers (after you've had more practice) will count more than earlier papers, but I don't put a fixed percentage on particular papers. Six of these papers we will write together, with set due dates (two of these will be the midterm, on Oct. 17, and the final, on Dec. 10). The other four will come from your own reading and ideas and can be turned in when you (and your group) decide you are ready to submit them; two of these independent papers are due before the midterm, and the other two by December 5. Do not submit more than one paper per class; and read the comments on your previous paper before submitting the next one.

Reading assignments will be given out in chunks for each unit, at the beginning of each unit; I will make some required assignments and poll you to decide on others. If you find a reading you'd like to share with the class, bring it to me in advance and I'll have it duplicated. (Please include a bibliographic reference.) Each unit will have a critical goal and a stylistic goal, and these will move from basic to more sophisticated techniques so that by the end of the semester you will be writing (we hope) with intelligence and verve.

SCHEDULE

Unit 1 Sept. 3–Sept. 19
Goals: Mastering strategies for effective critical reading
Discovering your writing strengths and weaknesses
Dates: Writing group day Sept. 17
Paper 1 due Sept. 19

Unit 2 Sept. 24–Oct. 3
Goals: Writing to an audience
Understanding the differences between student and professional writing
Dates: Writing group days Sept. 26 & Oct. 1
Paper 2 due Oct. 3
Conferences will be scheduled individually in this unit.

Unit 3 Oct. 8–Oct. 17
Goals: Writing logically
Cutting the fat from your prose
Dates: Writing group day Oct. 15
Paper 3 (HOURLY) written in class Oct. 17.
Independent papers 4 and 5 must be turned in by Oct. 17.

Unit 4 Oct. 22–Nov. 5
Goals: Writing persuasively
Polishing your style
Dates: Folder checks Oct. 22
Writing group days Oct. 31 & Nov. 3
Paper 6 due Nov. 5
Conferences for the folder checks will be scheduled individually in this unit.

Unit 5 Nov. 7–Nov. 28
Goals: Writing synthetically
Expanding your options; writing under time pressure
Dates: Writing group days Nov. 19 & 24
NCTE convention Nov. 21; NO CLASS. Work on independent papers.
Paper 7 due Nov. 26
Thanksgiving Nov. 28; NO CLASS

Unit 6 Dec. 3–10
Goals: Review and Evaluation
Preparing to write your way out of the course
Dates: Writing group days Dec. 3 & Dec. 5
Independent papers 8 and 9 due by Dec. 5
Paper 10 (FINAL) written in class on Dec. 10

Paper Preparation   Papers should be typed with a legible ribbon, double-spaced, on nonerasable bond (correction tape and fluid exist for a reason). Legible word-processor printouts (with dark ribbons and on white paper) are also quite acceptable. Amateurish typing that has been neatly corrected is perfectly acceptable. (I use correction fluid in the spray-paragraph size myself). *Any* sort of uncorrected paper is unacceptable. Follow the guidelines in the *SF Handbook* for writing, documenting, and presenting your paper. If you do not do so, I'll return the paper to you ungraded for you to prepare correctly. There is no need to put your papers in fancy binders or covers; one reliable staple in the upper left hand corner is all that is required. There *is* a need for your name and student number, a title, page numbers, and very careful proofreading and correction. If you wish to bring outlines or drafts of your papers to my office, I'll be glad to discuss them with you.

It's important to have the syllabus typed and ready to hand out on the first day of class and to have extras for the students who will join your class in the first few weeks of the term. A few students may be intimidated by all this information, but most are grateful to know what to expect; to them it is evidence of your professionalism. Your department, too, will appreciate having your policies laid out in case of a later grade appeal or problem. It's helpful to have the syllabus duplicated on colored paper; students are less likely to lose pink or green sheets in the welter of paper they accummulate at the beginning of the semester. Now, with syllabus in hand, we can consider how you'll teach your course.

CHAPTER 7
CONDUCTING CLASSES

Too often, writing classes turn into classes where the teacher talks about writing while the students twiddle their thumbs in boredom. Nothing could be less productive. If one new maxim has entered the composition classroom as a result of all the research in the last thirty years, it's this: we learn to write by writing. Not by talking about writing, not be filling in blanks in workbooks, not by admiring set pieces of "good" writing — but by taking pen or pencil or keyboard in hand and actually making meaning in language. Most experienced writing teachers set aside regular class time for writing — in journals, on drafts, as reactions to readings, in freewritings, and so forth. My classes begin — except on workshop days — with 5–10 minutes of some writing activity every day. (I write with my class to reinforce my identity as a member of this community of writers.) For me, this is an absolute necessity; if we don't start by focusing on writing, I end up talking too much about writing. A writing start helps me and protects my students.

The sections that follow describe a number of techniques you can use in conducting classes, beginning with the first day of class. These are tips based on my experience and the experiences of a number of other writing teachers. If you want further suggestions for classroom practices, ask your colleagues. Almost every teacher has one "sure-fire" discussion starter or idea of how to get students engaged with some tough essay. Collegiality is one of the most important reference sources for the teaching of writing.

THE FIRST DAY OF CLASS

Almost every teacher, no matter how wizened a veteran, has nightmares about the first day of class. We walk down endless corridors unable to find our classroom, or find ourselves naked facing a room full of students, or suddenly in a foreign country unable to speak the language. These attacks of nerves are understandable. After all, teaching is a performance; every actor gets butterflies. And there's a lot of pressure on us: *we* have to teach these students to write, to succeed at our school, to become effective communicators. Studies show that one of the most important environmental factors in the writing classroom is the relation between teacher and student; we want that relationship to start well. With all this pressure, opening the classroom door becomes an act of supreme courage!

But relax. There are no documented cases of students eating a teacher on the first day of class, just as there are no cases that prove a bad first day of class ever killed a student, either. The first day is a time for both students and teachers to find out a little about each other, to establish a tone for the course, and to exchange some basic information. Once you conquer the sweaty palms and stomach gymnastics, in fact, you're likely to discover that the first class isn't long enough for everything you want to do.

Some elements of the first class are pretty basic. You'll want to introduce yourself, trying to give a sense of your personal and professional qualifications for teaching the course. This is sometimes a problem for new teachers, because they think students will not respect a TA or part-time faculty member. I tell them I've been a writer for over fifteen years (this goes back to my junior high days, but they don't need to know that). Students are very nervous on that first day, too; they want to know that you have experience with writing. So tell them. You can let them know a little about your writing subjects; I tell them I study English written before Shakespeare's time, especially writing by women, but I also mention that I work with doctors in editing medical manuscripts. I usually tell them that I have a Ph.D. (they love titles), collect classic detective novels and lousy jokes (which I sometimes inflict on my students), am married, and raise cats and seven varieties of tomatoes. I'm a person, just like they are; most students have no idea what an academic does outside the classroom. My openness invites them to tell me things as well; it begins the process of establishing a writing community in our classroom. I also tell students what I'd like to be called in the classroom (usually "Dr. T.," but some of my older students eventually adopt "Jo") so that they'll be a little less nervous in asking me questions.

But I cover a lot of business too. I hand out the syllabus, explain it, and answer questions on it paragraph by paragraph (even drawing a map for finding the bookstore, if necessary). I ask them to read it again after class and to bring in three written questions about it for the next class; this establishes some good habits of reviewing class material for the semester. Then I get some information from them by having them fill out a brief information sheet (illustrated below). This gets them writing quickly and provides me information about their schedules, possible time conflicts, and attitudes toward the course. Then I make the assignment for the second class meeting: besides constructing three questions about the syllabus and buying the books, I ask them to write down as full a list as they can of everything they do when they have a paper to write—from the day it's assigned to the day it's turned in. This will provide an opening for discussion of the writing process in the second class.

I also elicit a writing sample to confirm their placement in the class. In the past I've used passages from Caroline Bird's *The Case Against College* or from Arthur Hoppe's *The Good Old Medieval University* as writing prompts. This semester I'm going to use this as my first writing "assignment." I'll duplicate it on a large sheet of paper so that students have plenty of room to respond.

In his bestselling book *Cultural Literacy*, E.D. Hirsch quotes a newspaper writer's complaints about the "cultural illiteracy" of America's young people. Here's part of that complaint:

> I have not yet found one single student in Los Angeles, in either college or high school, who could tell me the years when World War II was fought. Nor have I found one who could tell me the years when World War I was fought. Nor have I found one who knew when the American Civil War was fought. . . .
>
> Only two could approximately identify Thomas Jefferson. Only one could place the date of the Declaration of Independence. None could name even one of the first ten amendments to the Constitution or connect them with the Bill of Rights. . . .
>
> On and on it went. On and on it goes. I have mixed up episodes of ignorance of facts with ignorance of concepts because it seems to me that here is a connection. . . . The kids I saw (and there may be lots of others who are different) are not mentally prepared to continue the society because they basically do not understand the society well enough to value it. (pp. 6-7)

These are serious charges about the "illiteracy" of your generation. How would you answer Hirsch's charges? [I am not going to grade this piece of writing, but please try to do your best on it. I want to see how well you organize, develop, and present your ideas in writing so that I can tailor this course to your needs.] Use both sides of the paper if you like; put your name at the top.

The goal of such a prompt, of course, is to provoke an engaged, thoughtful response, to get the student to commit some ideas to paper. I don't want a "safe" topic like "What I Did On My Summer Vacation" or "My Favorite English Teacher," because students usually rehash old bromides or try to write "what the teacher wants to hear." (These are the sorts of topics that cause Macrorie's most hated disease, Engfish.) Many other provocative statements could be used here; I know one large writing program that will use Allan Bloom's attack on rock-and-roll (*The Closing of the American Mind* especially pp. 78–81) as its prompt for the orientation writing sample this fall. The writing sample can set a tone for the writing course; it's never too early to ask students to read and think critically, to use their brains to prompt good writing.

Student Information Sheet

Name _____   Student ID# _____

Campus Mailbox _____   Local Phone _____

Local Address _____   College Advisor _____
_____

What other courses are you taking this semester?

What extracurricular time commitments do you have this semester (sports, activities, jobs, home responsibilities, whatever)?

What do you think you reading and writing strengths are?

What areas of reading and writing would you like to improve?

Aside from school assignments, what kinds of reading and writing do you do?

Tell me some distinguishing things about you to help me associate your name with you, the person.

CLASS DISCUSSIONS

Getting students to talk in class isn't difficult. Getting them to talk about what you *want* them to talk about, on the other hand, takes some strategic planning. Many factors may influence students' willingness to talk: the weather is "too nice" for class, the World Series is in progress, it's midterm week and students are burned out, and so forth, Occasionally you'll have to throw your carefully planned discusssion notes out and improvise. If the class wants to talk about baseball, have them argue the pros and cons of the designated hitter rule, or playing the World Series in daytime, or write columns imitating their favorite sportswriter. (If you don't think baseball is a literary subject, just poll writers and literary critics on the Cubs and Red Sox. You'll change your mind quickly!)

A short note here about lesson plans. Depending on your background, you'll either think these essential or never have seen one. Most teachers use some kind of written notes for class, even if those notes wouldn't pass muster in an educational methods class. Too many things happen in class and too often discussion ranges in unexpected directions for you to rely on memory alone. At minimum, your notes should outline the day's goals, the topics you want to cover, and any announcements or reminders you have for the class. (I make announcements *after* we write, to avoid repetitions for latecomers.) If the goals for the day include discussion of readings (see below), some notes about the points you want to make, along with the appropriate page numbers, will save many wasted moments of thumbing madly through the text. Often you can lay out a week's class on one sheet (see the example included) to help organize discussion; then you only need tick off the topics you've covered to keep track of your goals. If you need more detailed notes, by all means make them. But try to avoid writing out full lectures which you read word-for-word to your students. Remember that flexibilty as well as structure is needed in conducting classes.

There's no substitute when planning a discussion for knowing the material. This means you have to read the texts thoroughly, marked passages for close examination, and highlighted examples and techniques you want to point out. It helps to know something about the author and original context of essays and other works; that's why there are instructor's manuals. Try to anticipate the questions that will arise from a text; I write mine out, just as I ask my students to (they are asked to bring at least three written questions on the readings to class). Questioning the text is a very productive way of starting a discussion.

Of course, the questions have to be carefully worded. Nothing kills a budding discussion like a question that implies its own answer: "This was a pretty weak essay, don't you think?" Yes/no questions ("Does Mead use good examples?") are also dampening. Students worry that teachers, in conducting class discussions, are secretly checking that students have read the essay, or ensuring that they agree with the teacher, or are trying to embarrass the student. Starting from the text's perplexities fosters instead an attitude of exploration, of shared attempts to solve the problems a text poses. Don't be afraid to play devil's advocate in starting discussions; tell your students you'll do this. Sometimes offbeat questions can provoke lively engagement. In the last few semesters I've taught a number of essays that present essentially selfish positions (we should end welfare or foreign aid or Medicaid to the chronically ill) and begun discussions with questions like "What religion do you think this author follows?" When students

Course Name/Number/Term _____
Week of: _____   Goals:

Class I	Class 2	Class 3
Assignment:		
Announcements:		
Writing:		
Discussion:		
Reinforcement Activities:		
Next Assignment:		
Handed Out:		
Handed In:		
Notes:		

hesitantly answer "Christian" or "Jewish," I ask "What about the Judeo-Christian notion of 'I am my brother's keeper'?" By playing devil's advocate in this way, I force students to turn the essays inside out, to start from the opposite tack and consider how the author has shaped her argument. Often with a provocative essay and some surprising opening questions, you won't have to say much in the class, just act as traffic cop for answers. If only all classes went this well!

Sometimes, though, you'll need to do more. If students come up with the seed of an idea, you'll need to encourage the students, and their classmates, to develop it, to think out loud. If a student's response seems way off line, you may have to gently redirect it; phrases like "I didn't get that from the essay. Is there a particular passage in it that led you to led you to that conclusion?" or "That's a different approach. Do any of the rest of you want to react to that?" Certainly you don't want to ridicule a student or intimidate her so that she won't speak out again. Likewise, you want to encourage students to respect each other; try to keep them from showing their exasperation. If one or two students habitually try to dominate class discussion, you'll have to intervene to permit other students to respond. One way is to appoint the dominators as temporary discussion emcees while you act as "scribe," recording responses on the board; give them the responsibility of calling on other students. (You won't want to do this all the time because it may lead to charges of favoritism, but the experience usually makes the dominators more willing to allow other students to speak.) A word or two privately after class may also be necessary; assure the student you know *she's* doing the work and need her help to encourage others.

The most important role you can play in these discussions is that of facilitator; you're helping students reach understanding of the material. Often you'll be rephrasing what students have said or turning it into a new question. You can draw out shy students ("Lisa, you're frowning back there; do you disagree with what we're saying?") or simply recognize those who want to join the discussion. (Obviously this works best if you know the students' names!) Sometimes you can draw a consensus ("Ok, then, we agree Syfer's essay doesn't seem very appropriate for 1987") and use that to move on to a new topic or facet of the discussion ("If you were going to revise this essay for *Ms.* in 1988, what would you put in it?") These questions are particularly useful when you need to shift the focus from content to writing strategies.

Gradually you'll become more comfortable in conducting class discussions and will find that the "good days" happen far more often than the bad. Often, using writing to prompt discussion will help you find this comfort. Asking students to read and discuss their written responses to reading will often get a discussion off right. If discussion bogs down or hits an impasse, you can ask students to stop and write about it for a few minutes ("Okay, I want everybody to stop and make two lists—one of all the reasons to provide dialysis to the elderly and one of all the reasons to deny dialysis."). This kind of "thinking out loud on paper," as one of my students called it, often clears the air and allows discussions to proceed productively.

WORKING IN GROUPS

Not all discussion has to involve the whole class. Sometimes you'll want to teach in smaller groups, through one-on-one conferences, small editing groups, or larger workshop sessions. These take a little practice to become used to, on the part of both teachers and students. Usually these activities involve the critiquing of a piece of writing—sometimes published or completed essays, but most often drafts in progress. You'll need to teach your students what to do in such workshops, but once they feel confident with the process they often achieve remarkable results.

Each size of group activity is best suited to a different issue. Large workshops—the whole class—are best suited for global issues: support of a thesis, evaluation standards, and the like. Usually you'll duplicate one or two student papers and discuss them with the whole class. An overhead projector can be very useful for such discussions. At the beginning of the semester you may wish to use papers from another section or from a text so that students don't feel self-conscious about criticizing them. If you're going to use papers from your own students, make sure that all students have one analyzed in the large group before the end of the semester; don't just single a few out.

Large group workshops teach students how to look at overall pieces of discourse, a technique most of them fail to use in revision. They also teach students to look at a piece of discourse as a teacher (evaluator) looks at it. Start with some basic questions: What's the point of this paper? Who are the readers supposed to be? What are some things this writer does well? Then you can move to slightly smaller issues—the assertions backing up the thesis, the examples supporting a definition, the descriptive details that create the mood. Finally you can move toward identifying problem areas: What points in this paper should the writer revise before turning it in? Are there other things she should bring up? Should she leave any of this out? If questions get asked frequently, you may wish to make up a list that students can consult as they revise their own work. (I use the *Framework for Judging*, discussed below.)

After large workshops, students are usually ready to begin in small groups. Here they can examine the local concerns caused by larger issues. If, for instance, the text seems choppy or unorganized, they can experiment with rearranged paragraphs. If the thesis is underdeveloped, they can suggest new examples or analysis. If the style is too wordy, they can help each other tighten the prose. In essence, they're coping with two questions for each draft they examine: "What works?" and "What needs work?"

The composition of small groups requires care on your part. Somehow you have to mix strong and weak students, aggressive and shy ones, in cells of three or four students who will work together and help each other. For the first few sessions, you may want to give out specific lists of questions to ask. (A sample list is given below, pp. 40–41.) And you'll have to monitor discussion carefully to make sure it hasn't veered around to a sociology exam or a Bon Jovi concert.

Most group sessions work like this: One student reads his draft aloud, while other group members read along on copies. Then comes the response period. The group members first tell the writer what they think works in the draft. The writer then identifies two or three areas he wants help with, and the group responds with suggestions. The writer asks for clarification, if that's necessary. Finally, the group raises other questions it has about the draft and tries to help the writer answer them (often these come from the group's own experiences in previous papers). The writer is not bound to accept all the group's suggestions, but should be encouraged to think of them as the response of potential members of the audience for that piece of writing. Then another member of the group reads her draft, and the process begins again.

At the beginning of the semester you'll want to make these sessions short, to help students get the feel of the procedure. You may want to analyze one draft together as a class for ten minutes, then break up into small groups with five minutes or so for each draft. Then you can reassemble in the large group to talk about matters of general concern. If this is going to be the case, students should circulate their drafts in the previous class, so that they can be read in advance. Later in the semester you may wish to spend entire classes in groupwork, letting students spend more time reading and responding. Your job in these classes is to move from group to group, answering questions, serving as a member of the audience, and keeping attention focused on the task at hand.

There are some inevitable problems involved in group teaching. Some students will forget to bring drafts. Your syllabus should make clear that this is a responsibility, just as turning in papers on time is. Some teachers lower grades on the final papers if no drafts appeared. You need to make clear to students that drafts are *not* optional. Some students talk too much, or too little, or offer destructive criticism. You'll have to tinker with group chemistry if this is the case. Put all the talkers in one group, so that they can't dominate the discussion. Put the shy students together and force them to talk. Speak privately to students who are not cooperating, and be sure they've had the chance to have the whole class criticize their work; this increases cooperation markedly. You're the authority in the classroom; you need to exert control. Sometimes students talk about the content of drafts, not the way they were written, or won't talk about the drafts at all. You'll need to monitor their discussion and perhaps focus their thinking. Make them write out their comments or consider why an audience would find the subject more interesting than the presentation. Don't let them gossip and waste time. Sometimes you'll have to crudely remind them that the quality of their workshop performance will influence their grades; that usually gets their attention.

Here's a sample group revision checklist.

1. What are this paper's strengths right now?
2. As a reader, what about this paper gets your attention?
3. What big issues in the paper need work? Circle or read them, and try to give a few suggestions for improvement.

4. Based on your own experience and instincts (and the successes and problems you've had), make three concrete suggestions that will help the author improve this paper.

I find it very useful to give students a written description of writing groups and discuss it with them at an early class period. This gives them an idea of what to expect and helps them approach the strategy productively. Below is an example of the handout I provide.

WRITING GROUPS

Working in a writing group will be a little different from the groupwork you have done before. First, you have different responsibilities: to give careful, thoughtful advice to your fellow group members. Second, you have different rights: to expect careful, thoughtful feedback from your fellow group members. This is serious business; you can only expect to get as much, and as useful help, as you contribute. So you must have a draft ready for group workdays, and come prepared to help others. Failure to do so not only deprives your partners of your help, but will also lower your grade on the final paper.

For draft days, make sure you furnish a readable draft in advance. Put the drafts in the box by my office door by 5 p.m. the day before the workshop; make sure they go in the folder for *your* group. Pick up the drafts from the other members of the group and read them before the draft workshop. This will prepare you to give and receive the most possible help.

When working in a group, first establish the day's priorities: what do you have to accomplish today (reading everyone's draft, proofreading everyone's final copy, planning everyone's next paper, or whatever)? Estimate the amount of time needed, then divide it up equitably; each member is entitled to a fair share of the time. Let one group member be the timekeeper each session; he or she is responsible for keeping the discussion moving and making sure no one is denied fair time. Take turns being timekeeper.

After you divide up the time, pick a draft to start discussing. The writer of that paper should tell you what he/she is trying to accomplish in the paper, what areas he/she thinks are coming along well, and what areas he/she particularly wants help with. In response, the group should begin by telling the writer what is good/strong/well-done in the paper. Then offer advice on the matters for which the writer can strengthen the weak spots. The writer should ask you questions to get your suggestions clear in his/her mind and is free to accept only those suggestions he/she agrees with.

You will have time to review each other's papers at least once in each workshop session. If you finish early, start incorporating some of the suggested changes into your draft and ask the other members of your group what they think of them. The rest of the period can be spent finishing the other work on the agenda, proofing, working on individual problems, drafting/brainstorming/discussing other papers, conferring with me, or writing. When you need advice, call on another member of your group for help. As you learn to trust each other, you will be able to work more effectively as a group; you may choose to meet outside the class (perhaps on the night before a paper is due) to work or just to socialize. At any rate, working in a writing group should increase your confidence—and your skills—in writing and working together. If you are uncomfortable in your particular group, see me privately. I'll do what I can to adjust groups or group dynamics to provide the best writing environment for everyone.

If you want more information about using groupwork, consult the works in the bibliography by Peter Elbow, Roger Garrison, and Don Murray. These three teachers have become experts in the field, and their publications are full of helpful tips on technique. Garrison in particular is an authority on the third kind of group teaching, conference teaching. This strategy works best when class members are at many different competency levels, since you can individualize instruction, or when you wish to establish (or have established) a strong rapport with your students. Some teachers spend the entire semester in one-to-one teaching; most of those have the luxury of small classes. Other instructors incorporate one-to-one techniques in small doses, usually combining them with larger groupwork and discussions.

In such situations, the teacher holds brief (1-10 minute) conferences with each writer at four or five stages in a paper's development. Each conference has a clear goal: information gathering, central plan, organization, sentences and grammar, and editing. This kind of intervention tends to raise grades and limit the number of papers submitted; most teachers balance it with papers written without help.

Another kind of conference that has proven useful in writing courses is the "progress report" conference. After every few papers, the instructor and student sit down for perhaps fifteen minutes to discuss the student's progress to date. They try to identify the competencies the student has already mastered and the goals the student wishes to achieve in the next few papers. Students can ask questions about the teacher's comments on papers, discuss problems with the editing log (about which, see below, p. 70), and review plans for subsequent papers. I try to hold these about three times a semester and usually cancel a class in the week I hold them. Some words of advice: when you make your conference appointments, schedule a break at least every two hours to "decompress." Make notes in advance so that you'll know what points you want to make with each student; I keep these in their file folders and check them off as we cover them. (See the example below.) Keeps fluids and throat lozenges on hand, because you'll do a lot of talking. And leave yourself some free time once the conferences end, because they will exhaust you.

Here's an example of a student progress record I keep, along with the student's information sheet and other work, in files in my office. (You might also keep all the progress records in a binder so that you can take them home when grading papers.)

Name _____

Diagnostic
    Strengths:

    Student's goals:

    Proposed goals:

Paper 1
    Strengths:

    Problems:

    Goals set in comment:

Conference date
    Points I want to make:

    Points students made:

    Goals student set:

Paper 2
    Strengths:

    Problems:

    Goals set in comment:

Paper 3
   Strengths:

   Problems:

   Goals set in comment:

etc. . . .

Conference 2 date
   Points I want to make:

   Points students made:

   Goals student set:

etc. . . .

Exit conference date
   My assessment of student's performance:

   Student's assessment of performace:

   Recommendations:

After some experimenting, you'll find the right mixture of writing, discussion, and groupwork for your own teaching style. But you must always keep flexibility in mind. Some classes will never be comfortable with groupwork; others will resist discussion but flourish in small groups. Don't be afraid to vary the types of techniques you use and to change the pace; nothing is more deadly in *any* course than monotony. For every writing goal there are probably twenty ways of conducting class to achieve it. The makeup of your class and your rapport with the students determine best what techniques you'll use and when. If you feel dissatisfied with a particular technique, you might consider inviting a colleague to observe one of your classes. Sometimes a neutral observer can see ways in which you can better use time, or move discussions along, or encourage small groups; when you're involved with your students, it's hard to develop an objective view alone. You can also poll students on what techniques most help them; some of these strategies are discussed in the section on evaluation, below.

CHAPTER 8
DESIGNING WRITING ASSIGNMENTS

At the heart of any composition course are the actual pieces of writing that students complete. These provide opportunities to practice the closed competencies students have studied and to attempt to incorporate those closed competencies into open structures. In short, writing assignments let students see how far they've come in achieving their goals. But if assignments are to serve this purpose, the instructor must design them with care. The writing assignment must create a purposeful rhetorical situation and invite students to use that situation to create meaning in language. This takes—like everything else in teaching composition—an understanding of the writing process and careful planning.

First, writing assignments can't be made at random. They must form part of a sequence that helps students achieve the short- and long-term goals of the course. If the goal of a particular section of the course is to have students develop inductive arguments, then the writing assignment must create a situation where induction is appropriate. It should also ask students to use strategies or skills they have learned previously, to build on those achievements, to complicate their writing. If you identified your class goals clearly in the planning process and set up your syllabus to achieve those goals, then sequencing your writing assignments should come more easily; you already have a theoretical framework in place.

Second, writing assignments must be made in a context. Too often students are given assignments whose constraints are not made clear. One of my students recently asked me for help with a paper for another literature class. The assignment was one sentence: "Write a paper about the most interesting aspect of *Paradise Lost*." No wonder the student was bewildered! What kind of paper—critical analysis, explication, argument, personal interpretation? Who decides what the "most interesting aspect" is—the student, the teacher, some critic? Aspect in what context—structural, poetic, literary critical, historical, theological? How long should the paper be? Can the student consult outside sources? What kind of documentation is required? When is it due? How will the teacher evaluate it? Is it too late to drop the course?

We've all seen assignments like this, of course; many of us have had to write them. Experience has taught us that the first thing we do with an assignment like that is bombard the teacher with questions like those in the previous paragraph. But inexperienced students don't know that they can do that; many will try to wrestle with the assignment as given, and many will despair. It's not their fault; they're not stupid, as they may believe when they fail with the assignment. No, the assignment is at fault. It is completely arhetorical; it doesn't provide an indication of the context needed for successful completion.

Third, assignments must be concrete. A key assumption in the design of writing assignments is that they *should* be written out and distributed to students well in advance of the due date. It's only fair to students to know exactly what is expected; and it will save you the phone calls on the night before the due date when students ask "What exactly did you want us to do in this paper?" If duplication is a problem in your teaching situation (budgets are tight everywhere), write the assignment clearly out on the board, and see that students copy it carefully. Review the key points (goals, physical constraints, procedures) to make sure all students know what is expected. And make sure the assignment is distributed far enough in advance of the due date for students to complete it successfully. Adjust your evaluation standards accordingly: your criteria will be different if students have one night to complete a writing task than if they have a month.

The following list can be used as a guideline for composing writing assignments. It identifies four fields of information that a good assignment should cover. It also suggests places where less specificity, rather than more, may be helpful. When you cover these four fields, your students should have enough information to tackle the assignment.

Physical Constraints. When is the assignment due? When are drafts due? What form is it to be in (essay, lab report, editorial, etc.)? What would be a reasonable length? Must it be typed? Should all scratchwork be submitted? What kind of documentation should be used?

Discourse Context. What is the topic, subject, or principle behind the assignment? Has the instructor specified an exact topic, or is the student supposed to find a topic by narrowing down the subject area? If so, what kinds of narrowing might be profitable? What kinds of skills are students expected to demonstrate? Who is the audience? For what purpose is the author writing? What questions or problems does the assignment raise?

Resources. Where in the text can the student seek help? What class discusssions are relevant? Are there particular kinds of prewriting, drafting, and/or revising activities that will be helpful? May the student seek outside help from fellow students, authorities, and librarians? Is the student expected to consult secondary scholarship? If so, what kind(s)?

Evaluation Criteria.   What will determine success or failure in completing this assignment? Will students have an opportunity to receive feedback before they submit the assignment for a grade?

Here are two sample writing assignments that follow these guidelines in more or less detail. The first is from a freshman composition class; the second is from a course in contemporary American government (I am grateful to Robert Shore for this assignment).

Paper 5: Review
Due Monday, November 12 (note change in syllabus)
Class draft critique Monday Nov. 5; Rough draft session Wednesday, November 7
Length: 3–5 typed pages

One of the most frequent writing tasks in the professional world is that of giving informed opinions. Whether these be evaluations of programs, personnel, proposals, policies, or subjective reactions to restaurants, movies, works of art, or the like, this is a type of writing you are likely to be called on to do, so it'll be useful for you to practice it.

In this paper, I'd like you to give your opinion of something—the something is up to you, though I'd like you to run the subject by me verbally if you think it's "off the wall." It should be a review that can be published—whether in the print media, circulated by memo around the company, or what have you. You'll probably want to stick to something manageable and local—the Chapel Hill transit system, for example, not Amtrak. Use your best judgment—pick a subject you know well. If you're reviewing some policy or procedure from work, you might ask your supervisor if (s)he has any examples around you can examine. But the only real "research" this assignment requires is deciding on appropriate criteria for judging and gathering information on how well your subject meets its criteria.

Jackie Berke in *Twenty Questions for the Writer,* 3rd ed. (San Diego: Harcourt Brace Jovanovich, 1980, on reserve), reminds us that most reviews have a four-part structure:
  Introduction (generally catchy)
  Description of the subject
    A. What it is formally (book, movie, Mexican restaurant, affirmative action plan)

    B. What it is about
Evaluation: To what extent it fulfills or fails to fulfill its purpose
    A. Its strengths
    B. Its weaknesses (or vice-versa for a negative review)
Conclusion)

This structure will work well for almost any type of review you need to write, from the letter of recommendation to a course evaluation booklet to the evaluation of an employee training program to the review of La Chat Petite. You must pick a specific subject, decide on a set of tests for judging it, gather evidence objectively, and then organize that evidence (details and examples) into a subjective review.

For resources, you have the reserve readings in *Twenty Questions, New Strategy of Style* and *On Writing Well*; I suggest you consult them. We'll critique some student samples in class next time, and since reviews rarely run over 1200 words, we'll have time to look at three rough drafts in class on Monday.

In evaluating your review, I'll consider the clarity of your presentation, paragraph and sentence development, lack of lard, and your ability to select an appropriate tone of voice and style in explaining your criteria and presenting your conclusions to your audience.

Assignment 2
    We have used the Gramm-Rudman-Hollings debate in class to discuss the Constitutional theory of separation of powers. For this paper, I would like you to choose a contemporary (since 1981) federal political issue other than GRH that involved all three branches of government. Describe its development and resolution (if it's had one) to begin your paper, then use this issue to consider how well (or poorly) the separation of powers doctrine worked in this case. From your evaluation, conclude by recommending what changes (if any) you find necessary in the separation doctrine.

    To find information about your topic, I recommend consulting the *Reader's Guide* and similar indexes in the library. (Remember that they're about three months behind the times, so Ollie North's testimony won't be indexed yet.) Note whether your sources are biased or neutral. Document any source material you use following the recommendations in Turabian (on reserve). The paper should be from 8 to 12 typed pages, not including notes and bibliography, and is due in class on Monday Aug. 10. Grades will be based on the complexity of the issue selected, the clarity with which you present material and marshal your argument, and the persuasiveness of your presentation. And yes—spelling, punctuation, and "grammar stuff" count. This *is* college.

Both these assignments succeed because they carefully place the writing task in a context; the students can tell what the instructor wants them to demonstrate, yet are allowed considerable freedom in choosing how to fulfill their requirements. Consider the possible alternatives: "Write a review of some person, place, entertainment, course, or other tiem that can succeed or fail; use a contemporary federal political issue to show what aspects (if any) of the separation of powers doctrine should be changed." Assignments like the ones shown challenge students to succeed rather than doom them to fail. They also encourage students to use narrow competencies to reach broader ones, to achieve growth in writing. Goal-directed writing assignments like these are the true backbone of writing courses.

It takes time to design writing assignments that help students reach their writing goals, but it is time well spent. Not until you've seen an entire class misinterpret—and botch—a writing assignment can you really appreciate how worthwhile the time spent in working up a good assignment is. If it weren't for the harm done to the students involved, who almost always do their best to meet even the worst assignments and suffer the penalty for bad ones in grades, it might almost serve teachers right to have to read twenty-five or fifty papers on "The Definition of Friendship" or "The Causes of the Civil War." Some teachers come away from such experiences blaming their students; most, though, will honestly wonder what went wrong. Usually the students were asked to write without context or an understanding of their goals. If your assignments cover the four fields outlined above, you should be spared the agonies of grading papers you should never have assigned.

CHAPTER 9
INTERVENING IN THE WRITING PROCESS

The writing process is a complex matter; it varies for each writer, on each writing occasion. So it's hard to generalize about teaching techniques that "improve" the writing process. Probably the best we can do is to help students develop a repertoire of strategies to use in writing and help them learn when and where the strategies work best for them. Though the process is recursive, it can be best discussed in a linear fashion, so that's how this section will proceed. You'll have to emphasize to your students, however, that it's never the "wrong" time to call on one of the stages; invention may be part of the revision techniques on a final draft. (Ask how many of them make changes in wording and sentences as they type their final papers; most do, an illustration of revision still in progress as they complete their editing and presentation.)

PREWRITING ACTIVITIES

Prewriting, or invention, has drawn a great deal of scholarly attention; in fact, it might be said to have been *the* rhetorical subject of composition scholarship in the early and mid-1970s. There are many methods of teaching invention strategies, with many opportunities for groupwork, discussion, and one-on-one conference teaching. Prewriting can be seductive: many classes get so involved with it that they neglect *writing*. You and the students must remember that prewriting is a way for *finding things to say* in writing; it's not a substitute for composing written texts.

Prewriting strategies fall into two very large, ill-defined categories: unstructured and structured. Unstructured prewriting works best when students are trying to find a topic or form; it helps them find new material, to make new connections, to pursue (in Passmore's and Murray's term) surprise. Structured prewriting works best when the

50

topic or form is known or has been assigned; it helps students discover what they know and need to know about their writing subject and to make sense of the material they've found. The techniques for both kinds of prewriting are closed competencies; most students can learn to use them. But when they use them to develop new knowledge, or to structure their knowledge in a different way, these strategies become gateways to open competencies and to better writing. As teachers, we want our students to know about as many of these gateways as possible; we have to be careful, however, not to swamp them with all the techniques. You may need to introduce the techniques in pairs or triads—perhaps mixing unstructured and structured kinds—by choosing those that seem best suited to the assignment students currently are completing. At the same time you'll want to encourage students to try other methods, so that they don't limit themselves and their chances of discovery. There are few if any instances where prewriting should be graded; it's successful only insofar as it helps students find things to say in their larger papers. But you'll probably want to collect it along with the finished papers to see what kinds of prewriting the students are doing and to suggest alternate or more advanced strategies to help them develop their skills.

Unstructured Prewriting Strategies

Brainstorming.   Brainstorming allows writers, either singly or in groups, to explore many possible facets of a topic. The idea is to list all the ideas that come to mind when a writer thinks about a subject. The ideas may be wild, or superficial, or barely related to the subject; often teachers will need to help students probe more deeply into the subject. If the class or a writing group conducts the brainstorming session, the teacher or a group member acts as scribe, recording all the ideas on the board or on paper. The recorder has the job of asking "What do you mean? Can you be more specific? Any examples?" If the student proceeds alone, she scribbles ideas or perhaps records them on a tape recorder (brainstorming seems to work best visually) and must ask herself the probing questions. Either way, the ideas should come quickly and the suggesters shouldn't worry about grammar, spelling or syntactic completeness. Those come at a much later state. Once the brainstormed lists are complete, students can connect and sort ideas by circling and drawing lines (called a subject chart) or by recasting their lists.

Freewriting.   Freewriting, perhaps the best known of unstructured prewriting methods, encourages students to get their ideas on paper without worrying about editing their writing. As Peter Elbow defines it,

> The idea is simply to write for ten minutes (later on, perhaps fifteen or twenty). Don't stop for anything. Go quickly without rushing. Never stop to look back, to cross something out, to wonder how to spell something, to wonder what word or thought to use, or to think about what you are doing. If you can't think of a word or a spelling, just use a squiggle or else write, "I can't think of it." Just put down something. The easiest thing is just to put down whatever is in

your mind. If you get stuck it's fine to write "I can't think what to say, I can't think what to say" as many times as you want: or repeat the last word you wrote over and over again: or anything else. The only requirement is that you *never* stop. (1973, p. 3)

Advocates of freewriting such as Elbow and Macrorie recommend it because it lets students free themselves of pretensions (what Macrorie calls "Engfish") and worries about correctness. Instead they can pursue ideas, chain reactions, surprise. Freewriting takes practice; you'll probably want to encourage students to use it several times a week, moving from shorter sessions (4–5 minutes) at first into longer sessions. (The longer students freewrite, in theory, the deeper they will explore a subject and the better the results. This isn't always the case; while you won't want to grade freewriting, you'll want to keep an eye on what students do with it so that it's used productively.)

Not all students are comfortable starting freewriting from scratch; you may want to provide a suggestive word or phrase the first time or two to help students get started. And you may wish to incorporate student response; students, for instance, can exchange freewritings after five minutes or so, review them, and discuss the ideas they liked and those they think the writer could explore further. This process can be repeated as many as six or seven times to encourage students to dig deep into their ideas. If students are working in writing circles, they may stop after five or ten minutes, pass their prewritings on to the student on their left, and let *that* writer read and continue the prewriting with her ideas. This process is repeated until each writer in the group has contributed to each piece of freewriting. The original writer is frequently quite surprised by the many new directions other writers found in her original ideas and can proceed to develop this new material. If the writer is working alone, you may want him to stop every five or ten minutes, review what has been produced, and circle a few words, phrases, or a sentence that seems most interesting – a hot spot. This hot spot then becomes the starting point for a subsequent freewriting. The process can be repeated as often as the student finds it productive.

Freewriting can often help students who are intimidated by the blank page or who suffer from certain kinds of writing blocks. It also helps the students who feel they have "nothing to say"; when they see they've filled up an entire page or more in just a few minutes, they're often encouraged to produce even more writing.

Perception Busters.   Often, students forget how many ways there are to view a particular subject. Exercises in developing perceptual skills may help students break out of old patterns and find new ways of viewing their subjects. Ask students to draw something they're sure they know – such as the dial on a telephone or the gauges on the dashboard of their cars. Then have them compare their sketches to the real thing; where are the differences? Have them describe some familiar setting – their room, the classroom, a local watering hole – as specifically as possible, then ask them to revise the description for someone who has been blind since birth. What does the classroom look like from the point of view of that bee banging against the light fixture? How does the cafeteria look from the server's side of the line? Encourage students, too, to play devil's advocate; if they're going to be arguing for a position, have them freewrite about the other side, about comparisons and contrasts and precedents for their positions; have them pick the celebrity endorser who will do commercials for their position ("Hi! This is Lawrence Taylor for the Handgun Owners Association. . . . .") When students break the barriers of habit, learn to use all of their senses, and see other perspectives, they take giant strides toward learning and applying their new knowledge.

Journal Keeping.   We're used to the notion of "literary" writers keeping journals — Thoreau, Woolf, and others have taught us how valuable such records can be as writers develop their work. So it shouldn't surprise us that students can also profit from keeping journals, using them to record ideas and events, work out pieces of writing, and come to terms with their lives. Students generally need a little guidance when they start with the journal; they need to realize the difference between journals and diaries and personal calendars, for instance. You might also want to set a schedule for writing: make an entry every day you're not in class, or write five days a week for at least ten minutes. You can determine how students use the journals by suggesting that error logs (see below, p. 83) or progress charts be kept as part of them; you may have to provide a list of ten or fifteen "fallback" prompts for students to start from on those days when they can't find inspiration.

Generally students will take journals seriously. You'll find a lot of thoughtful material, both material for papers and material that the student is daring to share with you. When you read and respond to journals (which you should do, although you shouldn't grade them), you'll need to make serious comments. Some of these will focus on writing matters — possible subjects for papers, interesting words or descriptions or points of view the writer might want to exploit, or reinforcement of the student's abilities. The personal matters require a different kind of response. Students should feel free to staple pages shut or write "Don't Read!!!" at the top of the page and expect to have their privacy respected. Sometimes students will use journals to test you; they'll fill an entry with vulgarities or other offensive material. Usually the best response to these is silence the first time around; if such entries continue, you'll want to discuss the journal with the student.

The confessional entries — where the student tells you his hopes or fears or traumatic experiences — require a careful rhetorical response. They're an expression of trust; you may be the first adult with whom the student has dared shared these feelings. You can't simply respond with a marginal "Interesting" or "I know how you feel"; this violates the trust the student has offered. I usually thank the students for sharing the experiences with me, for trusting me, and encourage them to go on working the problem out in writing, to help them gain perspective. Sometimes, if the problem seems really serious, I'll suggest that the student and I have a cup of coffee and discuss it. You may be the only teacher in a position, for instance, to detect students in real academic trouble or in need of counseling; sometimes you may be the only help that student is willing to seek, and you'll have to encourage the student to seek other outlets. Such roles aren't generally included in the job descriptions of writing teachers, but if you encourage personal, honest writing, you may find yourself teaching and supporting students outside the classroom situation.

Commonplace Books.   Personal journals aren't the only kinds of writing notebooks students can keep. Often students will benefit from keeping old-fashioned commonplace books, where they not only record observations and summarize readings, but copy down words, phrases, and passages of writing they admire. Like the journals, such commonplace books can become treasure houses for students in search of paper topics to plunder, as well as collections of models they might imitate. If students are to keep commonplace books, you can encourage them to expand their range. Students may want to include only items from *People* magazine or from rock lyrics; you can direct them, gently, to alternate sources as well. It's best to encourage students actually to copy out the model; this makes them more aware of the words they copy than if they cut and paste in entries. If you use this prewriting technique, you might want to leave some classtime occasionally for students to share their most recent "gems."

Discussion.   With all the emphasis on pen and ink techniques, we sometimes forget how important a technique *talking* is for writers. In groups or conferences, or perhaps in brainstorming sessions with the whole class, a writer can explore her topic and receive feedback from other writers. This might also involve discussion of an essay, if students are writing about a reading, or discussion of a sample student paper where the writer faced a similar subject or situation. If students are writing narratives, they might try interviewing each other and "ghostwriting" each other's tales as a prewriting activity; if they are writing description or narration they might try to present it as a reporter for Action News or *Sixty Minutes*. Role playing can help students get started with writing; you might have them work with "actual" situations or work from fantasy. I sometimes give my students the nursery rhyme "Jack and Jill" and assign them roles: one describes the situation as a *Dragnet*-style cop, another as Jill's mother, another as an insurance investigator, another as a politician seeking reelection in Jack's district, another as a scriptwriter for *Moonlighting* or *Magnum P.I.*, and so forth. Simply talking *about* writing isn't productive; but students and teachers can use talking as a way to move into writing.

Structure Prewriting Strategies

Outlining.   To judge from many older writing textbooks, the formal outline is the only kind of prewriting a student need do. The student picks a topic, immediately constructs a perfectly parallel sentence outline, and goes on blithely to write her draft. Baloney. As most of us have discovered in our own writing, we outline *after* we have text to outline, not before. But students can use outlining productively if they already have some information about their topic. The outline need not be formal, in complete sentences with Roman and Arabic numerals neatly in place. Students can use outlines to shape rough chunks of their material, to see what they have already gathered and what they still need to find out. At the revising stage, students can use outlines, again rough, to find digressions, unsupported or underdeveloped points, and to test the sequence of their ideas. If your department requires that students learn the formal outline, it's best to teach it as a separate rhetorical form and to divorce it from the kinds of scratch outlines that help students generate and organize material. (Some word processing programs, such as WordPerfect, will do the formal outlining for students, complete with appropriate indentations and Roman numerals; all the student needs to do is fill in the sentence or heading. Such technolgoy can be a boon if your program requires formal outlining; let your students know about it.)

Heuristics. Most structured invention techniques form heuristics, lists of questions that direct students toward particular goals. These techniques may be close-ended, eliciting only a certain kind of answer, or open-ended, allowing students to explore a topic in a structured way. Since heuristics generally direct students along someone else's lines of thought (you or someone else makes up the questions), they should always be paired with unstructured techniques, so that the student's own ideas get included. Many leading rhetoricians have published long sets of heuristics for invention; some of these are summarized below, and references for others are provided. (In adapting these for classes, many teachers follow Tom Lehrer's sarcastic advice in *Lobachevsky:* "Plagiarize, plagiarize; never let another's work escape your eyes. But call it 'research'.") If you should choose to use these techniques in class, be sure you abide by the copyright law (described below, p. 92).

1. *The Journalist's Questions.* Most of us are familiar with the journalistic "recipe" for writing the lead to a story: Who, What, When, Where, Why, and How. Variations on these questions ("Who are the contras? What are they fighting for? When and where were they formed? Why does the U.S. government support them? How do they operate?") can lead students to explore facets of their topics that they wouldn't otherwise consider. Usually these questions won't have right or wrong answers; ideally, many will lead to follow-up questions as the student explores the topic in more depth. Literary critics will recognize these as the basis of Kenneth Burke's "dramatistic" theory of analysis: What was done (act)? Where or when did it take place (scene)? Who did it (actor)? Why was it done (purpose)? How was it done (agency)? The journalist's questions work well with brainstroming and perceptual blockbusting to open up new possibilities for writers.

2. *Classical* topoi *and their descendants.* Classical rhetoric developed an elaborate set of *topoi* or locations where material for arguments could be found. Modern adaptations of the *topoi* adapt their questioning strategies for exposition, narration, and other modes as well. One of the most fully developed *topoi* heuristics is that found in Elizabeth Cowan Neeld's *Writing*, 2nd edition, pp. 46–48 (her label "Aristotelian" is somewhat

of a misnomer). You might not want to use such an elaborate heuristic at first, but to pick and choose questions to help students develop their topics before graudally introducing them to the whole system. Likewise, if students are writing about readings (fictional or nonfictional), they may find Edward P.J. Corbett's adaptation of the *topoi* to readings useful (*The Little Handbook* (1977), pp. 186–221). Thomas Boley presents a brief but effective list of questions for persuasive writing in "A Heuristic for Persuasion," *CCC* 30 (1979), pp. 187–191. And Richard L. Larson provides perhaps the most complex of all heuristics in "Discovery Through Questioning," *CE* 30 (1968), pp. 126–134. Of course, you can also design your own heuristics to focus on a class' particular needs. Start simple; add on questions as students are able to handle more material. (Students may also develop their own heuristics based on their strengths and weaknesses; these can spur productive conference discussions.)

3. *Range and Variation.* In the late 1960s, three rhetoricians – Richard Young, Alton Becker, and Kenneth Pick – adapted the terminology and methods of modern physics to invention strategies. Their "tagmemic" method (from the Greek verb "to arrange") encourages writers to see their subjects not just as static objects or entities but as processes and parts of larger systems. Writers using tagmemic invention look at the subject's identifying characteristics (called "contrast"), the amount of changes it will tolerate before it becomes something else (called "variation"), and its role in the larger systems in which it plays a part (called "distribution"). For instance, a Mercedes Benz 560 SEL has certain features of design, engineering, and equipment that make it unique. They give it its contrast. Some of these features and options can be varied or left off, but at a certain point, the car becomes a different kind of Mercedes – a 420 or a 300, or the Mercedes 560 of a previous year. The limits to which a 560 can be modified and still remain a 560 are its variation. Finally, the 560 SEL plays a part in a number of systems: all the Mercedes models, German-engineered products, targets of protectionist quotas, status symbols for the rich. These systems represent the 560's distribution, the worlds in which it plays a part.

Many authors have tried to include tagmemics in texts, but the method has never been widely popular; nevertheless it does work in the classroom. Among text adaptations of it you might find useful are W. Ross Winterowd's in *Contemporary Rhetoric*; Janice Lauer, et al.'s in *Four Worlds of Writing*; and Dean Memering and Frank O'Hare's in *The Writer's Work*. Charles Kneupper's article "Revising the Tagmemic Heuristic" (*CCC*, 31 (1980), pp. 160–168) also provides a number of suggestions for using this multifaceted invention strategy in the classroom. Freewriting and journal keeping work well with tagmemics.

Research.   Although we seldom think of research as an invention tactic outside of the research paper, reading and asking questions of a subject are often the most productive ways for students to find and organize material on their topics. Book research can provide facts, figures, authorities, and perspectives the student didn't know. Talking to experts can be even more rewarding; an expert's interview can add eyewitness testimony and illustrative ancedotes to facts, figures, and printed sources. The student who is writing about the jogging craze, for instance, might talk to a running shoe salesman, an orthopedist, a track coach, and both inexperienced and experienced joggers as she gathers material. The student writing about medical school admissions can talk to an admissions counselor, students undergoing the process, and students who already are in medical school. Macrorie calls this process "I-search" rather than research, because there are live people involved, and therefore the subject becomes more real to the writer. As with heuristics, you'll have to encourage the student to provide her own answers as well as those she finds through reading and interviews; journals, freewriting, and discussion work well as preliminaries to research prewriting.

With all these techniques, students can quite easily spend an entire semester prewriting, simply generating material. But that's not the goal of a writing class. At some point, the student must *do* something with this wealth of material: sort it, thin it out (sometimes easier said than done), and start shaping it: "face the white bull of the page," as Hemingway would say. That's drafting—the next step in the writing process.

DRAFTING SUPPORT

"I love being a writer. What I can't stand is the paperwork." Whether we attribute this quote to the writer Peter DeVries or the imaginary poet Gowan McGland (from the film *Reuben, Reuben*), most of us share the sentiment: writing stops being fun when we have to do it. This is why drafting is such a lonely job. Before we can revise, reshape, rewrite, and retire, we have to put words on paper. Many students panic at this stage; they either slam material down on paper without much thought and refuse to change it ("It's there; it'll do") or avoid as long as possible the drafting of the paper ("It's not due until Friday and today's only Wednesday"). We can't really *force* students to draft, but we can provide them with some strategies and support while they do battle with language.

First, we can reduce the intimidation factor by introducing students to what Donald Murray and others call a "zero-draft." This essentially is an extended freewriting: students write down their ideas hastily, without stopping to edit or revise, putting in squiggles or stars in areas they want to fill out later, skipping the introduction and conclusion if those are trouble spots (for many inexperienced writers, they are). The goal is simply to get a couple of sheets of writing together, so that the writer can begin working; they're private, safe places to put down ideas. (One of my students calls these "hamburger" drafts "because you add the mustard and stuff later.") Sometimes students do better with zero drafts if they're not written on loose leaf paper; many like old sheets of computer printout if it's available. Some students will want to put each "chunk" of their papers on a separate sheet so that the chunks can be shuffled to determine the best possible order of ideas. Encourage students to experiment; techniques that seemed far-fetched often prove most successful.

Second, we can make sure students know what it *is* they're trying to draft. If students are writing reviews, make sure they know what reviews look like, what sorts of elements go into them and what kinds of structures could be used. If students have discussed the assignment together and have looked at a few sample papers, they'll understand better "what the teacher is looking for"; this gives them more concrete goals to aim at and may help them draft more effectively.

Third, we can try to discourage premature editing. Many students paralyze their drafting by trying to edit each word and sentence as it moves onto paper; then they complain "Oh, I can't remember what I was going to say next" because they've totally destroyed their trains of thought. Try to get such students to stick to freewriting rules in their zero drafts; if they hit a spot that isn't "right," suggest they put a star or check in the margin, circle the offending word or phrase, or just leave a blank, and go on recording their ideas first. Compulsive editors find this difficult and you'll have to encourage them, perhaps through the comments on papers, to try new ways to liberate their creativity.

Fourth, we can provide a supportive environment for drafting. Discuss with the class how drafting methods differ; I draft some things sitting at the computer with two cats sitting on the mantelpiece, the stereo on, and a cup of tea at hand. Other things—usually pieces of writing I'm not sure about—I draft in pencil, on yellow legal pads, alone, and in silence. What sorts of enviornments do they use to write in? What do they do when they hit a block? (The answers to this one will *really* surprise you.) Does anyone talk into a tape recorder? Talk to herself? Need a Springsteen album playing to be creative? Students feel better about drafting when they realize that everyone has difficulties some—if not all—of the time. They've been indoctrinated by the "blithely outline and briskly draft" propaganda that older texts promoted. When they realize that there's nothing wrong with them for producing texts in different manners, often the barricades begin to crumble.

Finally, we can provide practice in drafting. After all, in many situations students will have to draft quickly: on essay exams, during the LSAT, in the office. So short practice sessions, where students examine a drafting strategy and then apply it, or practice in the journal, will help students learn to "get on with it." In ideal classrooms described in theoretical tomes, students have all the time in the world to find material and incubate it. In the real world, the test may be over in twenty minutes; that letter may have to be in the 2:30 mail. The more student resistance to drafting is lowered, the more likely they are to meet their deadlines.

A common student misunderstanding is that they need only write *one* draft, which they tinker with a bit and submit as is to the teacher. This is a notion you'll have to dispel. Some parts of a text do remain the same from incubation to final submission; the more of these, the easier the writer's task. Of course, this requires that the writer produce suitable material the first time out; most of us just aren't that good unless we've practiced a great deal. Students may need two, three, or four drafts—even more—to arrive at language that meets their goals. This is fine: Hemingway rewrote the last, painfully beautiful page of *A Farewell to Arms* thirty-nine times "to get the words right." Most of us don't need that many drafts, but it's nice to know that we're not the only ones who struggle.

I try to encourage beginning writers to go through at least five drafts of a piece of writing: a zero draft; a shaping draft (where students work on structure, audience, and voice); a style draft (where they tinker with paragraphing, sentence structure, and word choice); an editing draft (where they work on mechanical and format problems); and the final draft they submit. Each draft encourages them to focus on particular kinds of revising, which enables them to revise more thoroughly. By late in the semester, many can combine the zero and shape drafts and the style and editing drafts but they still go through at least three distinct versions before they submit the paper (and draftwork) for a grade. For group workshops I ask them to bring at least a style draft; if time permits, I schedule shorter group sessions on editing drafts. (These requirements have several practical ramifications. The student has to start the paper well in advance of the due date, so I get fewer hasty papers; and it cuts down on instances of plagiarism, since I require and examine so many drafts.) Some students will proudly proclaim that they "draft in their heads"; unless you're an accomplished telepathist, you'll have to require their drafts on paper.

REVISING STRATEGIES

When writers move from the drafting to the revising stage of a piece of writing, they shift perspective radically. Heretofore they have been the creator, the parent, the controller of the words. Students who have difficulty producing texts in fact become protectors of their words; after all the effort spent in getting that language on paper, they're not about to omit or change the fruits of their labors. Thus, when we ask them to turn about, become members of their own audience, challenge, examine, and change the language they've produced, it's no surprise that they become defensive, confused, and recalcitrant. Revision seems to them an attack on their own best efforts, not an attempt to refine and improve their performances. In teaching revision, then, we have to stress the necessity of reseeing their work, of thinking as a member of the audience, of getting outside of their personal involvement with their compositions. I like to give students a piece of advice attributed to Oscar Wilde: "Criticize your own writing as if your worst enemy had written it." Students might not need to be this hostile—but Wilde's advice can be well taken.

Many students, in fact, misunderstand what revision is. They think of it as "fixing" or "correcting"; that is, finding what they've done "wrong" and remedying the problem before the teacher with his red pen comes along. Nancy Sommers has discovered that students often don't have the word "revision" in their writing vocabularies; it's a teacher's word. Students use terms such as scratch out and do over, review, redo, mark out, and slash and throw out (1980, p. 381). These indicate how limited a version of revision they understand.

So one of the first things to teach in revision is what the word means and what the process can involve. To use Sommers' definition, revision is "a sequence of changes in a composition—changes which are initiated by cues and occur continually throughout the writing of a work" (1980, p. 380). For students, Sommers argues, these changes are largely rewording, as if changing a word or two may guarantee success or failure on an assignment. But she also finds that experienced writers start from the other end; their key phrases include finding a framework, taking apart and putting back together, reworking, chiseling, and the like. They work with ideas, not just words, to ensure the success of their writings (pp. 383–384). This means revising starts with the large concerns in the draft: what is the writer trying to do? How well have her efforts succeeded? What kind of audience is she trying to reach? and so forth. The smaller concerns, such as word choice, punctuation, and spelling, come at the very tail end of revision. They shouldn't be the only revising activity that goes on. Sometimes it helps students to see revision in process; show them some of your own drafts, other student examples, even literary manuscripts. Seeing can be believing.

Revising Global Issues

Questions of purpose, audience, and structure can be productively addressed in large group workshops first. Show students a paper that is weak in one or more of these areas (you might want to "sabotage" a paper for demonstration purposes) and ask them "What do you think this writer wanted to do in this paper? Who do you think he imagined as his readers? How can you tell? Is he talking to a different audience than he imagined?" From there, you can ask more specific questions. "How, would you describe the shape of this paper? What do you think about the order of his ideas? How would you tinker with them? Could you arrange them in a better way? Should there be a different form here?" (If you'll notice, these follow the order in the Framework for Judging below, p. 84.) Help students focus on these larger issues; show them that this is where revising begins. Then they can break into smaller groups of 3–4 students and share drafts; in such a system, each student will get two or three sets of responses to these questions, outside perspectives on her work. She should feel free to ask questions of her readers: "Why don't you think I'm talking to you? Where did you get lost on page 2?" These sessions help writers see their own texts as other readers—if not their worst enemies—see them.

Sometimes structure can be a hard topic for students. If your department requires that students write in a number of modes or in several prescribed forms, students will generally struggle through; the mode or form is generally determined in the assignment, and like it or not, the student must wrestle with it. But what about open topics, or when students find that their apporach to a topic just won't "fit" into the assigned mode or form? Here you have several alternatives. For open topics, both prewriting and classical heuristics might come into play to help students decide what form their paper is going to take. They might also consider some "recipes" for paper structure such as Frank D'Angelo's "paradigms." He argues that most paper structures represent patterns of thought, and that students can learn to use these patterns to arrange ideas according to the intentions they have. D'Angelo's paradigms are too long to list here; you can find them in his *Conceptual Theory of Rhetoric* (1975) or conveniently summarized in Lindemann (1987), pp. 166–169.

One structure you may want to discuss with your students is that old war-horse, the five-paragraph theme. Many students learned this generic writing structure (introduction, three paragraphs of development, conclusion) in secondary school. For some limited topics it works; it's quite useful on essay exams and the LSAT and for short pieces of exposition. But students need to know that there are many other ways to organize pieces of writing, and that they needn't try to confine all of their ideas to five cramped boxes.

When students want to write something that doesn't fit into the prescribed structure, you have some tough decisions to make. When students really show interest in a piece of writing, I want to encourage, not discourage them. So I temporize. If they want to write in a mode we'll be covering later in the semester, I tell them to get their ideas down in a zero draft and save it for that later paper, suggesting that they develop the ideas in journal entries and freewritings in the meantime. Then we try to find another topic that fits the current assignment. If they want to write in a form that doesn't really fit in the class – for instance, a science-fiction spoof in an argument class or the analysis of a novel in an exposition class – I will agree to read and comment on it, but not count it for a grade. I remind the student that she has to show competencies in a number of areas the school has defined; those are the minimum. But since I'm glad she's making meaning in language, I'd enjoy the chance to read what else she's written. (This has on one occasion landed me with the 600-page handwritten draft of an experimental novel, but for the most part I've enjoyed my students' other production.) These situations don't arise often, but when they do, try to stay as flexible as you can.

Revising Paragraphs

The question of large structures inevitably leads to discussion of smaller ones, particularly paragraphs. Inductive teaching, letting students examine samples and learn some techniques from what they find, seems to work best here. For instance, take that old stalking horse, the topic sentence. Most of our students were taught, as we were, that "good" paragraphs have clear topic sentences supported by several sentences of development and ended with a firm recapitulation of the topic sentence. But only about half the paragraphs in published writing seem to work this way (the seminal article on the subject is Richard Braddock's "The Frequency and Placement of Topic Sentences in Expository Prose," *RTE,* 8 (1974), pp. 287–302; his numbers can be duplicated roughly in the prose of doctors, lawyers, biochemists, and literary critics, according to examinations my students have conducted over the years). Have students examine paragraphs from a number of sources—textbooks, novels, newspapers, magazines, instruction manuals, coffee table books, and so on. How many topic sentences do they find? When they start to wrestle with the "topic-less" paragraphs, how do they describe the structures they find? Do the paragraphs use statement and comment, question and answer, problem and solution, or other organizing principles? Can they paraphrase a topic sentence, even if one is not expressed? Here you can bring in the notion of the controlling idea: just about all good paragraphs have one of these (transitions may be an exception), even if it's not stated explicitly.

These discoveries about topic sentences can lead to new strategies for paragraphing. For instance, students might try to pinpoint the relationship between writer and audience when topic sentences are used; usually they are found in situations where the audience knows less than the writer (such as in textbooks or instruction manuals). How might that affect students' decisions about their paragraphs? And how long are good paragraphs? I once had a student who indented every seventh sentence; she explained it worked more often than it didn't (actually, she'd learned to cram her ideas into boxes of that size). Students are amazed to find one-sentence paragraphs or, if skimming periodicals like the *New Yorker,* paragraphs of a page and more. Students can decide when one-sentence paragraphs work (as transitions, when making snide or summary remarks, in narrow-columned newspapers, etc.) and when they don't (when they provide an opinion without support, when they're the introduction to a paper, etc.) Likewise, they can decide what the relationship between the writer and audience is that permits longer paragraphs (the writer trusts the audience's knowledge, interest, and/or intelligence) and can develop some intelligent rules of thumb for each piece of writing ("My readers won't have heard any of these terms before so I'm going to break things up into small chunks for them to handle"). Encourage paragraph dissection and recombination by students; let them experiment with several different structures and lengths of paragraphs to get the feel of each. Let them see, too, that while the paragraph may present a "complete idea" (whatever that may be), they may need several paragraphs on that same idea, from different perspectives, to treat it thoroughly in the paper. I encourage students to think of the body of their paper in "chunks" of discourse rather than in paragraphs; a chunk can contain one or many paragraphs, depending on the complexity of the idea discussed. This allows students to keep a sense of form without feeling constrained by a five or however many paragraph structure.

Simply knowing how a paragraph may be shaped, however, doesn't always help students know what to put in their paragraphs or how to arrange this material. Here some strategies developed from transformational-generative grammar may prove very useful. For example, Francis Christensen's "generative rhetoric of the paragraph" (1967) suggests that most paragraphs work through subordination and coordination. That is, they start with a general statement, then paraphrase, elaborate on, or modify it. Christensen describes the directions his paragraphs take as "levels of generality."

Sentences are numbered to show how specific the information they contain is; the most general information is level 1, and each subsequent level of specificity is given a higher number. Sentences that represent about the same level of generality (which are often rhetorically parallel or coordinate) have the same numbers. Here's a paragraph from Allan Bloom's bestseller *The Closing of the American Mind,* arranged to show Christensen's levels:

1. What Aristophanes satirizes is the exterior of science, how the scientist appears to the nonscientist.
    2. He can only hint at the dignity of what the scientist does.
        3. His Socrates is not individualized; he is not *the* Socrates we know.
        3. He is a member of the species philosopher, student of nature, particularly of astronomy.
            4. The first known member of this species was Thales.
                5. He was the first man to have seen the cause of, and to predict, an eclipse of the sun.
                    6. This means that he figured out that the heavens move in regular ways that accord with mathematical reasoning.
                    6. He was able to reason from visible effects to invisible causes and speculate about the intelligible order of nature as a whole.
                        7. He at that moment became aware that his mind was in accord with the principles of nature, that he was the microcosm. (p. 270)

Students can practice analyzing their own and other students' paragraphs to see what kinds of levels are reflected. Many students, for example, will only attempt one or two levels of generality in a paragraph; they don't probe their ideas in great detail. These students might be encouraged to revise by adding more examples, details, and specific explanations to make their paragraphs more three-dimensional. Likewise, students might tie the levels of generality to D'Angeleo's paradigms or other models of structure to create templates for paragraphs: A comparison-contrast paragraph arranges its levels so, or a narrative paragraph arranges its levels so. (Students must be warned to use such strategies as starting points and to vary them; otherwise the paragraphs will seem machine-produced and have very little appeal.) These strategies can lead to new paragraph-length hypotheses: a paragraph is long enough if it contains enough material and enough specifics for the particular readers. Encourage students to play with these and other structures to find out what paragraphs really can do.

Revising Sentences

Sentences, too, need attention in the revising process. Most students play it safe with their sentences; the shorter the better, they feel, because the possiblity for error is less. Many students have done little reading aloud, so they haven't learned to perceive sentence rhythms and the effects of variation on those rhythms. They're used to spoken sentences—often short, snappy, and incomplete ("Less filling! Tastes great!"). They may have had exposure to loose, periodic, and cumulative sentences in the lower grades, but most simply don't know what those labels mean, or how to employ those strategies.

The revising stage can offer students the opportunity to experiment with their sentences, to take risks without fear of punishment. In recent years, "sentence combining," a set of strategies enabling students to generate longer, more complex sentences, has been very popular with some teachers for this stage. However, as with prewriting, teachers and students can get carried away with sentence combining. Doing the exercises (mostly using someone's else prose) can be fun, and students seem to enjoy the activities; but they are no substitute for the students writing their own sentences and applying the techniques to their own sentences as part of a larger writing assignment.

Sentence combining arose from applications of transformational-generative grammar principles to classroom practices. Researchers such as Kellogg Hunt and Frank O'Hare determined that encouraging students to expand sentences by coordinating (adding on), deleting (eliminating repeated words), and embedding (inserting new information into a main clause) enabled them to write complex, fluent sentences without having to master elaborate grammatical terminology. The practice they recommended was giving students a base sentence and several other sentences of information to incorporate in the base sentence; then students experiment with various ways to combine the information.

In most sentence-combining instruction, students learn various kinds of combinations, starting with relatively simple coordination and subordination using conjunctions. Then they progress to removing repeated elements, embedding information as adjectives and phrases, culminating in "advanced" strategies such as adverbials and absolutes. They're provided with the information to combine (in most cases) so that they will focus on the structures they are trying to produce. After they control the structures, they are introduced to the punctuation conventions the new sentences require. Students are rewarded for taking risks, for trying new combinations, and are generally not "punished" for punctuation faults until they have mastered the patterns structurally. Of course, the problem here is that they are operating on someone else's prose, not their own. You can remedy this by asking them to imitate sentences using their own ideas, or to "decombine" or practice combining on sentences from their own papers. (Reading notebooks and journals provides a great deal of material for them to operate upon.)

Here's an example of the kind of exercise Hunt suggests:

Rock videos have drawn criticism.
The criticism has been recent.
The criticism says videos exploit women.
The criticism says videos promote violence.
The criticism says videos cause antisocial behavior.

The criticism comes from conservatives.
The criticism comes from parents.
The criticism comes from religious leaders.
The criticism comes from some musicians.

Students using coordination might initially produce versions such as:

Rock videos have drawn criticism recently. Conservatives, parents, religious leaders, and some musicians say videos exploit women, promote violence, and cause antisocial behavior.

Later, using subordination, deletion, and other strategies, they may progress even further to sentences such as:

Recently, parents, conservatives, religious leaders, and even some musicians have criticized rock videos for exploiting women, promoting violence, and causing antisocial behavior.

To demonstrate how students can improve after just a little practice with sentence combining, here are two samples from a student's work. She is working with the "aluminum test," one of Hunt's sample passages to challenge sentence combining ability. The first sample was completed about three weeks into the semester, before we had begun working on sentences. The second sample was completed two weeks later, after we had spent about 30 minutes in each of four classes practicing together.

Directions: Read this passage all the way through. You will notice that the sentences are short and choppy. Study the passage, and then rewrite it in a better way. You may combine sentences, change the order of words, and omit words that are repeated too many times. But try not to leave out any of the information.

Aluminum is a metal. It is abundant. It has many uses. It comes from bauxite. Bauxite is an ore. Bauxite looks like clay. Bauxite contains aluminum. It contains several other substances. Workmen extract these other substances from the bauxite. They put it in tanks. Pressure is in the tanks. The other substances form a mass. They remove the mass. They use filters. A liquid remains. They put it through several other processes. It finally yields a chemical. The chemical is powdery. It is white. The chemical is alumina. It is a mixture. It contains aluminum. It contains oxygen. Workmen separate the aluminum from the oxygen. They use electricity. They finally produce a metal. The metal is light. It has a luster. The luster is bright. The luster is silvery. This metal comes in many forms.

Before
Aluminum is an abundant metal with many uses. Aluminum is manufactured from a clay-like ore called bauxite. Bauxite contains several other substances besides aluminum and workmen must extract these substances. To do this they put the bauxite in pressurized tanks and wait for the other substances to form a mass. When the mass is formed it is removed with the aid of filters. What remains is a liquid. They put the liquid through several other processes until it finally yields a white, powdery chemical called alumina. Alumina is a mixture which contains aluminum and oxygen. Workmen then use electricity to separate the aluminum from the oxygen. This separation finally produces a light, bright, silvery metal. The metal is one with great luster and it comes in many forms.

After
Aluminum is an abundant metal with many uses, manufactured from a claylike ore, bauxite, which contains several other substances besides the aluminum which must be extracted. To do this workmen place the bauxite in pressurized tanks and wait for the other substances to form a mass which is removed with the aid of filters, leaving a liquid that is put through several other processes until it finally yields a white, powdery chemical called alumina containing aluminum and oxygen. Workmen then use electricity to separate the two elements, finally producing a light, bright, silvery metal with great luster coming in many forms.

There are many texts that include sentence combining exercises; some are devoted entirely to the technique. If you're interested in learning more about it, you might wish to consult *Sentence Combining and the Teaching of Writing*, an anthology compiled by Donald Daiker, Andrew Kerek, and Max Morenberg; Steven Witte's review of this book (*CCC*, 31 (1980), pp. 433–437) makes some wise suggestions about how the method might be used more productively in classes. Francis Christensen has also applied similar principles to develop a "generative rhetoric of the sentence" (much like generative rhetoric of the paragraph); it's described in *CCC*, 14 (1963), pp. 155–161, an article that is frequently reprinted.

Students can incorporate sentence strategies in a number of ways. One of the best is to have them read passages aloud to groups; if the sentences sound choppy or get too tangled up to be followed, the group can suggest ways the writer might revise them. Students can be encouraged to pick two or three paragraphs in a draft and try to combine sentences in them; gradually this can be expanded to pages and to the whole draft. Group readings can also help uncomplicate overcombined sentences and to find faulty connections ("You said 'because' here but you're talking about a contradiction. Wouldn't 'But' be better?"or "About every fifth word when you read that sounded like 'and'. Did I hear you right?") Students need to be reminded that sentence work is a *revising*, not a *drafting* activity; they shouldn't start tinkering with sentences until after they have the zero draft completed. With practice, sentences may start coming out in combined form; but it's not "wrong" to draft in choppy or imcomplete sentences and refine them later.

Revising Words

Finally, in revision students need to consider words. Most of our students have fairly limited academic vocabularies; they've read little and have received little encouragement to expand their linguistic resources. But they actually know a great deal about words; one of your chief jobs is teaching them how to tap that knowledge productively. For instance, though students may not be familiar with the terms "connotation" and "denotation," thay can tell you the difference between "fat," "plump," "overweight," "obese," and "lardball." You might give them a number of terms (usually neutral) and ask them to provide varieties of ways to express those terms (usually positive and negative) as a way of introducing connotations and denotation. They may have been introduced to the thesaurus but have few ideas how to use it; you can teach them to cross-check in the dictionary by "gussying up" plain statements with synonyms from the thesaurus, or let them try the process themselves (in such experiments, "Twinkle, twinkle, little star," becomes "Scintillate, scintillate, asteroidal nimific" and "Happy birthday to you" becomes "Permit me to express my best wishes for the felicitous celebration of your natal anniversay").

Such exercises inevitably raise questions of purpose and audience: when and why would a writer want to use these strategies? What happens when "tax increase" becomes "revenue enhancement"? What effects do different connotations or phrasings have on different readers? Students may wish to examine advertisements, published examples (the school bulletin is usually full of excellent examples), junk mail, and other kinds of written products to develop their sensitivity to language manipulation. (For instance, what are "light" potatao chips? What is "diet" lasagne?) Where you can, use good student examples to show students that they can manipulate language just like the professionals. Dictionary work can also be included in these definitions: who puts those usage labels on words? Does the student's dictionary tell her when to use "nauseous" and when to use "nauseated," for instance? (I won't go into the question of dictionary authority here, but students may ask you about it—especially if they note that members of a dictionary's usage board have been dead for many years. I usually tell students that these experts were consulted by Ouija board.)

Another problem students sometimes face with language comes from the many varieties of American English. Some students will know what "homebody" or "bumbershoot" or "woodpussy" will mean; the Southern student's "branch," however, is the Northeastern student's "creek." To get a hoagie in a Denver delicatessan, a Philadelphia student has to ask for a sub; in other parts of the country this sandwich is called a submarine, a grinder, and a poorboy (though afficianados will claim each has a distinct identiy). Some students have been made to feel somewhat ashamed of their home languages; they feel there's something "wrong" with them because their language doesn't match that of some anchorperson or soap opera star or teacher. Of course, nothing could be further from the truth; all of our students need to know this, just as they need to know how to call on the particular varieties of language required in special discourse situations.

Exercises to strengthen the students' fluency in both kinds of discourse can be helpful. For instance, students may wish to compile a dictionary of student slang, then analyze their findings as evidence of social or political attitudes. They might collect dialect examples (some excellent suggestions are given in Roger Shuy's *Discovering American Dialects* (1967) if you want model surveys). Their results could be incorporated into family or community histories or analyses of how certain ethnic groups influenced the American language. "Code switching," the ability to shift into different varieties of English at different times for different purposes, is a considerable linguistic achievement. Students can experiment with inserting bits of nonacademic language in academic papers, or vice-versa, and speculate on the effect of these on the audience (for instance, how would an audience react to an argument against cutting aid to dependent children that concluded "The reasons for cutting aid to these children stink—like a day-old diaper"?).

Students who have serious dialect interference problems, however, might need some private or outside help to identify the areas where their home language is in conflict with academic language. Such situations are best handled in private conferences, where you and the student can work one-on-one in developing new hypotheses. If you have such students in your classes, check whether your school offers extra help for these students; they may need it.

All of these discussions about language can be conducted without much reference to elaborate grammatical terminlogy. Once the students have mastered the ideas, you might wish to introduce them to some of the terminology ("The name for these good and bad rephrasings of a word is 'connotation'; that's what you look under in the index of your book"). It's far more important, however, that students learn to use their own language, to develop their own repertoires, than that they master a cluster of latinate labels. Likewise, they should be working with their own words, not filling out exercises in a book or running through someone else's drills. Remember: we learn to write by writing. If they want to learn to use language effectively, they have to be creating language.

In revising words, students can apply the techniques used for sentence revision. Reading passages aloud and discussing the word choices with other students seem to have best effect ("It sounds weird when you say you could have barfed when he said that;" or "I like calling those people 'parasitic' in the second paragraph"). Students might begin experiments with connotation a few paragraphs at a time, expanding gradually to the whole paper as they grow more confident. Encourage them to ransack their freewritings, journals, and reading notebooks for words or phrases that might give their meanings new force. They may overuse the thesaurus at first; teach them how to cross-reference the synonyms in the dictionary to make sure the one they've chosen is appropriate. Botching a few word choices shouldn't make or break a paper; but finding good ones, as Mark Twain wrote, is like knowing "the difference between a lightning bug and the lightning."

EDITING AND PRESENTATION

It's a sad fact that most writing instruction gets focused on etiquette: the editing and presentation of ideas. Sometimes teachers concentrate on these areas to the exclusion of finding, developing, and organizing ideas entirely. The result can be described by a line from *My Fair Lady:* "[They] don't care what you do, actually, as long as you pronounce it properly." Of course, editing and presentation are important; they have a lot to do with the reader's reaction to a piece of writing. But their place is last; they involve the applications of a set of closed competencies that nearly all students can master with time. Learning to edit is no substitute for learning to write.

Grammar and Punctuation

The most frequently-raised editing concern is grammar; in fact, some people mean "learning standard grammar" when they say "learning to write." The two are not the same. "Grammar" can have a number of meanings; Patrick Hartwell identified five in his article "Grammar, Grammars, and the Teaching of Grammar" (1985). In most writing courses, grammar means "school grammar," the rules for punctuation, spelling, and syntax. These can be presented in a number of ways.

The most common way of presenting grammar for many years was to have students memorize rules and do exercises in workbooks. Somehow, the theory went, students would internalize these drills and their grammar, as manifested in the papers they wrote, would improve. But years of studies (summarized neatly by Hartwell) have failed to prove that this is the case, and experience, as the Wife of Bath could have told us, reinforces our awareness of this. We've all known the students who were letter-perfect on the drills in the text, yet couldn't prevent comma splices or dangling modifiers in their own writing. Students apparently learn better by having their writing diagnosed, keeping an error log, and learning to predict the situations where errors may occur so that they can check them carefully. Usually they do this best working one-on-one with the teacher or in small groups; there are few instances where the teacher has to lecture on grammar to the whole group.

Teachers may want to help students by providing some inductive exercises. If a number of students seem to be having problems with placing the comma in compound sentences joined by a subordinator, the instructor might duplicate a number of these and ask students to determine where the commas go. Then the teacher can provide another list of samples, some punctuated incorrectly, and ask the class to decide which need correction. (I make these lists up by taking sentences from student papers; I'll sabotage some and correct others if needed, to get sufficient examples. If you keep a ditto master in your typewriter or grade papers near your computer keyboard, you can make these exercises up as you grade—another time-saver.) Finally, the students can examine their error logs and current drafts to see if they've applied the rule properly. Induction—figuring the rule out, practicing it, and applying it—seems to offer students a better chance of learning to correct their most common errors. (Such exercises also work for common problems such as faulty agreement, verb complications, and homonym detection. They're very versatile.) Each student can develop his personal "editing checklist" (often confirmed in conference with you) to identify his particular grammar demons. Not only does such a technique help students in the writing class, but often they carry it over into other courses.

Grammatical and punctuation problems, too, can be a sign of growth; often the etiquette falls by the wayside as students try new sentence patterns and rhythms. Since most students don't make these mistakes deliberately (although some make them carelessly), teachers shouldn't penalize them too severely—at least not the first time they occur. Some teachers in the past would give a student a failing grade if a paper contained more than a certain number of misspelled words or grammatical errors. This is certainly counterproductive; it tells the student that presentation, not content or skill, is what the teacher values. In fact, Maxine Hairston's research (incorporated in *The Scott, Foresman Handbook for Writers*) suggests that readers can dismiss some mistakes quite easily; only a few are regarded as serious offenses. While you want your students to observe the etiquette of academic discourse, it needn't be your first priority.

Spelling

Spelling is another problem that gets some people very agitated. In fact, spelling is another closed skill that students learn with differing degrees of mastery; much has to do with the kinds and amount of instruction they received as young children and much with the amount of reading they've done. Students can learn to conquer spelling demons in the same way they master grammatical problems: learning to recognize the words and spelling situations that give them problems and developing strategies to correct them. Many students, for instance, spell "by ear"; they try to record how the word sounds. Unfortunately, the many pronunciation changes in English language history have left sound as an unreliable guide to spelling. Students who have this problem may be able to diagnose the sound or sounds they habitually misspell: the unstressed vowel /ə/ and the consonant cluster /ĵ/ are prime culprits here. Sometimes they overgeneralize a rule, doubling a consonant or changing a vowel where such is not required. The teacher can help the student use error logs to find such situations and to work out revising strategies (such as reading aloud and checking the spelling of all words with suspect sounds) that will help the student overcome the problems.

Other students may not have learned (or have learned imperfectly) some basic spelling rules, such as those for vowel clusters. Often a short review of the rule by the teacher, and some practice on the student's own writing, are enough to help the student conquer the problem. Many students today rely on spelling-checker computer programs. These are fine as far as they go, but since the student can't always take the computer along, it's far better for the student to master the rules and use the spellchecker as a timesaver.

Almost everyone has a few words she misspells consistently. I show students a history paper I wrote as a college sophomore, in which I misspelled the word *privilege* twenty-four times in four pages. (I spelled it the same way the TA had on the assignment sheet, but that still didn't make it right.) That's a word I still look up, along with *judgment*. These have become part of my personal editing strategies; I know I have to check. Students may have similar spelling problems (such as *arguement* for *argument* or *develope* for *develop*); there's nothing wrong with adding these words to their personal editing checklists.

Format and Presentation

Format, the physical layout of a student's paper, can provide unusual problems for students. Not all will have access to typewriters, for example; those who do may not know much about using the typewriter. And when computers are introduced into the picture, the possibilities for foul-ups become immeasurable.

It's important that students understand what format you require for each assignment. Many schools will have a format guide or policy sheet that spells out the constraints on paper presentation. If your department doesn't have such a guide, you can usually find one in a class text. Basically, students should be required to produce legible, double-spaced texts (skipping lines if handwritten), in dark ink on one side of a page. For some, this means investing a few dollars in a new typewriter ribbon for their family's 1957 Smith Corona; you're well within your rights to ask them to do so. Others may be using school-provided computing equipment; depending on the quality of maintenance, the printout may be easily readable or palimpsest (some students may have to photocopy their printouts to get readable print). Remind students that if you can't read their work, you can't give them a grade; they, not you, will suffer for it.

Students often don't know what an essay or review or memorandum or research paper should look like. When you review samples, then, it pays to spend a few minutes noting particular features of the layout ("The footnote number is a little above the line;" "Notice that paragraphs in business letters don't get indented"). If students are using computers, you can suggest they ask the computer attendants how to set up "macros" or "style sheets" that will automatically format their papers, putting page numbers, footnotes, and the like in the proper places. (Some computer centers maintain such style aids on a master disk and will allow students to copy them directly onto their own disks.)

Students also show a tendency to waste money in the purchase of fancy folders in which to present their papers. These are not only unnecessary but are frequently unwieldy. A staple that holds all the pages together is usually sufficient. If your students will be submitting notes and drafts, you might want them to make a one-time investment in a closable folder or padded mailing envelope, in which they can submit their papers and all the preparation materials. This helps them organize their work and, just as importantly, may prevent sheets from getting lost while they're scattered about your desk.

Proofreading

Proofreading is one the simplest closed competencies in writing, but one that few students have learned. When they reread their papers (usually just before class) they see what they *intended* to put on the page, not what's actually there. As a result, static from surface errors can end up detracting from good work. So students generally appreciate some tips for proofreading. Here are a few that work well.

1. *Give it time.* Once you've finished typing or copying your final draft, set it aside for a few hours (overnight is ideal) and go do something else. Let your short-term memory empty out. When you come back to the paper, you'll be more likely to see what is there than what you wanted to put there.
2. *Proofread in several directions.* First start from the last word and read the paper backward to check for misspellings and typos. *Then* read the paper from first word to last to check for omitted words and punctuation problems. Hold a blank sheet over the paper so that you can only see one word at a time. This will keep your eyes from jumping ahead. Go slowly; skimming won't work. Refer to your error log to remind yourself of the special problems you're working on.
3. *Correct carefully, using one line to cross out mistakes and printing in changes carefully in black ink* (or matching ink, if the paper is handwritten). If you use correction fluid, make sure you're using the right kind. The alcohol in typewriter correction fluid dissolves most pen and felt-tip ink. There's correction fluid made especially for ink; use it instead. In a crisis, typewriter correction fluid can be thinned with nail-polish remover; ink correction fluid can be thinned with water. Brush the fluid on lightly and let it dry; you can add a second coat if needed.
4. *Consider using a backup proofreader if proofreading is a real problem for you and if your teacher permits.* You're still responsible for finding and correcting your own problems, but if using a computer program or another set of eyes helps you catch more problems, you'll benefit in the long run. (Make sure you add problems your outside proofreaders find to your error log so that you can begin to handle those problems yourself.)
5. *The more tired you are, the more mistakes you'll make.* In such cases, it's particularly imperative you proofread carefully; you may have accidentally left out sentences or even whole paragraphs. You might want to keep your draft handy as you proofread the final copy to make sure this isn't the case.

CHAPTER 10
EVALUATING FINISHED PRODUCTS

At some time, of couse, all the work that you and students put in has to be judged — and in the final analysis, you'll be the one who has to make the judgments and assign the grade. This is one of the hardest parts of your job as a writing teacher, but it's also one of the most essential. And you needn't do it alone; there are ways to have students do a good deal of the preliminary work for you and to set standards that enable you and students to agree upon grades. Essentially, the grading task has three parts: identifying strengths and weaknesses, suggesting remedies and new goals, and conducting the whole process quickly. Let's look at each of these elements in turn.

IDENTIFYING STRENGTHS AND COPING WITH ERROR

Most students will give you an honest effort. They will use the strategies they know to complete an assignment well and — let's be frank — to win your approval in the form of a high grade. But the efforts notwithstanding, students will have differing degrees of success with an assignment. And your reactions will have to differ accordingly.

Any writing effort will have strengths, even if they are few and sometimes hard to find. It's essential to identify these; not only do they show what goals have been attained, but also help the students see which competencies they can apply to different situations. Even if the strength you praise is a very mundane one ("Gerri, your format here looks very professional"), the positive encouragement may encourage the student: you liked *something* about her work. And, of course, the strengths often outweigh the weaknesses; then the problem is deciding what to praise. But what about the weaknesses? These, of course, are what most of us first see when we read a student paper. Nothing more encourages us to play deconstructive critic than a paper with ambiguities, gaps,

73

and faultily-observed conventions. And it *is* our job to alert our students to these problems so that their writing can improve. But the method of identifying such weaknesses need not be *destructive*, even if our technique is essentially deconstructive.

As trained readers of literature, of course, one of our touchstones is intentionality: we assume that features of a text are there on purpose and proceed to critique the text on that assumption. The late Mina Shaughnessy in her book *Errors and Expectations* did all of us a great service by reminding us that the intentionality of student texts is quite different than that of literary works. In a literary work the writer is in control; he or she adheres to or violates conventions based on deliberate decisions. Joyce and Faulkner and Walker violate many standards of "good English" just as Dickens and Hemingway and Woolf observe them; in each case we assume that the writer did so for a reason. But when students violate the etiquette of syntax or spelling or punctuation, Shaughnessy reminds us, we assume that they did so with the same kind of artistic control experienced writers wield. And this is not the case. Students rarely if ever make deliberate errors; they are trying to succeed. Often, however, they attempt syntactic structures or make linguistic choices over which they have imperfect control. They approximate control of discourse structures, narrow competencies, that they have not yet mastered fully. And so we must regard their errors and weaknesses not as intentions to fail; rather we must determine at what they were trying to succeed. We must not just identify and criticize their errors; we must analyze them and try to help students fulfill their true intentions.

David Bartholmae, applying some of Shaughnessy's observations to basic writers, argues that such error analysis can be a valuable diagnostic technique for instructors. "By . . . investigating and interpreting the patterns of error in [students'] writing, we can help them begin to see those errors as evidence of hypotheses or strategies they have formed and, as a consequence, put them in a position to change, experiment, imagine other strategies. Studying their own writing puts students in a position to see themselves as language users, rather than as victims of a language that uses them" (1980, p. 258.) If we are to teach in this manner, we have to suspend, a little, our natural tendencies to prejudge, to circle in red every error we can find. Instead, we have to look for patterns in the weaknesses a student shows. Is the student truly a "lousy speller," or does he consistently misspell the sound /ə/? Can the student truly not support an assertion, or does she think that quoting some authority by itself constitutes support? Is the student "illiterate," or is some other variety of English—Appalachian, Black English, Pennsylvania Dutch, whatever—intruding into his grapholect? Often you can begin to solve these problems in conference; ask the student about her hypothesis, then help her see how academic conventions require her to alter or refine it. Sometimes it's a matter of helping students appreciate fine distinctions in language: main clauses introduced by subordinate conjunctions are fragments; those introduced by conjunctive adverbs are not. Many times, in fact, errors and weaknesses are signs of growth. Often student papers submitted after sentence-combining practice are plagued with comma splices, as students struggle to master new syntactic patterns. Here the students are demonstrating the courage to try new techniques; penalizing them for failing on the first try to master the punctuation etiquette required will defeat your attempts to help them grow. Sometimes, of course, there will be true errors: a word transposed or omitted in copying, the fingers one key off on the keyboard, an embarrassing or amusing typo (such as "Shakespeare's play of love and punishment, *Romeo and Joliet*"). These represent failures of editing skills, language performance rather than language competence, and can be treated as such.

RESPONDING TO STUDENT WRITING

Once you've identified a particular text's strengths and weaknesses, you must convey this information to the student writer. Often this can be a touchy process; students may sometimes confuse criticism of their texts with personal criticism. So it's important to maintain an objective, supportive tone in your comments; the occasional snide remark or mild joke is likely to come back to haunt you in unexpected ways, as well as harm the rapport you've tried to build with the student. Instead, start by identifying what the student did well and can carry forward to subsequent papers. This encourages students to look back at the text, to reexamine it in terms of their own development. This can be done in your marginal remarks ("Your analysis of Sagan's statistics here convinces a reader that you know what *you're* talking about better than he does") or in your end comment ("Your careful examination of King's religious language gives your paper a great deal of credibility. In your subsequent papers you can use this sensitivity to language to support your own assertions"). Every writer likes to know she's succeeded; tell your students what competencies they show.

But of course, you're going to have to identify those weaknesses and errors as well. There are many ways you can do this; unfortunately, many intimidate students. If you circle or mark every mistake, and write long marginal screeds, the paper can sink in a sea of red (or green or whatever) ink; this gives the student the message "You'll never learn to write 'good English'." Or you can blur the margins with a number of cryptic symbols referring to sections of a handbook or to obscure proofreading rituals; this tells students "Only English teachers can learn all these rules." Or you can deliberately undermark, perhaps by putting checks in the margins of lines that contain errors, as Richard H. Haswell suggests (see his article below, p. 165). This puts the responsibility of finding and correcting errors on the student, and the teacher can judge the success of the student's efforts by reviewing the paper in conference. Probably the best method of identifying weaknesses is to mark only major concerns in detail and use minimal marking for questions of punctuation, grammar, spelling, and other mechanical etiuqette.

How would this work? Often in such a system, the marginal comments that identify weaknesses are questions or statements that lead students to examine the text more carefully ("Can you give a more precise description of the Lamborghini than 'nice' and 'neat'? What's your evidence for this point? Does your reader know what 'appreciated amortization' is?") Or they can describe your reaction as a reader ("I can't see the connection between these two ideas. Did you leave a step out?") Occasionally you may want to refer the student to a particular reference source ("Your footnotes should be in MLA form; see ch. 22 of the handbook"). Checks in the margin can direct student attention to mechanical weaknesses. Such individual problems should be summed up as part of your end comment: "Often you provide a quote to support your assertions, but you rarely analyze the quotes to show how they fit into your argument. Where you do this, as on p. 3, it really strengthens your argument. Where you leave it out your argument is less persuasive—you make your readers infer the connections you see." "A lot of your checkmarks have to do with where commas go in complex sentences. Look at chapter 16 as you correct these problems."

Of course, you have to pick the issues you address in your end comment carefully. Two, or at most three, weaknesses are enough for a student to focus on for the next paper. Try to address the largest issues first; if the writer can't address an audience or formulate a thesis, spelling and colon placement are trivial problems. And often, as in the cases discussed above, the weaknesses are signs of growth. Even if the student has not yet learned to analyze evidence, he's learned to provide it; even if the student continues to make comma splices, she's learning to write more complex sentences. Your comments can be phrased to reflect these tentative steps of growth: "I'm glad you tried some of the sentence-combining we practiced. Now that you've learned the patterns, take a close look at where the punctuation goes so that you can use those elaborate sentences to their best effect." "You've picked really sharp quotations to back up your points. Next time push your skills one step further; follow up each of those quotes with a sentence or two of comment to help your audience see how they fit into your argument."

Finally, your response needs to help the writer set and reach new goals. These will usually involve conquering competencies that were mastered incompletely in the current text or moving on to apply those competencies in new contexts. Here is where the critical teaching in comments takes place: you want the student to move to a new level of achievement. The goals should be clearly expressed ("Now that you've mastered simple and compound sentences, it's time to move to complex ones"; "It's clear you can persuade an audience that basically agrees with you. Next time why don't you aim to persuade a mildly hostile audience?") And they should suggest clear strategies for achieving those goals ("Try brainstroming and using the journalist's questions to generate more details about your subject. Then you can have the luxury of picking and choosing which ones you want to use"; "Write down all the arguments objecting to your position you can think of, and try to find reasonable answers to those objections."). You may even find it necessary to offer a small reward to encourage timorous students to take risks ("Try to write some different kinds of sentence patterns; I won't 'mark off' if you don't quite master the punctuation next time.") Your response can also encourage students to reconsider their writing processes ("The drafts of this paper show you just changed a few words; you didn't revise much. Next time I want to see messy drafts—move paragraphs around, change sentences, scratch out! Don't settle for the first thing you can think of!").

In sum, your end comment should encourage the student not only to go back into this paper, but to move forward to the next. If you keep the tripartite structure—praise strengths, identify weaknesses, set goals—in mind, you'll find it relatively easy to write a coherent, goal-oriented end comment. Encourage students to discuss those comments with you before they submit their next paper; often a word or two of reinforcement or clarification can lead to quantum leaps in writing performance.

COPING WITH THE PAPER LOAD

At this point, you may well be objecting "How am I supposed to do all these things—running groups, intervening in processes, holding conferences, analyzing errors, writing long comments—and remain sane?" Good question—and probably the most vexing one writing teachers face. There's no way of avoiding it: grading papers takes time, lots of it, time that you'd far rather spend reading or working on your own scholarship or having a personal life or just enjoying fresh air and natural light. The best way to speed up the grading process, then, is to reduce the amount of grading you have to do. Several techniques will help you achieve this goal.

First, you can reduce the number of assignments you actually put letter grades on by allowing students to select, say, five of nine papers completed in the semester to submit as a portfolio for the class. The problems with this strategy involve quantity *and* quality; rather than mark twenty-five papers nine times a semester, you'll have to mark one-hundred twenty-five at one time. If you teach multiple sections, the problem can be magnified. You may wish to lessen the burden by marking two papers at midsemester and the others at the end of term or by otherwise adjusting the due dates to meet your own—and the class—needs. Likewise, you'll still need to provide students with feedback on the individual papers, so they know what points to work on and which papers to revise as their "best".

Another possibility is to work individually with students on the development of papers. You could "evaluate" some papers in one-to-one conferences, assigning verbal grades of "excellent," "very good," "fair," and the like. Since these grades will likely be high, reflecting your evaluation of the project at many stages, you might then assign letter grades only to papers students produce independently, alternating conference and independent papers. This strategy reduces by half the number of written comments you must produce; its drawback is the amount of time such conference teaching requires.

A different kind of workload reduction can be achieved by letting your students do some of the work for you. When students work effectively in small and large groups, they can identify writing problems at the draft stage and help their fellow students remedy weaknesses. Group proofreading sessions likewise can find and solve many mechancial problems before they reach your desk. If you train the groups to look for the kinds of problems students are having, they can do a great deal of the diagnostic work for each other. You'll occasionally have to correct a faulty diagnosis, but will generally save time in this manner. If all students have access to computer facilities, you can encourage them to use spellchecker programs and perhaps a few of the stylistic diagnostic programs as well. (Unfortunately, few of the latter are of real practical use for collegiate discourse.) Students with cognitive problems can be referred to various kinds of campus assistance (about which see below, p. 97).

Another way in which students can help you with grading is to encourage them to set the standard for achievement in the class. You can use a model such as the framework for judging (discussed below, p. 84) or your school's description of letter grades, if it provides once. Or, early in the semester, you can have students develop sets of criteria that characterize average, above average, below average, and excellent writing; then hold them to these in assigning grades. Duplicate the criteria and distribute them to the class members; use them to develop goals in assignments, to develop groupwork heuristics, and to support your comments. Below is the set of goals developed by one of my freshman writing classes two weeks into the course; they are challenging, even more so because the students developed them with only a few hints and leading questions from me. The wording is theirs.

The members of English 101:L4 agree that these are our standards for writing in this class:

Average Writing (C to C+) has
    a sense of organization (transitions, thesis, etc.)
    adequate word choice and grammar
    average style—not great but not really rough
    some repetition
    some sketchy or missing development
    some boring sentence structure
    sometimes a weak intro or conclusion
    a "vanilla" writer writing for a "vanilla" audience

Above Average Writing (B to B+) has
    the strengths of average writing and more clarity
    a structure that really works but doesn't stick out
    good research, support, background, or details as needed
    a sense that the writer knows what he's doing and is addressing real people

few mechanical problems
sharp, almost professional appearance
proofreading
a good intro and conclusion

Below Average Writing (D) has
all of the weaknesses of avearage writing and roughness
cliches or other thoughtless word use
little sense of purpose or organization or support
little sense of who's the writer or the readers
problems with style, mechanics, and/or proofreading
the characteristics of a rush job—sloppiness, skimpiness, and
disorganization

Excellent Writing (A) has
the strengths of above-average writing and flow
a real sense of the writer's competence
a real sense of the writer's purpose
something memorable
really careful language use and style
a positive impact on the audience
a "professional" feel to it

Unsuccessful Writing (F) has
many problems, such as
the below-average problems, only worse
failure to meet the assignment
plagiarism
excessive lateness
a sense that the writer was unwilling or unable or unorganized or all
of these things

I ask each of my writing classes to develop a list like this (this is an exceptionally good one); then, with each paper, I ask them to include a note describing which of the standards they feel they've met and which they are having trouble meeting. Then I can address my comments to those points. Students frequently underestimate their performance at first, but as the semester progresses, many predict their grades quite accurately.

In the end, of course, you have to grade some papers. For the beginning teacher this can be a time-consuming and excruciating process; novices frequently spend an hour or more on each paper. If you have a heavy course load or large enrollment; the task can seem impossible. In time, you'll learn to move more quickly, but still will need to spend at least 15–20 minutes on a 500–700 word paper. What follows are some practical tips to help you speed the grading process.

1. *Start with carefully designed assignments and give the students enough time to complete the assignment successfully.* The clearer the assignment, the fewer variables left for you to cope with; the more adequate the time, the fewer hasty or careless errors you (should) have to contend with.

2. *Be realistic when telling students when they'll get papers back.* Many authorities insist that teachers return papers at the first class meeting after the assignments are submitted. Sometimes, if the papers are short enough and the classes small enough, and the instructor's life uncomplicated enough, this is possible. Certainly it's ideal. But life is what happens while you make ideal plans. Two class meetings—or a week—is more realistic. The students need at lease one class meeting to review your comments and suggestions on one paper before submitting their next effort—and more time is helpful if they need a conference to discuss those comments with you. Schedule papers far enough apart to let you grade them carefully; and don't make promises you can't keep.

3. *Not all papers must be new assignments.* Often students may profit from revising and reshaping an earlier paper, either one of their own choosing or one that you suggest they revise. Such assignments teach students the crucial importance of revising while giving you time to hold conferences, attend to individual problems, and design subsequent assignments.

4. *Set a schedule for your grading and keep it.* If you must grade 50 papers in 5 days, that's ten a day. At a half-hour per paper (a good beginner's rate), that's six hours of grading a day (you'll need a break or two to maintain your concentration). Resign yourself to setting the VCR, sending out for pizza, and becoming a hermit for that time. If the papers come in before a weekend, you'll have more time for your grading; it is possible to do 50 papers in two days, though your sanity at the end will be in serious jeopardy.

5. *Set reasonable time limits.* Buy a timer and be ruthless about paying attention to it. Allow yourself a maximum time per paper—25 or 30 minutes for an average (500–700 word) paper for a beginner, 15–20 minutes as you get more experienced. Read the paper through once in its entirety before you mark *anything,* even minor mechanical errors. This allows you to assess the biggest strengths and weaknesses, to target your attention. Reread the paper, making your minimal marks and marginal comments. Then skim it one more time and compose your endnote. (Sometimes the endnotes written by beginning teachers are a page or longer; you'll learn to control this with experience.) Again, the three-part formula—strengths, a few weaknesses, goals/strategies—can help you compose a response quickly. Often you'll find yourself calling on stock phrases to compose your endnotes; students rarely compare comments, so you needn't worry too much if every third endnote contains a sentence or two such as "Kelli, one of the strongest things about this paper are the quotes you use to support your

opinions;" or "The quotes you've chosen, Jim, really offer strong support for your assertions." As long as the comments are appropriate for the student's paper, you needn't concern yourself unnecessarily with the originality of the sentiment. After all, students are shooting for similar goals; naturally, some will have similar successes and weaknesses.

If you have clear grading standards, put a letter grade on the paper after you've written your endnote; if not, sort it into roughly-defined piles: the good ones, the okay ones, the problem ones, and go back to assign a grade later. If your time runs out, finish your note immediately and move on. If the paper is a real disaster, set it aside; you'll want time to write a thoughtful note later. If you finish early, take a quick stretch and move on; you'll want that time later. Don't turn the endnote into a justification or apology for a low grade; use it as a chance to teach the student ways to improve. If you feel that assigning a very low grade would be detrimental to the student's progress, you can always mark it "No grade pending conference," discuss the paper with the student, and grade it after the student has revised it further. This is a solution that works best when used sparingly and privately; otherwise you'll have B+ students clamoring for a chance to rewrite papers to get an A.

6. *Keep good records.* Don't just put the grade on the paper; record it in your gradebook or progress folder immediately. If you're keeping a progress chart like the one shown above (p. 43) for conferences, make a few sketchy notes now; you can go back and elaborate later if necessary. If you forget to record grades now you'll eventually find yourself in the position of returning a set of papers without recording the grades; then you have to go through all sorts of conniptions to get the papers back to record the grades. Such a time-consuming annoyance can be avoided by keeping records carefully from the beginning.

Evaluating individual written products is a matter of seeing how well students have reached imtermediate goals in the course. It can't be done on the bell curve; writing progress is too individual a process for that. While you'll want to apply the same standards to all students, you'll probably have to allow some leeway in measuring achievement. Students who master narrow competencies (such as mechanics or syntactic variety) quickly should receive credit for these successes, but should probably be judged more on how they master more open matters—audience manipulation, voice, development, and so on. Students who have a great deal of difficulty mastering the narrow competencies—those who come from particularly weak backgrounds or who have dialect interference problems, for example—may have excellent ideas but difficulty in presenting them. They should be rewarded for the content of their papers but encouraged to master the conventions of academic discourse as well. Make it clear to students that you're not evaluating how well they compete *against* other students but how much progress they're making in achieving the goals set for all students.

You'll also have to guard against biased reactions to certain students. Too often we find ourselves saying "Oh, here' Renée's paper; it'll be another good one;" or "Oh dear, let's see what kind of disaster Dana's committed this time;" or "Chris has been such a know-it-all in class lately; I'll show him he still has things to learn." It's human to make these prejudgments, but to teach effectively you have to set them aside as you mark the actual paper and consider its strengths and weaknesses as objectively as you can. (This is another reason why making evaluation criteria part of the assignment can help you; it assures each paper a fair reading.) Likewise, you may be tempted to reward a student's effort on a paper rather than the product he actually produces ("This just doesn't hold together but he worked so hard; look at all these drafts!"); such sympathy may be human, but it's not going to help the student. Giving good grades for effort rather than for results provides students with a false assessment of their achievements. It's dishonest. Better to withhold a grade pending a conference and revision in such cases than to artificially inflate such student's expectations.

Of course there are other kinds of evaluations that need to be made in writing courses. The next section will discuss those in more detail.

CHAPTER 11
EVALUATING THE WRITING COURSE

A writing course is made up of three elements—the student writers, the instructor, and the course of instruction. The performance of each of these has to be assessed to determine the course's effectiveness. Tradtionally such evaluations are carried out only at the end of the course; the drawback to such a tradition is that nothing can be done to remedy any weaknesses of the course for those students and that instructor in that particular situation. So the description of evaluation below will vary a bit from the tradition to describe some kinds of evaluation that can take place while the class is in progress.

EVALUATING STUDENT PERFORMANCE

Beyond writing comments on individual student papers, there are several other productive ways of keeping the student informed about her progress and helping her improve her writing throughout the semester. One is the error log. This technique asks students to keep a log of all the checkmarks on graded papers, sorting them out into categories such as spelling, punctuation, syntax, format, and content problems. The student records each checkmark in the appropriate category, along with a correction. Then periodically (most easily in conferences) the instructor reviews the log with the student and helps him see the patterns his errors take. For instance, there may be confusion about the spelling of words containing the sound /ĵ/; are they spelled -dge or -ge? As the student perceives the pattern of errors, the instructor can help her develop a private editing checklist that focuses her attention on the situations that lead to those errors. A frequent comma-splicer, for instance, might learn to examine commas before clauses beginning with "however" if this has been the occasion for error in the past. By keeping error logs, students learn to diagnose and rememdy their most common writing problems, techniques that will be very useful when they leave the writing class and have no teacher to point out the weak spots.

Heuristics are another technique that students can use to evaluate their own writing and alter their writing processes. These may be impressionistic lists of goals to achieve, such as the class standards for grading described above, or they may be more rigidly structured lists such as Robert Bain's "Framework for Judging" (1974). This list, which Bain has since modified in courses at the University of North Carolina at Chapel Hill to incorporate nonsexist language and external concerns, begins with global writing concerns of purpose, structure, and audience and moves to smaller concerns such as support, language, choice, and mechanics, ending finally at concerns outside the actual writing process. Students can use this to judge progress on a particular draft; moreover, if certain points (such as audience address or sentence structure) are habitual weak spots, the teacher and student working together can identify strategies to remedy individual weaknesses. Thus a student who often has problems with developing support may be encouraged to try several extra types of prewriting as he gathers material for a paper; a student who has trouble with paragraph development may ask all the paragraph questions for each chunk of her paper. Here is Bain's modified framework.

A Framework for Judging†

1. A writer promises to do something. What does the writer of this paper promise to do? Can we state that promise in our own words. Does the writer keep that promise? If not, where and why does the writer fail to do so?

2. Is there a perceivable order to the presentation of the writer's feelings and ideas? Can we follow and describe that order? Does that order of presentation show how the writer has felt and thought about the subject? If we cannot follow the order of the presentation, where does the writer lose us and why? Can we suggest better strategies than those the writer has chosen? If so, how and why?

3. What seems to be the writer's attitude toward the audience—playful, sarcastic, condescending, serious? What does the writer's attitude toward the audience say about the relationship between that writer and the audience?

4. Has the writer omitted any important details or arguments that would contribute to our understanding of the writer's understanding and feel-

---

†CCC, 25 (1974): 307–309

ings? Has the writer included details or arguments not connected with the feelings and ideas under discussion? Where could the writer add to the paper and where subtract? How could the writer clarify these feelings and ideas?

5. Is the writer's attitude toward these feelings and ideas convincing? Is the writer filling space or writing about feelings and ideas which matter? How can we tell?

6. Is the language of the paper appropriate to the author's voice and subject? If the writer uses big words, is it done to show off or to help the reader better understand? Is the language fairly free of cliches, jargon, and worn-out words and phrases? If the writer bends or breaks the conventions of language (making up new words or running them together), are there reasons for doing so?

7. Does each paragraph signal clearly to the reader the direction in which the writer's ideas and feelings are moving? Does each paragraph develop and complete the idea it introduces? If we lose our way in a paragraph, where and why do we get lost?

8. Are the rhythms and patterns of sentences appropriate to the writer's subject and voice? If the sentences seem to be "Dick and Jane" sentences, how could the writer combine sentences to break up this pattern? If the sentences are so long the reader gets lost in them, where could the writer break them into shorter units? Does the writer use the passive voice excessively? If so, is that usage justified?

9. Has the writer observed the conventions of grammar, punctuation, spelling, and capitalization? If not, is there a good reason why the writer has not done so?

10. Does the writer's paper demonstrate the skills asked for by the assignment? That is, if the assignment calls for an argument, is there an argument in the paper?

11. Have any external circumstances such as late submission, nonstandard form, plagiarism, or the like, influenced the reader's reaction to the paper? If so, can the writer overcome that influence?

As mentioned above, students can evaluate their own progress through brief notes attached to the papers they submit. Students need only answer two or three questions, perhaps writing on the back of the paper itself or on a separate sheet: "What do you [the student] think has worked well in this paper? What in this paper gave you trouble? Are there goals or competencies you don't think you've achieved yet?" Students will usually answer those questions frankly, and you can see their responses to guide your evaluation of the text and to compose your endnote.

EVALUATING THE INSTRUCTOR'S PERFORMANCE

While we all like to think we're perfect—or nearly so—the sad truth is that many of us have areas of our teaching performance that could be shored up. It's hard to have the humility of Chaucer's Clerk, "Gladly wolde he lerne, and gladly teche"; yet that attitude is essential to teachning success. To do our best job in the classroom, we have to evaluate our strengths and weaknesses as honestly as we do those of our students. Thank heavens we don't have to do this alone; we have students and colleagues to help.

Student evaluations tell us one thing and one thing only: what the students *perceive* about our course. They're not experts in curriculum design or in the subject matter, but they are professional takers of courses. And their comments on evaluations tell us how we, and our courses, come across to them. If students think you tell too many bad jokes, or give out too many handouts, or really care about them, they'll say so when offered the chance. Listen to what they have to tell you, and ask for their honest response. Among my standard questions are "How can I make this course better? Which of your needs should I address more directly?" Sometimes I don't get a consensus in the answers, but I nearly always get thoughtful responses, to which I do pay attention.

Evaluations conducted by colleagues are another feature of most writing programs. This is done on a more-or-less formal basis, depending on the school. Some ask the teacher being observed to submit a lesson plan to the observer in advance, have the observer record what goes on in the classroom, and arrange for observer and observed to meet and discuss the results. Other programs have a colleague drop in on a class and write an informal letter to the chair or director summarizing what went on. Such evaluations may or may not be used in hiring, reappointment, and promotion decisions.

You may also ask for informal peer observation if there are factors in your classroom performance that you'd like to improve or just would like to have assessed objectively. Here you can invite a friend or officemate to sit in on a class, record what goes on (what you say and do, what the students say and do, and when), and discuss it with you. These informal observations are often good practice if you're due for a formal observation shortly; there's nothing like a dry run to sharpen things up. If your school offers videotaping services, you might like to have your performance videotaped. Once you get over the embarrassment of watching yourself on tape, you can usually find some habits to correct or methods to work on. (I was horrified, when I was first taped, to see how much I fiddled with my rings. I've about conquered that problem, but from my last taping I've discovered that I now fiddle with, and mutilate, paper clips instead, and that my students watch me do it. Another habit to kick.)

Although opinion varies, I think it's best to inform students in advance when you'll be observed and why. This reassures them that *they're* not being judged and often wins you some extra cooperation. Most will come to class on observation day ready and willing to talk; you may have trouble controlling discussion, instead of eliciting it! Even the quiet or distracting students usually contribute on observation days; somehow, students presume that how you perform depends on *them.* In these sessions, you may come as close to being a united writing community as you ever will be.

Self-evaluation is the hardest part of evaluating your performance. It's hard to put all the comments, criticism, praise, and suggestions in perspective, especially when these remarks are in conflict. Half the class may love workshops; the other half may loathe them. Half may want to write more in class, while the other half wants to discuss essays. How do you strike a balance? A reasonable solution is to look at the trends the comments suggest, compare them to your colleague's evaluations if available, and act on those suggestions that seem most reasonable to you. If you're perplexed, talk to an experienced teacher or your director and get some perspective. Evaluations, after all, don't really show what you do *badly*; they show you what you can do well and what you can do better.

Alas, not all evaluations are used in these ways. Many institutions, as noted, use them for hiring and promotion decisions. That's why you should always look at your student and colleague evaluations. If your department keeps them on file, add a short written response to them. You may wish to note special circumstances (the course was held from 8:00 to 9:30 p.m. in a small, unair-conditioned room, and the students rightly rebelled; evaluations were distributed on a religious holiday when 25 percent of the students were absent) and, more concretely, your reaction to any criticisms or suggestions. These show that you take your teaching performance seriously and that you can deal constructively with criticism. You might want to indicate actions you're not going to take, as well ("Students claimed I graded too harshly; however, as 75 percent made a B or higher, I'm not worried that I am habitually underrating their performances."). It's not a bad idea, too, to draw attention to the strengths students note, in a low-key way, if your evaluations will be read. If students think workshops and conferences help them, point this out; only this may counterbalance a colleague's expressed surprise at your "failure" to lecture.

ASSESSING COURSE EFFECTIVENESS

There are many ways you can assess the strengths and weaknesses of the course you teach; if you're prudent, you'll do this while the course is in progress, so that you can adjust the syllabus or your teaching methods to meet student needs and help them reach their goals. You may, for example, wish to begin the course with some kind of attitude survey or poll that examines students' attitudes toward writing and language to how these attitudes change (I often reap platitudes out of the "pop grammarians" books, such as "A good sentence never ends in a preposition" or "Never use 'I' in serious writing" or "All successful paragraphs have a clear topic sentence" and see how strongly my students agree or disagree). These reactions provide fruit for class discussion and often suggest some provocative writing prompts.

A short, anonymous, in-class evaluation can be conducted quickly during the semester to keep tabs on the class' perception of its progress. (A model for such an evaluation is below.) In a quarter-length course, this might be used once; in a semester-length course, it might be used twice. Anonymity encourages students to answer honestly. You should discuss the results with the class to assure them that their suggestions are valuable and tell them what changes (if any) you'll make in response to their comments.

Midterm Evaluation

Answer each question by circling the letters that best describe your position on each question. Feel free to use the back of this sheet to make other comments. DON'T put your name on this survey. DY = definite yes; Y = yes; NC = not certain; N = no; DN = definite no

1. I'm doing at least 80 percent of the reading.   DY   Y   NC   N   DN

2. I want to discuss the texts in more detail.   DY   Y   NC   N   DN

3. I have a clearer notion of what good writing involves.   DY   Y   NC   N   DN

4. Assignments and classwork have helped my writing to improve.   DY   Y   NC   N   DN

5. I find conferences helpful.   DY   Y   NC   N   DN

6. I find the writing groups helpful.   DY   Y   NC   N   DN

7. The comments on my papers are clear and helpful.   DY   Y   NC   N   DN

8. I feel free to ask questions, comment, and disagree.   DY   Y   NC   N   DN

9. I know what's expected of me on
   assignments.   DY Y NC N DN

10. I understand the goals I'm trying to
    reach.   DY Y NC N DN

11. I can cope with the workload.   DY Y NC N DN

12. I'm getting my money's worth from
    this course.   DY Y NC N DN

What techniques, competencies, and class techniques would you like to spend more time on? What would you like to do less of? How can I make this course better for you?

End-of-course evaluations have increased markedly in sophistication in recent years. The December 1982 issue of *College Composition and Communication* presented some of the most important aspects of the new research in evaluation, as well as some important caveats for how that information should be used. One of the most useful articles in that issue is one by Stephen Witte, John Daly, Lester Faigley, and William Koch. In it they describe an 80-item long evaluation and a 21-item short evaluation that have been tested and refined in writing courses nationwide. (A version of the short form is presented below.) But as important as these evaluations are, more important are the warnings that accompany them. The results can't just be calculated as raw scores; they must be calculated with standard deviations and assessed against a statistically vaild sample in order to have meaning. They shouldn't be used in isolation to determine a teacher's hiring, promotion, or salary; rather, they should be viewed as reflecting *student perception* of the teaching performance and judged accordingly. And, of course, they should be conducted anonymously to ensure honest response without fear of repercussion. Like all other evaluations, you should prepare a written response to what this evaluation tells you and others about your teaching performance.

Short Form Evaluation

Please follow your instructor's directions carefully as you fill out the identification section of the answer sheet. When you instructor tells you to begin, mark your responses to each item in the numbered spaces below. Use pencil and answer all of the questions, making sure that you record the answer to each question in the space that matches the number of the question. Items 22 to 26 are reserved for questions your instructor may wish to ask; these questions will be written on the board. Use the following code for recording your response:

1 = Strongly agree
2 = Agree
3 = Undecided
4 = Disagree
5 = Strongly disagree

A member of the class will collect your responses and turn them in to the departmental office. Your responses will in no way affect your grade, and your instructor will not see them until final grades are turned in.

1. My instructor in this course is a very good one.
2. My instructor in this course is one of the most helpful instructors I have ever had.
3. My instructor is intellectually stimulating.
4. My work in this course is evaluated fairly.
5. The instructor does a good job of teaching students how to write different kinds of papers.
6. The instructor is good about teaching students how to argue a thesis or position.
7. The instructor puts too much emphasis on "correct" grammar in student writing.
8. The instructor clearly connects what he or she teaches in class with the writing assignments he or she makes.
9. The instructor is good about teaching me how to evaluate my own papers so that I can better revise them.
10. The instructor is good about teaching me to consider the needs of my audience when I am thinking about a writing topic.
11. The instructor is good about using class time to help me as I am writing my papers.
12. The instructor spends too much time on some things and not enough time on other things.
13. In evaluating my writing, the instructor uses standards that are too high.
14. The instructor's comments on my papers are easy to understand.
15. The instructor is good about teaching me how to support main ideas in my papers through examples and specific details.
16. The instructor is good about encouraging me to join in class discussions.
17. The instructor does a good job of using examples of writing in teaching students how to write.

18. The instructor is good about trying to increase my confidence about writing.
19. What this course teaches is very useful to the student right now.
20. What I am learning in this course is valuable.
21. What this course teaches will be useful to its students in the future.
22. (Items 22 through 26)
23. are reserved for
24. additional questions
25. your instructor may have
26. for you.)

CHAPTER 12
SURVIVING AS A WRITING TEACHER

Teaching writing is a complicated process, and it has its own complex problems both within and outside your classroom. This section covers, although not in great depth, some of the most common problems you may face. Each campus may have its own ways of handling these; don't forget to consult your department's policy manual for its recommendations.

SPECIAL CONCERNS

Copyright

The most common need of writing teachers is a way to duplicate material: exercises, sample papers, student drafts, and outside readings. Whether it be by photocopying machine, duplicator, mimeograph, or printing station, we generate multiple copies of multiple pieces of writing for the educational benefit of our students. But we can't approach this naively; many of these sources are protected either explicitly or implicitly by copyright, a legal right that must be respected. Most libraries and professional copying centers have their own policies about making copies available within the copyright law and are usually quite willing to help you stay within the law; never hesitate to ask.

The "Fair Use" section of the copyright law says that libraries may put on reserve a single copy of the following at a faculty member's request: a chapter, an article, a short story, a graph, a chart, a picture, a short poem, an essay, or a book owned by the library. (Workbooks cannot be handled in this manner.) The faculty member may arrange to provide up to four more copies of those reserve materials, under the following circumstances:

—the number of copies is reasonable with regard to the total enrollment in the course, to a maximum of four copies;
—the library stamps the materials with a notice of copyright;
—the amount of material is "reasonable" in relation to the total amount of material required for the course ("reasonable" varies according to the nature of the course and subject matter and the level of the students taking it);
—the market (saleability) of the work is not harmed by making it available in photocopies (i.e., the author's royalties are not affected); and
—the instructor decides to use the material "spontaneously," so that there is not enough time to receive an answer from the publisher to a request to duplicate the material.

In practice, this means you *can* make a small number of published sources available to the students through your library without violating copyright. If they choose to photocopy one copy of the material for their own use at the library, they are also abiding by the law. However, if you want students to buy or otherwise obtain a large number of articles (usually handled through a commercial photocopying service), you must "clear copyright" for those sources. This is done by writing to the copyright owner (usually the publisher), describing how you want to use the material, and asking for permission. This is usually granted, although sometimes you will have to pay a small royalty (again, often collected and forwarded by the photocopying service). A sample letter for permission follows. Note that you must specify what you want to use, how much of it, how you will distribute it, when you want to use it, and what kind of use you will make of it (stress "educational purposes").

Permissions Department
Scott, Foresman and Company
1900 East Lake Avenue
Glenview, IL 60025

Dear Sir or Madam:

I would like permission to copy the following material for continued use in my English Composition classes in future terms:

Text: Elizabeth Cowan Neeld, *Writing*, 2nd edition, copyright 1986
Material to be copied: pages 43–48 ("Classical Invention")
Type of Reprint: Photocopy
Use: Supplementary teaching material for students' educational use
Distribution: 5 copies will be placed on reserve in the campus library;
    a typed summary will be distributed to students.

I have enclosed a self-addressed enveloped for your convenience in replying to this request. If I do not hear from you by two months from the date of this letter, I will assume that I have your permission.

Sincerely,

J.K. Tarvers
Assistant Professor

Although there have been rather fewer legal challenges, it's clear that student papers are also covered to some extent by copyright. Papers produced by students in your current class do not need copyright clearance; the exchange of student materials is an accepted pedagogical method. However, if you want to keep a copy of a student's paper to use in subsequent terms (or someday, perhaps, in an article or book,) it's best to obtain a simple copyright release from the student. Most students are flattered to be asked and grant the permission willingly; but they have the right to refuse and should feel free to do so if they wish. Here's a sample of a student paper release:

Student Name _____

Course Number, Name, and Semester _____

Description of Material to Be Used:

I would like to keep a copy of the work described above to use in subsequent terms and possibly in scholarly publication. If you are willing to let me use your work, please answer the questions below to tell me how you'd like it used. (Circle Yes or No).

1. Change the real names in the material   Yes   No
2. Correct minor errors before the material is used.   Yes   No
3. Give my [student's] name as the author.   Yes   No

Your signature

Your permanent (home) address

(Please print or write legibly)

Today's date

Thank you for your help!
J. K. Tarvers

Plagiarism

Instances of plagiarism, unfortunately, seem to be on the increase as students compete for higher grades and a better chance of success in the world (as they see it). Four kinds of student are likely to commit plagiarism: the lazy student, the desperate student, the grade-hungry student, and the ignorant student. Each must be handled differently. The lazy student sees a borrowed or purchased paper as a way of getting the grade without doing the work; you'll see this paper most often as the literary criticism paper or the research paper. The best remedy is prevention: require drafts, hold workshops and conferences, and have students submit their preliminary materials along with the finished paper. Be suspicious when students produce polished papers without the supporting materials. Few lazy students are willing to forge several sets of drafts for a paper, after all!

The desperate student is usually swamped by time, outside activities, personal circumstances, or a combination of the three. She may find it hard to submit a paper because two others are due that day, while she's working 25 hours a week to pay tuition. These students often turn to friends, school paper files, or outside vendors. Prevent these situations by giving students adequate time to complete assignments, setting mini-deadlines (such as draft workshops) to help them manage their time, and encouraging honesty. Tell students who are swamped to talk to you before the due date; obviously you can't mark all 25 papers the night they're submitted, so you can allow a student a little leeway taking in papers. Then encourage the student to uncomplicate his life a bit; burnout is not a good future!

The grade-hungry student sees grades as the only value in education. He's convinced that one B− will keep him from medical school or a lucrative career in investment banking or a scholarship. Encourage this student to be realistic; after all, if she plagiarizes and is caught, she'll receive a much lower grade (at some schools, an F for the course as well) than if she'd written the paper herself. All students can benefit from a de-emphasis of grades and a refocusing on goals, but some students won't be able to get those red letters out of their heads. Again, requiring drafts and keeping a close eye on student progress is the best remedy for such a problem.

Finally there's the student who really doesn't understand what plagiarism is and is usually horrified at such an accusation. Typically such students learned to "do research papers" in high school in a system that encouraged them to copy passages from books and encylodpedias and rewarded them for presenting as much copied material as possible. Footnoting, paraphrase, the use of quotation marks, and attribution of sources may never have been raised as issues. To remedy such problems, *teach* documentation; explain why a writer uses quotes (and when), why readers like to find attribution for sources, and how to write a correct footnote and bibliographic entry. Teach true paraphrasing (recasting both vocabulary and syntax) and summary as alternatives to quotation, again emphasizing the need for footnotes and attribution. Take time to explain where the quotation marks — double and single — go. This teaching can be handled inductively; use samples that allow students to infer how source material can be handled, then practice on examples to get the mechanics down. Check rough drafts for the handling of documentation and help students correct their errors. Most students are not only willing but quite able to handle sources correctly, and the recent simplifications of MLA documentation will help them be more accurate.

The best remedy against plagiarism, when all this is said and done, is still you; you know your students, how they write, and what they're writing about. If you see something which looks unfamiliar, ask your student about it (you may not want to actually use the word "plagiarism" unless you've found the source) in conference. (Some teachers like to have their officemates present at such a conference as an unobtrusive note-taker and witness.) A simple misunderstanding can be cleared up fairly easily. More serious cases will have be handled according to your school's established policy.

Outside help

In this age of consulting services, students can often find a number of outside aids to help them prepare their papers. These can range from formal tutoring services to "edit and type" agencies to the two-cent's worth of a student's roommate. You have to decide what you'll allow as outside help, based on the goals of your course. If students are expected to learn to edit and correct their own writing, you'll have to decide what kinds of editing help they can use: a tutor, a spellchecker, a typist. If they are supposed to learn to present their own work, will you accept papers copied by Mom, daughter, boyfriend, or paid professional? Make your decisions in advance and make them clear to students. Then abide by them.

Some students may have access to tutoring—through an athletic team, foreign students' office, minority services program, sorority development program, or whatever. If your students are getting tutoring, set limits on what kinds of help the tutor should be giving your student. For instance, tutors might help students with a number of paragraph development exercises, but shouldn't tell the student *how* to develop the second paragraph on p. 3 of his draft. You might suggest particular areas the tutor could focus on to help the student achieve her goals and ask for progress reports or mutual conferences so that you can coordinate your assistance. Some schools ask students, tutors, and teachers to write out a sort of contract that covers the responsibilities of all three. Remember that not all students can get access to a tutor, so be sure your evaluation is not biased in favor of (or against) such students.

CAMPUS SUPPORT

Most schools provide extracurricular support services for you and your students. It's worth a few moments of your time thumbing through the campus phone directory or school bulletin to find out about these, so that you can refer your students to them if needed. Your department may provide you with orientation materials that help you locate these resources; if not, your dean's or student affairs offices may be able to direct you. Among these services may be:

Counseling—These services may run from full psychological support (often offered through the infirmary) to advice for confused students to seminars on time-management and stress relief. At most schools, these services are free to students.

Tutoring—Some students, by virtue of membership in a campus "special interest group," may have access to free or inexpensive tutoring. Often such services are offered for minority, foreign, nontraditional (sometimes called "adult" or "returning students"), and handicapped students, as well as for athletes. Some other campus groups, such as Greek organizations, future teachers, and student government associations, may also provide outside help. If you refer a student to such a tutor, make sure you establish, clearly the kinds of help the student may accept on graded assignments.

Skill Centers—Many schools offer professional help in writing, reading, computer use, study skills, and cognitive development. The key is to find out what these centers are called and what services they offer. Writing centers or labs are usually administered through English departments; computer skills through the school's computer center; research paper skills through the library's reference department. Other skills—notetaking, reading comprehension and cognitive development, for instance—could be housed in a number of departments. If you can't find them immediately, see if your school has an academic services, student services, educational skills, or like-titled office. Sometimes the counseling center may house these services; at some schools, they are under the aegis of the school of education. (Of course, some schools don't offer them at all.) Don't be afraid to call the dean's office and ask if your school can provide any of these services to students.

THE PROFESSIONAL ENVIRONMENT

The biggest problem, unfortunately, that many writing teachers face comes not from the course or from the students. Rather, it comes from the institution in the form of nonrecognition of a teacher's professional status. Since some institutions still regard composition as a "service course," they feel justified in hiring part-time teachers but denying them faculty status (even library cards), benefits, and rights (such as offices, access to duplicating facilities, and even written contracts). Some members of literature faculties (and some whole departments) look down on, and snub outright, those who teach about creating written products instead of analyzing products already written. (Jay Robinson's article, included below, sums up these positions cogently.) Alas, there are many teachers who must endure such situations. They are unpleasant, but some teachers have no alternatives. And the economics of education don't seem to offer much hope for change.

In 1987, the Conference on College Composition and Communication (CCCC), the professional organization of college writing teachers, adopted the so-called "Wyoming Conference Resolution," which calls for establishment of grievance procedures for writing teachers and encourages better professional treatment of writing teachers by institutions. In the long run, this may have some effect; in the short term, things are not likely to get better quickly. Try, if you can, to act as a professional, even if your institution does not. Join the various professional organizations such as CCCC and NCTE; go to professional meetings; present your work. Do the best teaching you can. If your institution continues to mistreat you, take your valuable skills somewhere else, even outside of academe. *Illegitimum non carborundum* has long been the watchword of composition teachers; make it yours, too.

PART III
RESOURCES FOR WRITING TEACHERS

As the field of composition and rhetoric studies has expanded, so have the resources available for the writing teacher to consult. Below you'll find a sampling of what's out there for you to learn about. First come four essential position statements for writing teachers, detailing what many of us believe about home languages, what "English" as a field is, what writing teachers do, and what institutions should do to support their writing teachers. We hope these will be helpful not only as you develop your own course, but also as you try to strengthen the writing program at your school.

Next come nine articles on various aspects of teaching writing. With the exception of two, they are not otherwise anthologized. They were chosen to reflect some of the most up-to-date thinking on the topics this book discusses, to provide you with excellent follow-up bibliographies, and to give you a sense of the many perspectives and approaches that distinguish our profession. Emphasis was given to articles by experienced, current classroom teachers who are also scholars, since these most often represented a useful balance between theory and practice.

The following section lists a small, annotated scholar's bookshelf of basic works on the teaching of writing; a few articles have also slipped in. A relatively small investment could put them all in your library; and the list can be duplicated and handed to any friend, relative, or other generous soul who asks you what you want for Christmas, Hannukah, your birthday, or any other occasion for giving.

Finally, a bibliography lists the works cited in this text with a few additional titles bearing on its discussions. Books from the basic reference library are not included.

Students' Right to Their Own Language (excerpt)

Executive Committee of the Conference on College Composition
and Communication resolution, 1972

We affirm the students' right to their own patterns and varieties of language—the
dialects of their nurture or whatever dialects in which they find their own identity and
style. Language scholars long ago denied that the myth of a standard American dialect
has any validity. The claim that any one dialect is unacceptable amounts to an attempt
of one social group to exert its dominance over another. Such a claim leads to false
advice for speakers and writers, and immoral advice for humans. A nation proud of its
diverse heritage and its cultural and racial variety will preserve its heritage of dialects.
We affirm strongly that teachers must have the experiences and training that will enable
them to respect diversity and uphold the right of students to their own language.

Essentials of English:
A Document for Reflection and Dialogue

The following statement on the Essentials of English was prepared by the Commission on the English Curriculum and approved by the Executive Committee of the NCTE in October 1982. John C. Maxwell, Executive Director of NCTE, wrote of the new statement when he sent it to the editors of NCTE journals and to others:

The Executive Committee is indebted to the Commission on the English Curriculum (Elizabeth Cowan, Director) for its early work in defining the Essentials of English and to Jeff Golub of that Commission, who worked with President-Elect William Irmscher in arriving at a further draft. In all, there were four drafts of the statement, each one of them gone over painstakingly by staff, members of the Executive Committee, commission leaders, and others.

The statement is an elaboration of the spirit and intent of the "Essentials of Education," published several years ago. It seeks to contest the trend toward basics and minimums and to keep alive among the public and the profession the idea that an appropriate program in English language arts needs focus, balance, and purpose.

On the other hand, limitations of space in a pamphlet suitable for wide dissemination prevents complete description on that scope, and individual readers may not find all of their viewpoints reflected in the statement. Still, I think you'll find that it succeeds in its basic purpose. As a document for the public and all who are concerned about education, it will be more than helpful in stating what English is for those who have forgotten or need to be reminded. For the profession itself, it will affirm the importance of our mission.

In 1979, the National Council of Teachers of English joined a coalition of other professional associations to reaffirm the value of a balanced education by endorsing a statement entitled "The Essentials of Education." As one of the organizations committed to promoting academic excellence for all learners, we as teachers of English now submit our own statement identifying the ways in which the study of English contributes to the knowledge, understanding, and skills of those who will make up the society of the future.

ESSENTIALS OF ENGLISH

The study of English includes knowledge of the language itself, development of its use as a basic means of communication, and appreciation of its artistry as expressed in literature. Teachers of English trace the origins of the language in the past, study its development in the present, and recognize that continuing change in the future will keep the language and the literature alive, flexible and adaptable to the highest expression of which the human being is capable.

The use of English involves skills in reading, writing, speaking, listening and observing. The development of these skills is a lifelong process. The extent to which they are developed can influence an individual's ability to become self-sufficient and lead a productive life.

LANGUAGE

Language is a subject worthy of study in itself, but language in use always exists in a setting involving people and situations. Language is a primary way individuals communicate what they think and feel. They find self-identity through language, shape their knowledge and experience by means of it, and depend upon it as a lifelong resource for expressing their hopes and feelings.

Children acquire language at an early stage and internalize much of its grammar through use before formal training in school begins. Continuing attention to language makes students aware how language functions and helps them control and use it in increasingly effective ways. Language is therefore basic to learning in all disciplines. Skillful use of language may be the single most important means of realizing the overarching goal of education to develop informed, thinking citizens.

By studying language, students should

- learn how the English language has developed, continues to change, and survives because it is adaptable to new times
- understand that varieties of English usage are shaped by social, cultural, and geographical differences
- recognize that language is a powerful tool for thinking and learning
- become aware how grammar represents the orderliness of language and makes meaningful communication possible
- recognize how context—topic, purpose, audience—influences the structure and use of language
- understand how language can act as a unifying force among the citizens of a nation

LITERATURE

Literature is the verbal expression of the human imagination and one of the primary means by which a culture transmits itself. The reading and study of literature add a special dimension to students' lives by broadening their insights, allowing them to experience vicariously places, people, and events otherwise unavailable to them, and adding delight and wonder to their daily lives.

Through their study and enjoyment of literature, students should

- realize the importance of literature as a mirror of human experience, reflecting human motives, conflicts, and values
- be able to identify with fictional characters in human situations as a means of relating to others; gain insights from involvement with literature
- become aware of important writers representing diverse backgrounds and traditions in literature
- become familiar with masterpieces of literature, both past and present
- develop effective ways of talking and writing about varied forms of literature
- experience literature as a way to appreciate the rhythms and beauty of the language
- develop habits of reading that carry over into adult life

COMMUNICATION SKILLS

Communication is language in action, by which individuals participate in the affairs of society through reading, writing, speaking, listening, and using electronic media. The study of English develops fundamental communication skills that prepare students to engage in fluent and responsible communication and to analyze information that comes to them.

Reading

Students should

- recognize that reading functions in their lives as a pleasurable activity as well as a means of acquiring knowledge
- learn from the very beginning to approach reading as a search for meaning
- develop the necessary reading skills to comprehend material appearing in a variety of forms
- learn to read accurately and make valid inferences
- learn to judge literature critically on the basis of personal response and literary quality

Writing

Students should

- learn to write clearly and honestly
- recognize that writing is a way to learn and develop personally as well as a way to communicate with others

- learn ways to generate ideas for writing, to select and arrange them, to find appropriate modes for expressing them, and to evaluate and revise what they have written
- learn to adapt expression to various audiences
- learn the techniques of writing for appealing to others and persuading them
- develop their talents for creative and imaginative expression
- recognize that precision in punctuation, capitalization, spelling, and other elements of manuscript form is a part of the total effectiveness of writing

Speaking

Students should learn

- to speak clearly and expressively about their ideas and concerns
- to adapt words and strategies according to varying situations and audiences, from one-to-one conversations to formal, large-group settings
- to participate productively and harmoniously in both small and large groups
- to present arguments in orderly and convincing ways
- to interpret and assess various kinds of communication, including intonation, pause, gesture, and body language that accompany speaking

Listening

Students should
- learn that listening with understanding depends on determining a speaker's purpose
- learn to attend to detail and relate it to the overall purpose of the communication
- learn to evaluate the messages and effects of mass communication

Using Media

Students should

- become aware of the impact of technology on communication and recognize that electronic modes such as recording, film, television, videotape, and computers require special skills to understand their way to presenting information and experience
- realize that new modes of communication demand a new kind of literacy

THINKING SKILLS

Because thinking and language are closely linked, teachers of English have always held that one of their main duties is to teach students *how* to think. Thinking skills, involved in the study of all disciplines, are inherent in the reading, writing, speaking, listen ing, and observing involved in the study of English. The ability to analyze, classify, compare, formulate hypotheses, make inferences, and draw conclusions is essential to the reasoning processes of all adults. The capacity to solve problems, both rationally and intuitively, is a way to help students cope successfully with the experience of learning within the school setting and outside. These skills may be grouped in three major categories.

Creative Thinking

Students should learn

- that originality derives from the uniqueness of the individual's perception, not necessarily from an innate talent
- that inventiveness involves seeing new relationships
- that creative thinking derives from their ability not only to look, but to see; not only to hear, but to listen; not only to imitate, but to innovate; not only to observe, but to experience the excitement of fresh perception

Logical Thinking

Students should learn

- to create hypotheses and predict outcomes
- to test the validity of an assertion by examining the evidence
- to understand logical relationships
- to construct logical sequences and understand the conclusions to which they lead
- to detect fallacies in reasoning
- to recognize that "how to think" is different from "what to think"

Critical Thinking

Students should learn

- to ask questions in order to discover meaning
- to differentiate between subjective and objective viewpoints; to discriminate between opinion and fact
- to evaluate the intentions and messages of speakers and writers, especially attempts to manipulate the language in order to deceive
- to make judgments based on criteria that can be supported and explained

THE RESPONSIBILITY OF TEACHERS OF ENGLISH

The study of English offers varied opportunities for the individual to mature intellectually and emotionally. We believe in basic competency in English as a means by which the individual can acquire self-sufficiency and work independently in all disciplines. We believe further in challenges to both the analytical and creative capabilities of our students.

Toward accomplishing these aims, we as teachers of English hold ourselves responsible for

- helping all students become literate and capable of functioning in an increasingly complex society
- directing them to read and view materials appropriate to their abilities and interests
- encouraging them to exchange ideas, listen perceptively, and discuss vigorously
- urging them to write honestly in the spirit of open inquiry
- helping them expand their interests and reach thier fullest potential through language

By contributing in these ways, we hope to expand the capacities of the human intellect and to preserve the tradition of free thought in a democratic society.

Teaching Composition: A Position Statement

The NCTE Commission on Composition has prepared and adopted this position paper to state essential principles in the teaching of writing. The statement has been cleared for publication by the Executive Committee of the NCTE. It is an expression of the views of the Commission on Composition and does not represent an official NCTE position statement. The members of the Commission hope that this statement will guide teachers, parents, and administrators in understanding the power of writing and in teaching it effectively.

I. THE ACT OF WRITING

Writing is a powerful instrument of thought. In the act of composing, writers learn about themselves and their world and communicate their insights to others. Writing confers the power to grow personally and to effect change in the world.

The act of writing is accomplished through a process in which the writer imagines the audience, sets goals, develops ideas, produces notes, drafts, and a revised text, and edits to meet the audience's expectations. As the process unfolds, the writer may turn to any one of these activities at any time. We can teach students to write more effectively by encouraging them to make full use of the many activities that comprise the act of writing, not by focusing only on the final written product and its strengths and weaknesses.

II. THE PURPOSES FOR WRITING

In composing, the writer uses language to help an audience understand something the writer knows about the world. The specific purposes for writing vary widely, from discovering the writer's own feelings, to persuading others to a course of action, recreating experience imaginatively, reporting the results of observation, and more.

Writing assignments should reflect this range of purposes. Student writers should have the opportunity to define and pursue writing aims that are important to them. Student writers should also have the opportunity to use writing as an instrument of thought and learning across the curriculum and in the world beyond school.

III. THE SCENES FOR WRITING

In the classroom where writing is especially valued, students should be guided through the writing process; encouraged to write for themselves and for other students, as well as for the teacher; and urged to make use of writing as a mode of learning, as well as a means of reporting on what has been learned. The classroom where writing is especially valued should be a place where students will develop the full range of their composing powers. This classroom can also be the scene for learning in many academic areas, not only English.

Because frequent writing assignments and frequent individual attention from the teacher are essential to the writing classroom, writing classes should not be larger than twenty students.

Teachers in all academic areas who have not been trained to teach writing may need help in transforming their classrooms into scenes for writing. The writing teacher should provide leadership in explaining the importance of this transformation and in supplying resources to help bring it about.

IV. THE TEACHERS OF WRITING

Writing teachers should themselves be writers. Through experiencing the struggles and joys of writing, teachers learn that their students will need guidance and support throughout the writing process, not merely comments on the written product. Furthermore, writing teachers who write know that effective comments do not focus on pointing out errors, but go on to the more productive task of encouraging revision, which will help student writers to develop their ideas and to achieve greater clarity and honesty.

Writing teachers should be familiar with the current state of our knowledge about composition. They should know about the nature of the composing process; the relationship between reading and writing; the functions of writing in the world of work; the value of the classical rhetorical tradition; and more. Writing teachers should use this knowledge in their teaching, contribute to it in their scholarly activities, and participate in the professional organizations that are important sources of this knowledge.

The knowledgeable writing teacher can more persuasively lead colleagues in other academic areas to increased attention to writing in their classes. The knowledgeable teacher can also work more effectively with parents and administrators to promote good writing instruction.

V. THE MEANS OF WRITING INSTRUCTION

Students learn to write by writing. Guidance in the writing process and discussion of the students' own work should be the central means of writing instruction. Students should be encouraged to comment on each other's writing, as well as receiving frequent, prompt, individualized attention from the teacher. Reading what others have written, speaking about one's responses to their writing, and listening to the responses of others are important activities in the writing classroom. Textbooks and other instructional resources should be of secondary importance.

The evaluation of students' progress in writing should begin with the students' own written work. Writing ability cannot be adequately assessed by tests and other formal evaluation alone. Students should be given the opportunity to demonstrate their writing ability in work aimed at various purposes. Students should also be encouraged to develop the critical ability to evaluate their own work, so that they can become effective, independent writers in the world beyond school.

Position Statement on the Preparation and Professional Development of Teachers of Writing

CCCC Task Force on the Preparation of Teachers of Writing

To provide effective instruction in writing for learners at any age and at all academic levels, teachers need, first of all, experience in writing, and also some theoretical knowledge to guide classroom practice. To help meet this need, the Conference on College Composition and Communication presents this position statement. We hope it will be discussed and followed, in the preparation of teachers of writing at all levels, by college and university English departments, faculty of teacher preparation programs, faculty and administrators in elementary and secondary schools, and staffs of state departments of public instruction.

The recommendations offered here are consistent with those offered in earlier publications of NCTE and CCCC that deal with the preparation of teachers of writing, with findings of research on the composing process, and with studies on the teaching and learning of writing.

I

Programs for the preparation and continuing education of teachers of English and language arts, at all levels, should include opportunities for prospective and active teachers:

1. *to write,*
   (a) as a means of
      (1) developing, shaping, representing, and communicating our perceptions of our world, our experiences, our beliefs, and our identity,
      (2) finding sensory and aesthetic pleasure in working with and playing with language,
      (3) developing our various intellectual skills;
   (b) in a variety of forms, e.g.,
      (1) prose that attempts to express what we think, feel, and imagine,
      (2) poems representing experience and the fruits of imagination,
      (3) narratives: autobiographical, fictional, historical,
      (4) scripts for performance in class, on television, in film and radio,
      (5) informative records and reports;

(c) in response to a variety of authentic rhetorical situations in which our work will be read and responded to by others, including teachers, classmates, family, and friends; readers of school and community publications; audiences at public readings of our work.

2. *to read and respond to the writings of students, classmates, and colleagues,*
    (a) making supportive comments that express respect for others' ideas and feelings and encourage writers to use writing as a means of personal, academic, and professional growth,
    (b) asking probing questions that help writers see what they have not expressed clearly and convincingly and what they have not presented effectively (perhaps because their knowledge is limited, or their point of view is narrow, or they do not recognize the implications of what they say).
3. *to become perceptive readers of our own writing,* so that we can ask questions about, clarify, and reshape what we are trying to express.
4. *to study and teach writing as a process,*
    (a) by reflecting on how our own writing grows from initial idea to final draft;
    (b) by studying authors' journals and notebooks for indications of their composing processes, and by comparing successive drafts of their work;
    (c) by working with learners while they are composing:
        (1) exploring interests and experiences, and discovering subjects for writing,
        (2) composing first drafts,
        (3) rereading and reacting to their own writing, evaluating the clarity and effectiveness of their ideas,
        (4) responding to their own questions and reactions and those of other readers,
        (5) revising, throughout the steps above,
        (6) editing final drafts for punctuation, spelling, usage, and other conventions.
5. *to experience writing as a way of learning* which engages us in intellectual operations that enable or require us
    (a) to interpret what we experience and discover in light of what we already know, making connections, seeing relationships;
    (b) to re-shape impersonal data into knowledge that is meaningful to us personally;
    (c) to perform essential activities of mind such as analyzing, synthesizing, evaluating, testing, asserting;
    (d) to use what we already know in searching for what we don't know, making hypotheses, imagining new patterns.
6. *to learn to assess the progress of individual writers by responding to complete pieces of their writing and studying changes in their writing.*
7. *to study research and other scholarly work in the humanistic discipline of the teaching of writing, including research on*
    (a) the development of writing abilities and styles
    (b) the ways in which language "means"
    (c) the theory of discourse
    (d) how the English language works

(e) the composing processes of individual writers
(f) the rhetorical effects of different pieces of writing.
8. *to study writing in relation to other disciplines,*
   (a) to learn the insights offered by
      (1) applied linguistics (including language acquisition and development and second language learning sociolinguistics, including study of dialects; psycholinguistics—i.e., the study of the way human beings process language),
      (2) psychology: cognitive and interpersonal,
      (3) history and anthropology;
   (b) to learn what is asked of writers by professionals in other disciplines, including
      (1) the arts of language
      (2) the fine and performing arts
      (3) history
      (4) the social sciences
      (5) the natural sciences.

II

To enable teachers of English and lauguage arts to develop the practical and theoretical knowledge recommended here, CCCC urges

1. college and university English departments
   (a) to provide opportunities for the faculty to develop knowledge of theory and skill in the teaching of writing,
   (b) to develop undergraduate and graduate courses that offer the experiences enumerated in I,
   (c) to require that courses in literature students ask students to write, give them guidance in writing, give them supportive and probing responses to their writing, and encourage them to view writing as a way of reacting to and learning about literature;
2. faculty of teacher education programs
   (a) to provide prospective and active teachers the opportunities listed under I,
   (b) to assure that prospective and active teachers have the opportunities to work with individual learners and groups of learners, so that these teachers can apply what they are learning from the theories and practice of writing discussed in I,
   (c) to work with state departments of education in assuring that the emphases in I are incorporated into the criteria for
      (1) approving teacher education programs
      (2) certifying teachers of English;

3. teachers and administrators in elementary and secondary schools
   (a) to provide opportunities for all teachers of English and language arts to develop theoretical knowledge and skill as teachers of writing,
   (b) to encourage teachers to give their students the experiences with writing listed in I, 1–5,
   (c) to assist teachers in learning to respond to students' writing and assess their progress as writers;
4. staffs of state department of public instruction
   (a) to work with faculties in teacher education on assuring that the emphases in I are incorporated into the criteria for
       (1) approving teacher education programs and
       (2) certifying teachers of English,
   (b) to give moral and financial support to in-service programs in writing for elementary and secondary teachers of English.

Different Products, Different Processes:
A Theory About Writing

Maxine Hairston

Most people who have been working in composition theory in the past ten years would probably agree that the major change that has come about in the profession in that time is exemplified by the maxim, "Focus on the writing process, not on the written product." It is part of the new conventional wisdom of the profession, and certainly for most of us a welcome change from an approach to teaching writing that depended primarily on analysis and imitation of the written product. I want to suggest, however, that following our new maxim is not nearly as easy as one might think; nonfiction prose is not all alike and different kinds of writing are not done in the same way. In other words, "the process of writing" should not be taken to mean the same thing as "the writing process." Almost certainly, there is more than one.

It's been evident in the profession for some time that major researchers and teachers in the field cannot agree on what the writing process is or should be. Those teachers who belong to what Lester Faigley and others call the "literary" or "romantic" school of writing—for example, Donald Murray, Peter Elbow, and William Coles—believe that students are most likely to learn how to express what they know and feel if the teacher focuses primarily on finding ways to stimulate the students' inherent ability and need to write. (See Lester Faigley, Roger D. Cherry, David A. Jolliffe, and Anna R. Skinner, *Assessing Writers' Knowledge and Processes of Composing* [Norwood, NJ: Ablex Publishing Co., 1985], Chapter 1.) They think that writers discover their meaning by writing, and that, for the most part, they cannot know what to write nor how to write it until they actually begin to write something. They would say that students do not really *learn* how to write; rather they come to an understanding of what it means to write by actually engaging in the process. This school of teachers has little use for strategies or formulas or for the Aristotelian approach that would divide the writing process into stages of discovery, arrangement, and style.

The other important school of composition theorists has been categorized as the "classical school"; Faigley calls it the "cognitive school." Some of its chief proponents are Linda Flower, whose theories are cognitively based, Frank D'Angelo, whose theories draw heavily on classical rhetoric, and Sheridan Baker, whose influential textbooks focus on structure, classification, and strategies. These teachers claim that one can teach the process of writing because it resembles other cognitive and problem-solving operations. In their view, writing is an activity that can be analyzed and mapped (see Flower's work on protocol analysis), and teaching strategies can be devised. For them, making plans and carrying them out is a central part of writing. (See Linda Flower and John Hayes, "The Dynamics of Composing: Making Plans and Juggling Constraints," in *Cognitive Pro cesses in Writing*, ed. Lee Gregg and Erwin Steinberg [Hillsdale, NJ, Lawrence Erlbaum Associates, 1980].)

For some time I have realized that I accept the claims of both schools, and that I respect and draw on the work of theorists in each group. Frequently my own writing processes are intuitive and unpredictable; at other times, however, I write cognitively and deliberately, using rational problem-solving strategies. I have never felt any conflict between the methods. I also encourage students to take both approaches to writing. Sometimes I suggest that they should discover their topics through writing, but I also show them strategies for expressing what they already know. So more and more I believe that the romantic and classical theories about writing are not necessarily contradictory and that we should be able to construct a larger view of the writing process that would accommodate both theories. I want to propose such a view in conjunction with a hypothesis I have devised about different types of writing.

A THEORY ABOUT CLASSES OF WRITING

I believe that if we think about the various kinds of writing done by people who must do substantial amounts of writing in the course of their everyday lives, we will discover that it can be divided into at least three main categories. I designate those categories as *classes* of writing (I think one could also call them *types*), and I define them in this way.

Class I: Routine maintenance or MESSAGE *writing.* Just as we must engage in much everyday "maintenance" talk with other people in order to keep organizations and personal relationships functioning, almost all of us must also do considerable maintenance writing. In its briefest form, writing of this kind is simple communication about uncomplicated matters. For example, short memos and brief notes and messages to colleagues, friends, family, or tradespeople fit into this category. It might include notes to one's spouse to pick up the cleaning, an announcement of a committee meeting, a brief thank you note, or a list of tasks to be done. Much of the interoffice correspondence in business is Class I messages written solely to convey factual information. Although this kind of writing is often important, and one must sometimes take care with it to insure that it is accurate and clear, most literate people can handle Class I message writing with little difficulty. Arthur Applebee makes the same point in this column "Musing" in a recent issue of *Research in the Teaching of English* (Arthur Applebee, "Musings: Writing Processes, Revisited," *Research in the Teaching of English,* 19 [October, 1985], 213–215).

Class II: Extended, relatively complex writing that requires the writer's attention but is SELF-LIMITING; that is, before the writer begins to write, she already knows most of what she is going to write or she can easily retrieve the content from memory or known sources. The limits of the piece are set both by its having a specific content to be covered and by the constraints under which it is written; much Class II writing is done under tight time limits.

This self-limiting quality is the key characteristic of Class II writing; writers seldom discover significant new material as they write, although they may think of supporting examples or get fresh insights about organization or style. Their main task is to decide how to organize and present their ideas effectively for a particular audience. They may, however, discover their stance toward the piece as they are working or make adaptations in style or tone to suit the audience.

A typical example of Class II, self-limiting writing is the kind of informative article that professional writers write for general audiences; for instance, a feature article in a magazine like *Newsweek* about recent findings about the relation of diet to cancer. For that kind of writing, the content is known, provided by someone other than the writer or by research into existing data. Not only will the authors not discover ideas as they write, they shouldn't. Other self-limiting writing in magazines or journals might be a piece about the logistics of taking one's bicycle to Europe or about learning to adapt to living in a cold climate. The writer is not likely to generate fresh content or new ideas while working on such basically informative articles.

Some kinds of student writing that are likely to be Class II, self-limiting writing are research reports, technical papers, laboratory reports, case studies, or summaries and analyses of assigned readings. Writing samples for the Law School Admission Test certainly call for a student to do Class II writing, organizing and getting down already known information as efficiently as possible; so do competency examinations and most essay examinations. Much of the writing done in government or corporate offices is also content-limited, Class II writing—progress reports, program analyses, explanations of budgets, and reports on marketing trends.

In whatever situation writers are doing self-limiting, Class II writing, often they can organize it by traditional formulas: state the main idea, give supporting data, analyze problems that may arise, draw a conclusion, and make recommendations. Or sometimes they can use a question/answer pattern or a "who/what/why/when/where and how" format and shape the content into an acceptable piece of writing rather quickly. One of my colleagues calls this kind of writing "quick and dirty," but it is not always the case that the writer can dispose of Class II writing tasks with dispatch. One must sometimes invest considerable time and thought, particularly when the document is for an important audience and the tone must be exactly right. Nevertheless, most people who must write frequently in the course of their work can handle most Level II tasks without much trouble and turn out satisfactory writing on demand.

Class III: Extended REFLECTIVE writing in which the writer discovers much of his or her thought during the writing process. The writer begins with little more than an idea and what Sondra Perl calls a "felt sense" of what he or she wants to say, not knowing precisely where the paper is going or how the ideas will develop. The writer counts on both form and content emerging as the writing proceeds. Scholarly writing, speculative or exploratory articles, and reflective philosophical writing usually fall into the Class III category, as do many other kinds of serious and original writing. Class III writing often focuses on the future, and it is often persuasive.

Formulas are seldom useful for this kind of writing; rather the writer usually has to develop a piece through several drafts, doing substantial revision between each one. Often the writer who is working at Class III writing begins with a discovery draft written primarily for him or her self, and gradually shapes the piece for the audience, developing a voice and a rhetorical stance as she works. Writers working on Class III must often take risks because they are working at the edge of their abilities, operating in unfamiliar territory. Class III writing is usually the most difficult to do, even for experienced writers. It is also the most time-consuming and frustrating, but the most satisfying when it turns out well.

Fortunately, most of our everyday writing is not Class III writing. It costs too much in every way—in energy, in time, in commitment. Nevertheless, I suspect that it is their experiences with Class III writing that make people both hate and love to write.

EXCEPTIONS AND RESERVATIONS

Now as soon as I have established these categories, I have to say that I have reservations—I always do when I begin to dissect, classify, and label, and try to make things fit into neat boxes. Certainly the categories don't cover all kinds of nonfiction writing—for instance, how should I categorize what is an important kind of writing for me, the marginal notes I make when I do serious reading? How should I classify the summary abstracts I sometimes have to write? Nor is it always easy to decide into which category a piece of writing should fit. For instance, does a creative and persuasively-written grant proposal fit into Class II or Class III? Are all technical reports and scientific writing necessarily Class II writing? I suspect not. Rather it is probably the case that sometimes when an author is writing what clearly looks as if it is going to be a Class II document, something unexpected will emerge that moves the process to Class III for some sections. Similarly, an author could be composing at Class III and come to a section that called for a review of the literature or a summary; that would clearly be Class II writing that can be managed by Class II strategies.

So there is some overlapping and confusion. In fact, to illustrate such overlapping, it might be useful to arrange the classes of writing along a continuum that ranges from the extremes of Class I message writing at one end—shopping lists and notes to the postman—to the extremes of Class III *reflective* writing at the other end—for example, a speculative essay on why young people join cults. If one were to arrange a variety of documents along such a continuum, the result might look like this.

note to cleaners	announcement of a meeting	thank you note	minutes of a meeting	report on an accident	case study in nursing course	article on local historical event	progress report of inquiry committee	annual corporate report	article on new ski resorts	grant proposal for battered women's center	critical essay on Henry James	article on needed reforms in high schools	essay on New York City street people	article on implications of high illiteracy in the U.S.	reflective article on dangers of the human potential movement	personal essay on the psychological effects of suffering child abuse

Class I	Class II	Class III

Figure 1. A Continuum of Classes of Writing.

But however one attempts to describe the classes, the hypothesis obviously raises questions of definition and classification to which I do not have clear answers. By nature, the craft of writing is inexact and frequently messy and resistant to analysis; the products, also, are often too complex to dissect and categorize. Thus when one tries to squeeze either language processes or products into precise pigeonholes or lay them on a scale, loose ends and bothersome questions are going to remain. But if we are going to study language and try to understand how it works, we have to learn to live with ambiguities and ragged edges and trust our intuitions when measurements fail.

EXAMPLES OF THE CLASSES

My own experience as a writer and the queries I have made to friends about their writing reinforce my theory. By keeping a log of the kinds of writing I did over a 10-day period, I found that I did Class I writing so routinely that I scarely noticed it—notes to students taped to my office door, replies to requests for information, and so on. I also did a great deal of Class II writing: routine professional correspondence about committee work, responses to requests for information, an uncomplicated letter of recommendation for a student and a more difficult one for a tenure review, a manuscript evaluation for the editor of a journal, a letter of complaint to my congressman, and a letter declining to serve on a committee. In none of these writing tasks was I searching for content, although an idea occasionally came to me as I wrote, especially for the tenure letter. Mostly, however, I wrote quickly, hesitating only over word choice or sentence structure. I was definitely *not* making meaning as I wrote except in the sense of putting information in a form that others could understand and respond to. Most of my writing falls into this category.

But in the same period I was doing Class III writing for this article. Although I had some sense of what I wanted to say since I had talked about the theory with colleagues, I was feeling my way, reflecting as I worked and letting content emerge. I had a sketchy outline but used it mainly as a stimulus and a reminder to include certain points. In this instance, I *was* making meaning as I worked, and I do so in most of my professional writing for publication.

Three other frequent writers—two businessmen and a university administrator—who volunteered to keep logs for me also reported that almost all of their daily writing fell into the Class II category. The tasks included writing letters to colleagues, writing an explanation of policy, making notes for an oral presentation, requesting clarification on a budget, and so on. Usually when they started to write they knew what they were going to say and they said it quickly; their verbal skills and internalized knowledge of appropriate patterns enabled them to do routine, although important, writing with surface editing, but comparatively little real revising. One respondent, however, said that when he had to write a complex statement about communications policy, he had to draft it, redraft it, do a final copy, and then edit it. Although he knew essentially what he wanted to say, he invested considerable time and thought because it was important to strike exactly the right tone. So Class II writing isn't necessarily easy writing—perhaps what is surprising is that so many professionals can do it so well and so quickly.

I believe that a substantial part of the college writing that students do outside of English classes—and even much in English courses—is Class II, self-limiting writing. My students confirm this claim. Term papers in history or economics, problem analyses in engineering, and observation reports in astronomy fit this class; so do some analytical and critical papers. So does almost all of their writing that is done in testing situations. The ability to write such documents quickly and effectively is an essential academic skill for most students, just as the ability to produce a clear and forceful document quickly is an essential business skill for executives at IBM or the vice-president of a university. Class II writing is a critical kind of discourse that keeps our civilization running, and none of us should scorn it or denigrate the ability to do it well.

Class III writing is very different, but it is not necessarily better. Unfortunately, the words that I find useful for describing this kind of writing are, for an academic audience at least, words that seem to privilege the category—words like "reflective," "original," and "probing." Moreover, when people are doing this kind of writing, their processes are not predictable; often they cannot even be investigated or mapped, and that element of mystery makes Class III writing seem more connected to the subconscious and somehow more creative to us. We think of it as the kind of writing we admire and want to be doing—in fact, as the kind of writing we *should* be doing. I would maintain, however, the most of our day-to-day working writing is not Class III nor should it be; if it were, too often it wouldn't get done.

We also need to remember that Class III writing is not the exclusive providence of professional writers and academics; at times, people in government, business, and the professions, particularly those at the upper ranks, must also do reflective discovery writing as they shape an important policy statement or write a major speech. Judges might well be doing Class III writing as they write opinions, and administrators or elected officials might use it as they devise contingency plans or draft position statements on critical issues. Scientists writing grant proposals must also do reflective writing when they project results they hope to achieve and speculate about the impact of those results. In such instances, they are at least partially creating their meaning as they work.

I think the tasks that professionals must do in other fields can be categorized in a similar way. For example, an architect friend with more than thirty years of experience tells me that his projects require a variety of approaches. Sometimes when a client asks him to design a building, the elements of the assignment are straightforward and uncomplicated, and he can design a good building quickly, especially if he has done many other buildings of the same kind. He doesn't have to start from scratch and make many sketches to coax a fresh idea from his subconscious; he has a battery of reliable strategies to draw on that will help him produce a satisfactory design with relatively little effort and no loss of his artistic integrity. At other times, however, a client asks for the kind of building that presents a new design problem. Then he has to reflect, experiment, and keep his mind open to new solutions and new options. He has to discover what he wants to do as he works—he does *reflective* design. Of course, this latter kind of designing challenges him more and is more rewarding, but he couldn't work in that way all the time. It's exhausting and time-consuming, and therefore costly. Fortunately, in architecture as in writing, most projects don't require this kind of investment.

TEACHING THE DIFFERENT CLASSES OF WRITING

I think many of our problems in deciding how we should teach writing come from our failure to distinguish between Class II and Class III writing, to recognize that each class is important, and to acknowledge that most of our students need to be able to do both well. Unfortunately, many writing teachers seem to want to emphasize either one class or the other.

Some teachers focus almost entirely on Class II writing because they believe that what students need most in a writing course is to master formulas and strategies that will enable them to handle the essential everyday writings tasks that they will face in college and on the job. They stress that writing is a cognitive, problem-solving skill, and their goal in the class is to produce competent and confident writers. Such teachers may, however, also give their courses a strong rhetorical base, stressing analysis of audience and purpose and trying to give realistic case study assignments. Aware of widespread criticism of student writing, they favor a pragmatic approach; if they encourage reflective expressive writing in their classrooms, they are likely to confine it to students' journals and to personal experience papers done early in the term.

Others—and these seem to be in the majority today, or else they are more articulate—have no use for Class II writing, calling it formulaic and sterile. This kind of teacher, exemplified by Donald Murray, Peter Elbow, William Coles, and Ann Berthoff, believes that students should write to discover themselves and to make sense out of their world. They believe that we create meaning by writing, that meaning does not exist as a separate entity to be communicated by writing. They hold that the essential features of good writing are originality and an authentic voice. These teachers seem to believe that every time students write they should do Class III writing, spending substantial time on discovery and working through several drafts to find out what they mean. They imply that no other writing is worth doing.

I think writing teachers should pay attention to and draw from both schools of teaching writing, because both kinds of writing are not only worth doing, they are absolutely necessary. Writers who can do only one or the other are going to be handicapped, both in college and in their professional lives. In some ways, Class II writing is probably easier to teach than Class III. We can show students how to outline a paper for which they know the content, show them how to start a paragraph with a topic sentence and downshift into examples, or show them how to make a commitment and then follow through on it. We can also show them how to use some practical formulas—the five-paragraph theme works well at times, and so do thesis sentences. We can even profitably draw upon the maxims of classical rhetoric to teach Class II writing: the Aristotelian topics can work quite well here.

The problem with teaching Class II writing arises because, unlike professionals who are working at real writing with important content, students often choose topics that look easy and require little research, then they produce trivial writing that bores both them and the teacher. But that problem does not come from the kind of writing they are doing; doing Class II writing to shape content one already knows but is interested in into a clearly written and forcefully expressed paper can be a stimulating and satisfying task. The question, of course, is how one gets students to take their work seriously. In another article I have suggested some answers to that question ("Working with Advanced Writers," *CCC*, 35 [May, 1984], 196–208).

Class III writing is much harder to teach because we have no workable prescriptions for it and often cannot describe, either in an article or a textbook, just how one goes about simultaneously discovering, organizing, and then restructuring material. Students often get uncomfortable because they aren't used to the open-ended assignments for which the teacher seems to have no particular model in mind, and teachers often get uncomfortable because they fear that they are relinquishing control over their students' writing. And to a great extent they are. But when a class that focuses on Class III, reflective writing is successful, instructors are often delighted with the results. Some students rise above formulas and invest in their writing, and some will even get to the point of moving beyond writing for a grade to writing because they are committed to their topics. But some students are never comfortable with Class III writing, feeling that it's too risky, and even when given every encouragement to start with discovery drafts they will stick to writing what they know. And that, I think, is their choice and we shouldn't reproach them for making it. I find that I can be just as interested in reading and responding to a self-limiting, Class II paper about the distance runners of the Mayan culture as I am in a reflective, Class III paper written by a Mexican student about the inherent duality of Mexican culture. Each has it own particular appeal.

For several reasons I think many college English teachers tend to put too much pressure on their students to try to do the reflective, often personal writing of Class III. First, as teachers trained in literature, we tend to value expressive and reflective writing far more then we do practical, working writing, and we give that message to our students by the kinds of essays we assign and talk about. (A teacher in a workshop I was conducting commented that he now realized how much he confused his students by using a text that emphasized Class II writing but giving Class III essays as models.)

Second, we tend to associate Level II writing with what adminstrators and faculty from other departments often call "service courses"; understandably, most of us have little enthusiasm for doing that kind of teaching. What we need to realize is that because a certain kind of writing is useful, that doesn't mean that we're teaching it as a service. Third, because teachers are so desperately tired of reading the "Engfish" that comes from students doing Class II writing thoughtlessly, they want to try another approach, any approach that will jolt the students out of writing vapid, formulaic papers. Their literary biases draw them to the intuitive and romantic school of writing teachers, whose precepts they accept uncritically. They embrace the doctrine that good writing can develop only by the student's making a personal search for meaning through the course of several drafts.

I believe that doctrine is impractical, unrealistic, and, eventually, counterproductive. Students are sensible enough to know that writing doesn't always have to be a search for meaning, that often they know quite well what they want to say; their main problem is to get their content organized and down in acceptable form. They expect, reasonably enough I think, that their writing courses should help them to do that. Moreover, if they're perceptive, they know that their teachers are not spending much time struggling to produce the difficult and reflective writing they demand of their students. If those teachers always insist on Class III writing, they are going to lose credibility with their students. They will also lose their students' cooperation because few students are willing to work intensively on their writing all the time. They don't have the time to invest and, if pushed too much, they will just gush out overly emotional garbage that is as inauthentic and uninteresting as any routine, canned writing. Reflective writing can become pseudo-reflective writing with its own kind of clichés.

I think our goal in teaching writing should be to teach students to work comfortably in both classes of writing, to understand how the classes differ and when each is appropriate. We should also talk about our own writing, bringing in examples of the different classes and discussing the processes involved in each one. One class isn't better than another; each has its place, and each has its own kind of excellence. We should also show them how to move between Class II and Class III writing on some writing tasks—relying on discovery and intuition at some stages, but turning to strategies for getting down what they already know or applying problem-solving strategies at others.

I encourage all my students to think about the class of writing they are doing for an assignment and to work on some Class III writing before end of a semester so everyone can taste the joys of discovery writing. And I do not assume that everyone has to master Class II writing before moving on to Class III, although we sometimes think of that pattern as a natural progression. Some students who have trouble learning the patterns for Class II—or who disdain them—may move quickly to Class III and enjoy it. Others—and often these are the high achievers who are skillful Class II writers—resist working on Class III writing because they don't want to take the risks.

RESPONDING TO THE DIFFERENT LEVELS OF WRITING

We will persuade our students to do both classes of writing only if we can learn to adapt our responses to students' writing to suit the kind of writing on which they are working. When you are working on Class II writing, we should reward clarity, smooth style, and solid competence. We should comment on their organizational skills, their mastery of transitions, and their control of the conventions of writing. And we should insist on solid, significant content, reinforced by the weight of facts and by research, if necessary. Class II writing should always have the potential of teaching someone something; just because it is self-limiting doesn't mean that the *reader* already knows the content. So we must consistently refuse to accept trivia and generalizations, however smoothly written. We must always care about content.

But when students are working on Class III and taking risks by venturing into new territory, we have to remind ourselves that the more risks a learner takes, the more he or she is likely to make mistakes. Then we should ignore egocentricity and scrambled organization in a first draft while the student finds out what he or she wants to do, and we should deemphasize concerns about usage until a late stage of the paper. We also have to read reflective writing without preconceptions about how it should be done— after all, no one ever wrote that paper before and there is no model for it. If we don't, if we encourage students to innovate and work at the edge of their abilities and then penalize them for violating the conventions, we will surely discourage them from trying to write reflectively again.

So, as one might expect, good writing teachers turn out to be good rhetoricians who can adapt their responses and their guidance to the individual writer in a specific writing situation, and who can shift gears to do different kinds of teaching for different kinds of tasks. They are also the pragmatists who don't totally accept any one theory about writing or any single prescription for teaching it. They take what works wherever they can find it, always searching for new ideas that will give them new strategies for working with students and for meeting the whole spectrum of those students' needs.

Writing Research and the Writer

John R. Hayes and Linda S. Flower

ABSTRACT: One of the central aims of education is teaching students to communicate with the written word. Because a fundamental shift in emphasis has occurred from analysis of written products to investigation of writing processes themselves, research on writing now provides new insights that have important instructional implications. This "process movement" is based on cognitively oriented research and focuses on the interconnections among thinking, learning, and writing. Hayes and Flower argue that sound writing instruction should draw on a clear understanding of the organization of cognitive processes underlying the act of writing. They discuss research on three major writing processes: planning, sentence generation, and revision. Process-oriented instruction promises substantial guidance on teaching students to manage these processes of generating text, as they are writing.
—The Editors

Writing instruction used to be simpler. When we (the authors) learned to write in school, we were given good models to imitate, the opportunity to practice, and red-penciled corrections from the teacher. This kind of instruction is described as product oriented because it focuses on the written product the students produce rather than on the processes by which they produce them. One of the radical departures of current instruction is to reverse this orientation and to focus instead on writing processes. In process-oriented instruction, the teacher attempts to intervene in the writing process itself—to teach students what to do when they write. They do this by engaging the students in activities designed to improve specific writing skills. For example, students are trained in brainstorming to help them generate ideas for writing, and they are encouraged to get peer responses to their work to develop a better sense of audience.

Support for this "process movement" in composition has come in part from research in the cognitive processes that underly writing and from a new awareness of the connections between writing, thinking, and learning. Young, Becker, and Pike (1970) drew on the art of invention in classical rhetoric to describe the heuristic processes that underlie invention and persuasion and to argue for the value of teaching writing as rhetorical problem solving. Emig's (1971) landmark study of the writing of 12th graders anatomized the process in terms of time spent on planning, reading, outlining, revising, and so on. In our studies (Flower & Hayes, 1981; Hayes, Flower, Schriver, Stratman, & Carey, 1985), we have begun to model the organization of cognitive processes with particular emphasis on both planning and revision and to translate research into teachable problem-solving strategies (Flower, 1985).

Ideally, we would like instruction in writing to be informed by an accurate model of the cognitive processes that underlie writing. However, there is ample evidence that this has not always been the case. Rohman (1965) proposed a three-stage description of writing that was widely used in teaching. His stages were prewriting (e.g., idea generation and planning), writing (e.g., composing a draft), and rewriting (e.g., revising the draft). This stage model came under fire in the 1970s as an oversimplified version of the writing process that failed to recognize its recursive nature. That is, when people compose, the activities of prewriting, writing, and rewriting do not typically occur in fixed sequence but rather are interwoven with each other in a complex way. Visions of the writing process that focus on "activities" rather than on cognition continue to cause difficulty. Applebee (in press) has recently charged that much of the current process-based instruction is seriously limited by its preoccupation with a set of so-called "natural process" activities (e.g., the teacher regularly requires students to spend time on prewriting, journal keeping, free-writing, getting peer response, revising, etc.) Such procedures, he argued, fail to recognize the role of purpose in the writing process, which dictates whether a given process is even useful. For example, free writing, a procedure in which students are asked to write down whatever they think of and to keep writing without worry about quality of ideas, may seem pointless to students who already have a clear idea of what they want to say.

Process-oriented instruction is a new frontier we have only begun to enter. The exemplary experimental research of Bereiter and Scardamalia (1982) and Scardamalia and Bereiter (1983) illustrate the difficulty and the care that must go into constructing successful interventions. However, a recent meta-analysis of writing instruction research (Hillocks, 1984) suggests that process-oriented instruction (even in these early days) is already more successful than previous product-oriented instruction. Research may have played an important role in this success. As Applebee (in press) has noted, writing instruction is one area in which research has actually had a large and visible impact on teaching.

In this article, we attempt to characterize the present state of the field of adult (postsecondary) writing and to outline what we believe are the emerging trends and directions for future research. In particular, we will discuss the overall structure of the writing process and describe research on the major writing processes. (For a review of the developmental literature with a somewhat different focus, see Scardamalia & Bereiter, in press).

THE STUCTURE OF THE WRITING PROCESS

A number of important features of the writing process have been identified through research. We will discuss evidence that writing is goal directed, that writing goals are hierarchically organized, and that writers employ three major processes—planning, sentence generation, and revision—to accomplish these goals. Before doing this, though, it will be useful to describe the research methods used to reveal this information.

In our own attempts to characterize the writing process, we have employed a technique called protocol analysis (see Hayes & Flower, 1980). Protocol analysis has been widely used by psychologists to analyze complex task performance (see Ericcson & Simon, 1984). Protocol analysis starts with the collection of a "thinking aloud" protocol, that is, a person is asked to perform a task and to "think aloud" while performing it. In thinking-aloud studies of writing, the subject is asked not only to think aloud, but to read and write aloud as well. The writing tasks that have been studied by protocol analysis include short (hour-long) assignments completed under controlled laboratory conditions (Hayes & Flower, 1980) as well as extended (months-long) writing projects of a professional writer (Berkenkotter, 1983).

The data of thinking-aloud studies are contained in the verbatim transcript of the tape recording (with all the "um"s, pauses, and expletives) together with the essay and all the notes the writer has generated along the way. The transcript is called a protocol. These materials are then examined in considerable detail for evidence that may reveal something of the processes by which the writer has created the essay. In general, the data are very rich in such evidence. Subjects typically give many indications of their plans and goals, e.g., "I'll just jot down ideas as they come to me"; about strategies for dealing with the audience, e.g., "I'll write this as if I were one of them"; or about criteria for evaluation, e.g., "We better keep this simple." The analysis of this data is called *protocol analysis.*

Writing Is Goal Directed

Evidence that writing is goal directed is easy to find in protocols. Typically, writers comment on their major goals early in the writing session. For example, one writer who was asked to write about the role of women for a hostile audience, said, "If an audience were hostile, the worst thing to do would be to defend yourself—so I would try to humor them—to make them—uh—more sympathetic maybe." A second writer assigned this same topic said, "I'm trying to decide whether . . . I want to convince my audience of something specific about—uh—for instance, the Equal Rights Amendment or whether [I want to use] something general about [whether] women should have the same rights as men . . . and I also need to decide if I want to actively convince my audience or simply state my point of view." A few moments later she decided "I'll try to convince them of what it is like not to have certain rights." A third writer said "I'm not really trying to persuade these people of anything. I'm simply being descriptive . . . I'm saying, 'This is the way the world is.' " Because writing is goal directed, it may well be hazardous, as Applebee suggested, to try to teach writing subskills without giving students a context of reasonable writing goals.

Writing Goals Are Hierarchically Organized

When writers have identified their major goals, for example, the particular aspect of the topic they want to discuss and their general approach to the audience, they frequently identify subgoals on the route to these major goals. Indeed, the subgoals may in turn have their own subgoals. A writer whose main goal was to write about "worries" of a particular group set up subgoals to write about the subtopics "the political issue" and "the philosophical issue." Under each of these subtopics, the writer specified a list of three or four sub-subtopics. Thus, the major goal was expanded into a hierarchical structure of subgoals.

In the same way, a writer said that he was "simply being descriptive" elaborated his goal as follows: "I think what I really want is to present maybe one [point] with a lot of illustrations." He then went on to state the point and to develop a list of eight illustrations. In many cases, then, writers tell us in their "thinking aloud" protocols that their goals are hierarchically structured. Even if the writers didn't tell us explicitly though, there would still be plenty of evidence that writing processes are hierarchically organized. For example, many writers start writing sessions with a period of planning in which they try to develop an outline to write from. To do this they may first try to generate ideas freely. When they feel they have enough ideas, they try to organize them into an outline. Generating ideas and organizing them are parts of planning, and planning in turn is part of writing. Clearly these processes are hierarchically organized.

Writers Use Three Major Processes: Planning, Sentence Generation, and Revising

Research indicates that writers use three processes in achieving their goals; planning, sentence generation, and revising. In planning, the writer generates ideas and organizes them into a writing plan. In sentence generation, the writer produces formal sentences intended to be part of a draft. In revising, the writer attempts to improve a draft. Typically, these three processes are heavily interwoven. The interweaving has two causes: First, the writing task may be performed in parts, so that the writer plans, generates, and revises a first paragraph, then plans, generates, and revises a second paragraph, and so on. Second, the writing process may be applied recursively. For example, while revising, the writer may discover the need for a transitional paragraph. To write the paragraph, the writer invokes the whole writing process, that is, planning, generating, and revising, which are then nested within the revising process. In the remainder of this article, we will discuss research findings concerning these three major processes.

THE PLANNING PROCESS

If we were to build a model of planning in writing, we would want to consider, at least, the following three topics: the way people represent their knowledge, the sources of writing plans, and knowledge of writing strategies.

The Representation of Knowledge

The knowledge that a writer wants to express in a text may be stored in a wide variety of forms. Some knowledge is stored as language, perhaps in auditory form (e.g., a remembered proverb); some is stored as meanings that may be expressed in a variety of linguistic forms (e.g., "The dog is lively," or "Fido is bouncing off the walls"); some is stored as images or as skills that are harder to translate into language (e.g., the appearance of a particular facial expression or the skill of unbuttoning a coat button).

Because knowledge representations are diverse, the writing plans that writers construct to convey this knowledge must also be complex. Writing plans do not consist of knowledge representations of a single uniform type (Flower & Hayes, 1984); rather, writing plans appear to include information of at least three types: (a) pointers (in the form of cues or code words) to information that may be stored in many different forms such as schemas, episodes, images, and so on; (b) word images, perhaps in auditory form, of particular words or phrases that could be included in the text; and (c) goals that include such things as plans for affecting the audience, for creating connections, or content-free directions to the writer, such as "add an introduction" or "go back to the drawing board."

The Source of the Writing Plan

One obvious source of expert writing plans is a well-organized body of topic knowledge. Such knowledge can provide organizing concepts that aid the writer in selecting relevant information, for example, knowing what to notice in a baseball game (Spilich, Vesonder, Chiesi, & Voss, 1979).

One of the time-honored ways of improving student writing is to allow students to choose their own topics, in the hope of increasing both knowledge and motivation (Applebee, 1982; Britton, Burgess, Martin, McLeod, & Rosen, 1975; Shaughnessy, 1977). Yet it is commonplace that knowledge of a topic will not necessarily enable an individual to produce clear, much less effective writing. For instance, subject-matter experts, for example, programmers or computer scientists, have been notoriously ineffective in writing computer documentation. At least two factors appear to contribute to the problem. First, as we will discuss later, subject-matter experts' knowledge may itself make experts insensitive to the needs of readers less informed than themselves. Second, subject-matter experts may have inadequate rhetorical knowledge. That is, they may write poorly because they do not have command of effective writing formats at the sentence, paragraph, or whole text levels. Expert writers draw on textual conventions and genre patterns and other discourse schemas to give shape to their planning (Bracewell, Frederickson, & Frederickson, 1982; Olson, Mack, & Duffy, 1981; Schumacher, Klare, Cronin, & Moses, 1984). In the writing of children and in the construction of simple stories or highly conventionalized text (e.g., the thank-you note) such schemas appear to do a great deal of the work, offering a prefabricated plan for writing.

However, such rhetorical knowledge does not fully account for planning performance. The writing that older students and adults do typically calls for more complex, nonconventionalized plans unique to the immediate writing problem. As the writing task grows harder, then, less of the work can be done through the use of known formats, and the contribution of *problem solving strategies* increases. As in Voss, Greene, Post, and Penner (1983) studies of problem solvers in the social sciences, merely increasing the students' topic knowledge was insufficient to produce better analysts, because expert performance also depended on a repertory of strategies that included searching for constraints, consolidating the search, and testing hypotheses. It appears then that the writing plan has at least three sources: the writer's topic knowledge, the writer's knowledge of effective writing formats, and the writer's knowledge of strategies that support planning and problem solving when known writing formats are inadequate.

Strategic Knowledge

Because *strategic knowledge* plays such an important role in the more difficult or complex writing tasks, a model of writing would be quite incomplete if we did not consider it in detail. By strategic knowledge we mean a combination of three things: knowing how to define the writing task for oneself with appropriately demanding yet manageable goals; having a large body of high-level procedural knowledge on which to draw; and finally, being able to monitor and direct one's own writing process.

We can best illustrate the role strategic knowledge plays by comparing the goal-directed planning process we have observed in adults with the knowledge-telling strategy. Scardamalia and Bereiter (in press) have described in children.

Knowledge telling is a limited, but easily learned and efficient procedure that gets the job done for a wide variety of school writing tasks. In it, the writer's goal is simply to say what he or she knows about the topic, generating any information that is relevant to the topic rather than selecting and organizing that knowledge into a package designed for the reader. With writers who use this strategy, requests for an argument or an evaluative essay simply tend to elicit whatever the writer knows on the subject.

How does the expert planning process differ from knowledge telling? In children, the visible output (e.g., notes, etc.) and the mental "output" of planning appear to be nearly identical—the child generates a list of topics, content information, and actual language for use in the text. As students grow older, this written output can become more complex—the notes may include gists and goals that are then reordered before they appear in the text (Burtis, Bereiter, Scardamalia, & Tetroe, 1983). However, the more interesting and significant change occurs in the inner mental process of planning, that is, in the output we typically do not see and until recently have ignored in our description of good writing. Adult planning can be distinguished by four features (which themselves vary with the skill of the writer).

1. During planning writers construct an initial task representation and a body of goals that in turn guide and constrain their efforts to write.

2. The body of goals is no mere temporal list of instructions, but appears to work as a hierarchical structure. That is, writers set up top-level goals that they develop with plans and subgoals. At the same time, these goals are also connected in a network in which one action can carry out multiple goals and in which individual plans or goals can be linked by a web of associations to other parts of this network. In other words, the writer's goals themselves form a complex structure.

3. The network of goals is also a dynamic structure. It is built and developed and sometimes radically restructured at even the top levels, as the writer composes and responds to new ideas or to his or her own text. The relative salience of various parts of this structure will also change as the writer works. Priorities change; attention wanders; writers forget. However, writers often return to goals that they established earlier but had seemingly abandoned. Thus, writing goals may persist even if they are currently inactive. Modifying writing goals may be essential for good writing. Writers stymied by writer's block appear to have more difficulty changing goals and plans than do other writers (Rose, 1980).

4. The differences between the goal networks constructed by experts and those constructed by novices help explain why student writers regularly have such difficulty organizing their knowledge around a problem or question or developing a focus adapted to the reader and why planning itself can be a demanding cognitive process for all writers.

In a preliminary study of expert and novice adults, we found that experts tended to generate far more elaborated networks. The goals, subgoals, plans, and evaluative comments they gave themselves provided a richer problem, more alive to the constraints of the task and their own goals. Although the sheer elaboration of working goals can be a good indication of expert planning, it is an inadequate description of that expertise. What distinguished the experts from the novices most clearly was the difference in the integration of their plans. The experts created far more connections among their goals than did the novices.

THE SENTENCE GENERATION PROCESS

Because the writing plan consists largely of pointers to information and of instructions to the writer, a great deal of work must be done to translate the writing plan into formal prose. That work involves explaining briefly sketched ideas (e.g., "the philosophical issue"), interpreting nonverbal material in verbal form (e.g., "Just how did he look?"), and carrying out instructions (e.g., "Write a conclusion"). In a study of sentence generation, Kaufer, Hayes and Flower (1986) found evidence that the work involved in translating plans into text is substantial. They compared the lengths of writers' outlines with the lengths of their essays. Even for the most extensive outliners, the ideas noted in the outline were expanded on the average by a factor of eight in the final essay.

Kaufer et al. (1986) found that writers compose sentences in parts. Sentence parts were defined by pauses in the thinking-aloud protocols and averaged between 7 and 12 words in length. The following is a typical sentence-generating episode observed by Kaufer et al. The dashes indicate pauses of two seconds or more in the composing process. The writer is trying to describe her job.

> The best thing about it is (1)—what? (2) Something about using my mind (3)—it allows me the opportunity to (4)—uh—I want to write something about my ideas (5)—to put ideas into action (6)—or—to develop my ideas into (7)—what? (8)—into a meaningful form? (9) Oh, bleh!—say it allows me (10)—to use (11)—Na—allows me—scratch that. The best thing about it is that it allows me to use (12)—my mind and ideas in a productive way (13).

The proposed sentence parts in this episode were fragments 1, 4, 6, 7, 9, 11, and 13. Fragments 12 and 13 comprised the finished sentence that the writer included in her essay.

In general, experts and average writers constructed sentences in the same way. Both groups assembled sentence parts in a predominantly left to right fashion. That is, when writers proposed sentence parts, they were intended either to be added to the right of the last proposed sentence part, or they were intended to replace the last proposed sentence part. While producing a new draft, writers rarely revised sentence parts earlier than the one previously proposed. Further, both experts and average writers accepted about 75% of the sentence parts they proposed. That is, about 75% of the sentence parts mentioned in the thinking-aloud protocols were included in the written draft. The major differences between the two groups were (a) experts wrote significantly longer essays (786 words per essay) than average writers (464 words per essay) and (b) experts proposed significantly longer sentence parts (11.2 words per part) than average adult writers (7.3 words per part). This ability to work in larger units may be part of what it means to be a fluent writer.

THE REVISION PROCESS

When Murray (1978) said, "Writing is rewriting," he was dramatizing the important role that revision can play in writing. Unfortunately, many writers lack the skill to make effective use of revision in their own writing. Bracewell, Scardamalia, and Bereiter (1978) found that 4th graders hardly revise at all, that 8th graders' revisions hurt more than they help, and that for 12th graders, helpful revisions narrowly outnumbered harmful ones. Bridwell's (1980) results suggest greater effectiveness for for 12th graders' revisions than those of Bracewell et al. (1978). She found that 12th graders' second drafts were considerably better in "general merit" and mechanics than their first drafts. Pianko (1979) reported that college freshmen devote less than 9% of their composing time to reading and revising. Clearly, writers differ widely in the amount they revise. Holland,

Rose, Dean, and Dory (1985) reported that the difference between good and poor adult writers in the amount of time spent on revision depends on the particular writing task. In general, though, it appears that the more expert the writer, the greater the proportion of writing time the writer will spend in revision. We will outline some observations about the nature of revision and about differences between expert and novice revisers.

Experts Attend More to Global
Problems Than Do Novices

The literature suggests that experts and novices view revising in very different ways. Broadly, revision may be defined as the writer's attempt to improve the text. Within this definition, experts appear to attend systematically to different aspects of the text than do novices. There is considerable evidence that less experienced revisers focus their attention far more locally than do more experienced revisers. Stallard (1974) found that only 2.5% of 12th graders' revisions were focused above the word and sentence level. Bridwell (1980), who also studied 12th graders, found about 11% of revisions above the sentence level. Beach (1976), studying college juniors and seniors, found that students who revised extensively "tended to conceive of the paper in holistic terms" and to infer "general patterns of development" (p. 162.). Students who did not revise extensively "evaluated only separate bits" (p. 162) of their papers.

Sommers (1980) found that college freshmen understand the revision process as a rewording activity, that is, they concentrate on particular words apart from their role in the text. In contrast, experienced writers, such as journalists, editors, and academics, describe their primary objectives when revising as finding the form or shape of their argument. Further, Sommers found that the experienced writers have a secondary objective; a concern for their readership. Faigley and Witte (1983), who studied writers at various skill levels, found that experts were more likely to change meaning through revision than were novices. They observed that the revisions of inexperienced college writers resulted in changed meaning in 12% of cases; the revisions of experienced college writers, in 25% of cases; and the revisions of experienced adult writers, in 34% of cases. Hayes et al. (1985) found that experts and novices differed systematically in their implicit definitions of the revision task. Experts defined revision as a whole-text task. They tended to read the whole text through before beginning revision and created global goals to guide the revision process. Novices, in contrast, saw revision largely as a sentence-level task in which the goal was to improve individual words and phrases without modifying the text structure.

Writers Have Difficulty Detecting
Faults in Their Own Text

Barlett (1981) compared revision processes in fifth grade students who were revising both their own and other writers' texts. She found that when the children were revising their own texts, they were able to find 56% of missing subjects or predicates, but only

10% of faulty referring expressions. In contrast, when the children were revising the texts of other writers, they detected about half of each type of problem. Hull (1984) has found similar results for adult writers.

One possible explanation for these results is that writers' knowledge of their own texts makes it difficult for them to detect faults in those texts. If this explanation is correct, then we would expect that prior knowledge of the content of any text would make it more difficult for the reviser to detect faults in that text. To test this hypothesis, Hayes, Schriver, Spilka, and Blaustein (1986) asked revisers to underline parts of unclear texts that they judged would cause comprehension problems for readers who did not know the subject matter. In some conditions, the revisers had read and evaluated a clear version of the text before they evaluated the unclear version. Thus, they evaluated the unclear version with prior knowledge of its content. In other conditions, the revisers had no prior experience with the content of the text. On the average, revisers who had no prior knowledge of text content discovered 50% more problems in the unclear text than did revisers with prior knowledge.

The Cues That Initiate Revision

Several researchers have suggested that the cue or initiating condition for revision is a dissonance or incongruity between intention and execution. For example, Bridwell (1980) suggested that when rereading the text, "the writer may either verify what is on the page or perceive some dissonance" (p. 220). Perception of dissonance is the cue that may lead to a decision to change the text. According to Sommers (1980), "the anticipation of a reader's judgement causes a feeling of dissonance when the writer recognizes incongruities between intention and execution" (p. 385). It is this recognition, according to Sommers, that leads the writer to make revisions. According to Scardamalia and Bereiter (1983), who proposed the Compare, Diagnose, and Operate (CDO) model of revision,

> During the course of composition, two kinds of mental representation are built up and stored in long-term memory. These are a representation of the text as written up to the time, and a representation of the text as intended. The C.D.O. process is initiated by a perceived mismatch between these two representations. (p. 4)

Although the idea that revision is initiated by the discovery of a dissonance between intention and text is attractive, there are enough clear counterexamples to warn us that this explanation can only be a partial one. For example, there are many instances in which writers appear to have written what they intended to write, but decide to revise anyway because the act of writing has led them to discover something better to say. Writing stimulates discovery, and discovery can initiate revision in the absence of dissonance. More telling is the observation (Hayes et al., 1985) that revision may be applied not only to texts but also to plans for producing texts as well. Revision of a plan cannot be triggered by comparison of intention and text because, at this point, there is no text to compare to the plan. Rather, revision is triggered by the negative evaluation of a plan, for example, "Maybe I'll give them a list of principles. No, that would bore them to flinders!" A third sort of example may be observed when writers are revising other peoples' texts. In such cases, the reviser may be cued to revise by the difficulties he or she experiences in comprehending the writer's intention, the text, or both. Failure to comprehend either the writer's intention or the text would be a reason to revise whether text matched intention or not.

Revision, then, can be triggered not only by dissonance between intention and text but also by the discovery of better things to say, by the negative evaluation of a plan, and by failure to comprehend the text. Hayes et al. (1985) have attempted to incorporate these various revision triggers in a comprehensive model of the revision process.

Detection and Diagnosis of Text Problems

Hayes et al. (1985) found that experts detected about 1.6 times as many problems in a faulty text then did novices. Further, of the problems they detected, experts were able to diagnose 74% whereas novices were able to diagnose only 42%—a ratio of 1.7 to 1. Experts, then, showed a clear advantage over novices both in the detection and in the diagnosis of text problems. Superiority in these two skills gives experts much greater strategic flexibility in revision than novices have. To appreciate this point, one needs to recognize two important facts about revision.

1. *Diagnosis is not an obligatory step in revision.* Although diagnosis is heavily emphasized in composition classes, writers often revise without diagnosing. In many instances in Hayes et al. (1985), both expert and novice revisers detected problems in the text and rewrote the problematic sections apparently without bothering to diagnose the problems. We will call this approach to revision without diagnosis the "rewrite" strategy. The most common alternative strategy is to diagnose the text problems and to fix them. We will call this the "revise" strategy.

2. *Whether the rewrite or revise strategy is preferable depends on the text.* The rewrite strategy is generally preferable when (a) it is not important to save the original text, (b) there are many problems in the original text so that diagnosis involves much effort, or (c) the purpose of the text is clear and not problematic so that extracting the gist and inventing an alterntive text is easy. The revise strategy is preferable when (a) it is important to save as much of the original text as possible, (b) there are few problems in the text so that diagnosis is easy, or (c) the purpose of the text is unclear or problematic so that identification of the gist and inventing an alternative text is not easy. In such cases, diagnosis may provide the only effective means for identifying the gist or resolving problems and therefore for inventing an improved alternative text.

Because experts have strong skills in both detection and diagnosis, they can typically exercise either the rewrite or the revise strategy and therefore can choose the strategy they feel will be most effective. Novices, on the other hand, often find that their lack of skills limits their strategic choices. Experts, then, have more strategic options than do novices.

To revise a text for an audience is a very complex task. It requires the reviser to comprehend the goals of the text, to predict how well the text will accomplish those goals for the intended audience, and to propose better ways to accomplish those goals when the reviser perceives the text to be faulty. It is not obvious that expert revisers operating on their intuitions can accomplish this task optimally. Duffy, Curran, Sass (1983) found that when professional writing firms revised documents for clarity, the results were frequently disappointing when the original and revised documents were compared in tests of comprehension. Swaney, Janik, Bond, and Hayes (1981) asked a group of four document designers to revise four public documents so that they could be understood by a general audience. The designers invested about 100 hours in the project. Comprehension tests on the original and the revised documents showed that the designers' efforts had improved the comprehensibility of three of the documents but made the last one worse. Swaney et al. then revised this last document using protocol-aided revision. That is, they collected thinking-aloud protocols of readers attempting to comprehend the document and used these protocols to identify features of the text that required improvement. The document was then revised in the light of the protocols. After three revision cycles, the protocols revealed no further problems in the text. Comprehension tests showed that the text was now significantly clearer than the original (16% errors vs. 46% errors). This result is both a sensible one and a very practical one. It makes good common sense to go directly to the audience for information about readers' comprehension needs rather than relying on the writer's intuition. It is a very practical result because it can be applied quite directly to the improvement of documents. In fact, the above authors applied the technique to produce a prize-winning computer manual (Bond, Hayes, Janik, & Swaney, 1982).

Recently, Schriver (1984) constructed a set of lessons designed to increase the writer's sensitivity to readers' needs. In each lesson, students are asked to read a flawed text and to predict the sorts of troubles the reader would have in comprehending the text. Next, the students read a thinking-aloud protocol of a reader who is trying to comprehend the text. The students then revise their predictions of reader difficulties. The effect of instruction, that is, increased ability to predict reader problems, is evident after about six lessons and appears to transfer well to new texts.

CONCLUSIONS

Some of the results we have discussed can be translated directly into educational practice, but other results cannot be applied without further research. For example, it appears that protocol-aided revision could be applied not only to the revision of computer manuals but also to textbooks and instructional materials on a variety of topics, for example, statistics or history. On the other hand, although we have observed that experts define revision more globally than do novices, this fact cannot be translated directly into educational practice. It is exciting to speculate that we could improve students' revision performance by telling them, through words and examples, how experts revise and asking them to do the same. Such an improvement, achieved through changing the student's definition of the revision task, would be bought at a very small instructional cost. We have to recognize, however, that further research is required before we can recommend this sort of instruction for all students. Exposure to expert strategies might work for students who have the ability to recognize global problems and to fix them once they had been recognized. On the other hand, for students who lack these skills, the procedure might be ineffective or even harmful. Pushing students to use expert strategies too early may be like encouraging acrobats to start with the high wire. Good process instruction must be built on a sound understanding of the writing process and good diagnoses of developing writer's problems and needs.

Translating research into practice prematurely, then, can be counterproductive if research results are applied without sufficient caution. If research results are applied carefully, though, we feel that the new discoveries about the writing process will have a major impact on the effectiveness with which writing is taught. It has in fact already created a minor revolution. Teachers are extending their notion of how to teach writing from merely assigning and correcting to leading students through the full range of writing processes. This new perspective enables them to aid students in planning, exploring their own knowledge, identifying their audience, drafting, responding to peer critique, and revising.

Research in writing is beginning to show us the outlines of a theory of writing. It is giving us a much deeper understanding of the nature of writing processes and of how the writer uses them to produce text. In the near future, we can look forward to a very strong pedagogy based on a well-developed theory of writing.

References

Applebee, A. (1982). Writing and learning in school settings. In M. Nystrand (Ed.), *What writers know* (pp. 360–381). New York: Academic Press.

Applebee, A. (in press). Toward a post-process paradigm: Notes on the failure of process approaches to writing instruction. In D. Bartholomae & A. Petrosky (Eds.), *The teaching of writing,* Chicago, IL: National Society for the Study of Education.

Bartlett, E. J. (1981). *Learning to write: Some cognitive and linguistic components,* Washington, DC: Center for Applied Linguistics.

Beach, R. (1976). Self-evaluation strategies of extensive revisors and nonrevisors. *College Composition and Communication, 27,* 160–164.

Bereiter, C., & Scardamalia, M. (1982). From conversion to composition: The role of instruction in a developmental process. In R. Glaser (Ed.), *Advances in instructional psychology* (pp. 1–64). Hillsdale, NJ: Erlbaum.

Berkenkotter, C. (1983). Decisions and revisions: The planning strategies of a published writer. *College Composition and Communication, 34,* 156–169.

Bond, S., Hayes, J. R., Janik, C., & Swaney, J. (1982, August). *Introduction to CMU TOPS-20*. Pittsburgh, PA: Carnegie Mellon University.

Bracewell, R., Frederickson, C., & Frederickson, J. D. (1982). Cognitive processes in composing and comprehending discourse. *Educational Psychologist, 17,* 146–164.

Bracewell, R., Scardamalia, M., & Bereiter, C. (1978, October). The development of audience awareness in writing. *Resources in Education,* pp. 154–433.

Bridwell, L. S. (1980). Revising strategies in tweltfh grade students' transactional writing. *Research in the Teaching of English, 14*(3), 107–122.

Britton, J., Burgess, T., Martin, N., McLeod, A., & Rosen, H. (1975). *The development of writing abilities* (pp. 11–18). London: Macmillan.

Burtis, P. C., Bereiter, C., Scardamalia, M., & Tetroe, J. (1983). The development of planning in writing. In C. G. Wells & B. Kroll (Eds.), *Exploration of children's development in writing* (pp. 153–174). Chichester, England: Wiley.

Duffy, T., Curran, T., & Sass, D. (1983). Document design for technical job tasks: An evaluation. *Human Factors, 25,* 143–160.

Emig, J. (1971). *The composing process of twelfth graders*. Urbana, IL: National Council of Teachers of English.

Ericcson, K. A., & Simon, H. A. (1984). *Protocol analysis: Verbal reports as data.* Cambridge, MA: MIT Press.

Faigley, L., & Witte, S. (1983). Analyzing revision. *College Composition and Communication, 32,* 400–414.

Flower, L. S. (1985). *Problem-solving strategies for writing.* New York: Harcourt Brace Jovanovich.

Flower, L. S., & Hayes, J. R. (1981). A cognitive process theory of writing. *College Composition and Communication, 32,* 365–387.

Flower, L. S., & Hayes, J. R. (1984). Images, plans, and prose: The representation of meaning in writing. *Written Communication, 1,* 120–160.

Hayes, J. R., & Flower, L. S. (1980). Identifying the organization of writing processes. In L. Gregg & E. Steinberg (Eds.), *Cognitive processes in writing: An interdisciplinary approach.* Hillsdale, NJ: Erlbaum.

Hayes, J. R., Flower, L. S., Schriver, K., Stratman, J., & Carey, L. (1985). *Cognitive processes in revision* (Tech. Rep. No. 12). Pittsburgh, PA: Carnegie Mellon University, Communication Design Center.

Hayes, J. R., Schriver, K. A., Spilka, R., & Blaustein, A. (1986, March). *If it's clear to me it must be clear to them.* Paper presented at the Conference on College Composition and Communication, New Orleans, LA.

Hillocks, G. (1984). What works in teaching composition: A meta-analysis of experimental treatment studies. *American Journal of Education, 93,* 133–170.

Holland, M., Rose, A., Dean, R., & Dory, S. (1985). *Processes involved in writing effective procedural instructions* (Tech. Rep. No. 1-ONR). Washington, DC: American Institutes for Research.

Hull, G. (1984). *The editing process in writing: A performance study of experts and novices.* Unpublished doctoral dissertation, University of Pittsburgh, PA.

Kaufer, D., Hayes, J. R., & Flower, L. S. (1986). Composing written sentences. *Research in the Teaching of English, 20,* 121–140.

Murray, D. M. (1978). Internal revision: A process of discovery. In C. R. Cooper & L. Odell (Eds.), *Research on composing: Points of departure.* Urbana, IL: National Council of Teachers of English.

Olson, G., Mack, R., & Duffy, S. (1981). Cognitive aspects of genre. *Poetics, 10,* 283–315.

Pianko, S. (1979). Description of the composing process of college freshman writers. *Research in the Teaching of English, 13,* 5–22.

Rohman, G. (1965). Pre-writing: The stage of discovery in the writing process. *College Composition and Communication, 16,* 106–112.

Rose, M. (1980). Rigid rules, inflexible plans, and the stifling of language; a cognitivist analysis of writer's block. *College Composition and Communcation, 31,* 389–401.

Scardamalia, M., & Bereiter, C. (1983). The development of evaluative, diagnostic, and remedial capabilities in children's composing. In M. Martlew (Ed.), *The psychology of written language: A developmental approach.* London: Wiley.

Scardamalia, M., & Bereiter, C. (in press). Written composition. In M. Wittrock (Ed.), *Third handbook of research on teaching.* New York: Macmillan.

Schriver, K. (1984). *Revising computer documentation for comprehension: Ten lessons in protocol-aided revision* (Tech. Rep. No. 14). Pittsburgh, PA: Carnegie Mellon University, Communication Design Center.

Schumacher, G. M., Klare, G. R., Cronin, F. C., & Moses, J. D. (1984). Cognitive activities of beginning and advanced college writers: A pausal analysis. *Research in the Teaching of English, 18,* 169–187.

Shaughnessy, M. (1977). *Errors and Expectations: A guide for the teacher of basic writing.* New York: Oxford University Press.

Sommers, N. (1980). Revision strategies of student writers and experienced writers. *College Composition and Communication, 31,* 378–387.

Spilich, G. J., Vesonder, G. T., Chiesi, H. L., & Voss, J. F. (1979). Text processing of domain-related information for individuals with high- and low-domain knowledge. *Journal of Verbal Learning and Verbal Behavior, 18,* 275–290.

Stallard, C. (1974). An analysis of the writing behavior of good student writers. *Research in the Teaching of English, 8,* 206–218.

Swaney, J. H., Janik, C. J., Bond, S. J., & Hayes, J. R. (1981). *Editing for comprehension: Improving the process through reading protocols* (Tech. Rep. No. 14). Pittsburgh, PA: Carnegie Mellon University, Document Design Project.

Voss, J. F., Greene, T. R., Post, T. A., & Penner, B. C. (1983). Problem-solving skills in the social sciences. In G. H. Bower (Ed.), *The psychology of learning and motivation: Advances in research and theory* (Vol. 17, pp. 165–213). NY: Academic Press.

Young, R. E., Becker, A., & Pike, K. (1970). *Rhetoric: Discovery and change.* New York: Harcourt, Brace & World.

Writing and Knowing: Toward Redefining the Writing Process

James A. Reither

> Who is this that darkeneth counsel
> by words without knowledge?
> Job 38:2

Composition Studies was transformed when theorists, researchers, and teachers of writing began trying to find out what actually happens when people write. Over the last decade or so, members of the discipline have striven primarily to discover and teach the special kinds of thinking, the processes, that occur during composing.[1] The goal has been to replace a prescriptive pedagogy (select a subject, formulate a thesis, outline, write, proofread) with a descriptive discipline whose members study and teach "process not product." Although the methodologies of process research have been challenged, its contributions to our understanding of composing have been applauded by theorists and practitioners alike. The consensus has generally been that process researchers have done a good job of answering the questions they have asked. Still, some are beginning to point to questions that, if they've been raised at all, have certainly not been answered.

Richard Larson, for example, has asked, "How does the impulse to write arise?" And, "How does the writer identify the elements needed for a solution [to a rhetorical problem], retrieve from memory or find in some other source(s) the items needed in the solution, and then test the trial solution to see whether it answers the problem?" (250–251).

Lee Odell, in a Four Cs paper entitled "Reading and Writing in the Workplace," observed that our questions about composing and inquiry processes have tended to stay "too close to the text." Odell's own research has led him to conclude that writing and inquiry are often (if not always) "socially collaborative" and that invention, discovery, and inquiry are closely tied to institutional relationships and strategies. Interpersonal and institutional contexts are, according to Odell, far more important than our literature has acknowledged, and he urges us to study more closely these contexts and strategies as necessary components of writing and inquiry processes.

Taking a different tack, Patricia Bizzell has divided composition theorists and researchers into two theoretical camps—those "interested in the structure of language-learning and thinking processes in their earliest state, prior to social influence"; and those "more interested in the social processes whereby language-learning and thinking capabilities are shaped and used in particular communities" (215). Bizzell laments the dominance of the "inner-directed" camp, arguing that Flower and Hayes, for example, pay too little attention to the role of knowledge in composing (229), and that "what looks like a cognitive difference [between unskilled and skilled writers often] turns out to have a large social component" (233). She thus argues that student writing difficulties often stem not from faulty or inefficient composing processes but, rather, from unfamiliarity with academic discourse conventions. "What is underdeveloped," she suggests, "is their knowledge of the ways experience is constituted and interpreted in the academic discourse community . . ." (230).

One result, as John Gage notes, is that the classical concept of *stasis* has all but vanished from the textbooks. The typical writing situation, according to Gage, is one in which reader and writer already share knowledge, "and it is the difference between what they know that motivates the need for communication—in both directions—and which therefore compels the act of writing" (2). Our practice, however, is to "send students in search of something to intend, . . . as if intention itself were subject to free choice. Students do not begin writing in order to fulfill an intention; rather, they are assumed to begin intentionless to search for something to want to say" (2).

What Larson, Odell, Bizzell, and Gage all point to is the tendency in composition studies to think of writing as a process which begins with an impulse to put words on paper; and the issues they raise should lead us to wonder if our thinking is not being severely limited by a concept of process that explains only the cognitive processes that occur as people write. Their questions and observations remind us that writing is not merely a process that occurs within contexts. That is, writing and what writers do during writing cannot be artificially separated from the social-rhetorical situations in which writing gets done, from the conditions that enable writers to do what they do, and from the motives writers have for doing what they do. Writing is not to context what a fried egg is to its pan.[2] Writing is, in fact, one of those processes which, in its use, *creates* and *constitutes* its own contexts.

Assisted, however, by the notion that writing is itself a mode of learning and knowing, and by the popularity of such developments as the attacks on "Engfish" (with the concomitant emphasis on the values of expressive writing), process research—precisely because it has taught us so much—has bewitched and beguiled us into thinking of writing as a self-contained process that evolves essentially out of a relationship between writers and their emerging texts. That is, we conceptualize and teach writing on the "model of the individual writer shaping thought through language" (Bazerman, "Relationship" 657), as if the process began in the writer (perhaps with an experience of cognitive dissonance) and not in the writer's relationship to the world. In this truncated view, all writing—whether the writer is a seasoned veteran or a "placidly inexperienced nineteen-year-old" (Schor 72)—begins naturally and properly with probing the contents of the memory and the mind to discover the information, ideas, and language that are the substance of writing. This model of what happens when people write does not include, at least not centrally, any substantive coming to know beyond that which occurs as writers probe their own present experience and knowledge. Composition studies does not seriously attend to the ways writers know what other people know or to the ways mutual knowing motivates writing—does not seriously attend, that is, to the knowing without which cognitive dissonance is impossible.

The upshot is that we proceed as if students come to us already widely-experienced, widely-read, well-informed beings who need only learn how to do the kinds of thinking that will enable them to probe their experience and knowledge to discover what Rohman calls the "writing ideas" (106) for their compositions. We teach them to look heuristically into their own hearts, experiences, long-term memories, information- and idea-banks to discover what they have to say on the assigned or chosen subject. In so doing, we send several obviously problematic messages. One, identified by Bizzell, is that "once students are capable of cognitively sophisticated thinking and writing, they are ready to tackle the problems of a particular writing situation" (217). Another is that composing can be learned and done outside of full participation in the knowledge/discourse communities that motivate writing. Another is that other kinds of learning which can and do impel and give substance to writing—those, for example, that result from deliberate, purposeful learning through observation, reading, research, inquiry—are not really part of writing.[3] Yet another is that those kinds of learning have already occurred sufficiently to impel and "authorize" writing. That is, writers do not need to know what they are talking about: they can learn what they are talking about as they compose; they can write their way out of their ignorance.

We need to broaden our concept of what happens when people write. Writing is clearly a more multi-dimensioned process than current theory and practice would have us believe, and one that begins long before it is appropriate to commence working with strategies for invention. If we are going to teach our students to *need* to write, we will have to know much more than we do about the kinds of contexts that conduce— sometimes even force, certainly enable—the impulse to write. The "micro-theory" of process now current in composition studies needs to be expanded into a "macro-theory" encompassing activities, processes, and kinds of knowing that come into play before the impulse to write is even possible.

To bring about that expansion, we need to press some new questions; and we need to know more than we now know, not only about cognitive processes during compos- ing, but also about processes involved in coming to know generally. The focus of com- position studies is presently on the first three of the five parts of classical rhetoric—on invention, arrangement, and style. It is time to look for ways to bring *stasis* back into the process and to learn more about its role in writing. We should use case studies, ethnographic studies, longitudinal studies, textual analysis, thinking-aloud protocol analysis, to answer such questions as these: What is the precise role in composing of substantive knowing—of concentrated participation in a knowledge/discourse community; of, simply, a fund of information on and ideas about the subject at hand? What, in this regard, is the precise relation between writing and reading? Where do we get our language for talking about things? What exactly *are* discourse conventions,[4] where do they come from, and how do we learn them? Are writers who know a great deal—who have engaged in direct and indirect sorts of inquiry within specific knowledge/discourse communities—likely to be better or different writers? Are writers who *know how* to find out likely to be better or different? What happens when people conduct inquiry and research? How *do* writers acquire the authority that impels writing? What *kinds* of knowing, and what kinds of knowing how, enable and assist writing?

Bizzell (238–239), Elaine Maimon, and Kenneth Bruffee ("Peer Tutoring") all argue that we must analyze and teach the conventions of academic discourse. It seems clear, however, that that's not enough. To do that is to continue to confine students to the "impoverished" "meanings carried by the conventional rules of language" (Cooper 108). Bruffee, citing Richard Rorty, notes that "In normal discourse . . . everyone agrees on the 'set of conventions about what counts as a relevant contribution, what counts as a question, what counts as having a good argument for that answer or a good criticism of it' " (8). He goes on to say, rightly, that "Not to have mastered the normal discourse of a discipline, no matter how many 'facts' or data one may know, is not to be knowledgeable in that discipline" (9). But the obverse is equally true: What counts as a relevant contribution, question, answer, or criticism is determined not only by adherence to a set of discourse conventions, but also by such concerns as whether or not the contribution, question, answer, or criticism has already appeared in "the literature"—whether or not it is to the point, relevant, or timely. A writer addressing dead issues, posing questions already answered, or voicing irrelevant criticisms is judged ignorant and viewed as, at best, an initiate—not yet an insider, not yet a full member of the discipline. Rather more basically, what counts as relevant is a contribution in which the writer's version of "the facts of the matter" accords with the version held in general by the community addressed by the writing.

To belong to a discourse community is to belong to a knowledge community—an "inquiry community"; and the ways things are talked or written about are no more vital than the content of what's talked and written about. As Bruffee says, "Ordinary people write to inform and convince other people within the writer's own community. . . " (8). Because that's true, we must think not merely in terms of analysis and explanation; we must also think in terms of the other kinds of knowing required to belong to a community. We need to extend our understanding of the process of writing so that it will include not only experience- and memory-probing activities, but also inquiry strategies and techniques that will enable students to search beyond their own limited present experience and knowledge. We need to help students learn how to do the kinds of learning that will allow them, in their writing, to use what they *can* know, through effective inquiry, rather than suffer the limits of what they already know. We need to bring curiosity, the ability to conduct productive inquiry, and an obligation for substantive knowing into our model of the process of writing. To do that, we need to find ways to immerse writing students in academic knowledge/discourse communities so thay can write from within those communities.

The writing-across-the-curriculum movement, when it's done well, seems to have a chance of doing that. So also does Bruffee's own collaborative learning, if it can be untied from the notion of peer tutoring. As matters now stand, however, neither of these adequately addresses the problem of teaching students how to come to know so they can write literally as "knowledgeable peers" (Bruffee, "Peer Tutoring" 6) in academic communities. Neither gives students opportunities to "indwell" (Polanyi) an actual academic knowledge/discourse community, to learn, from the inside, its major questions, its governing assumptions, its language, its research methods, its evidential contexts, its forms, its discourse conventions, its major authors and its major texts—that is, its knowledge and its modes of knowing. Only this kind of immersion has a real chance of giving substance to their coming to know through composing.

The title of a course in which this immersion is to occur does not really matter. Neither does the name of the discipline or department in which the course is taught. It need not be a writing course. (In fact, obviously, this immersion need not occur in the context of a course at all. Most of us learned to do what we do on our own—perhaps in spite of the courses we took—and some students continue to do the same.) What does matter is that the course should be "organized as a collaborative investigation of a scholarly field rather than the delivery of a body of knowledge."[5]

As I have claimed above, discourse communities are also knowledge communities. The business of knowledge communities is inquiry—coming to know. In academia, inquiry necessarily begins with reading in the literature of a "scholarly field" (which may be almost anything: rhetoric or evolution, for instance; or deviant behavior, the literature of eighteenth-century England, the comedies of Shakespeare, Islamic religions, literacy, and so on). Because, in an essential way, the literature of a scholarly field *is* the scholarly field, reading in that literature is elemental to all other kinds and levels of investigation, including writing; and for all of us, but particularly for students, reading in the literature normally means library research. Furthermore, academic writing, reading, and inquiry are collaborative, social acts, social processes,[6] which not only result in, but also—and this is crucial—result *from,* social products: writing processes and written products are both elements of the *same social process.* Hence, academic writing, reading, and inquiry are inseparably linked; and all three are learned not by doing any one alone, but by doing them all at the same time. To "teach writing" is thus necessarily to ground writing in reading and inquiry.

In general terms, then, this immersion—this initiation—should image in important ways the "real world" of active, workaday academic inquirers. The course most effectively operates as a workshop[7] in which students read and write not merely for their teacher, but for themselves and for each other. In fact, students and teachers function best as co-investigators, with reading and writing being used collaboratively to conduct the inquiry. Organizing a course in this way allows an incredible range of reading activities—in everything from bibliographies to books; and a similar range of writing activities—from jotting down call numbers to writing formal articles of the sorts they are reading. What matters is that this should be language in use. In such a context, writing, reading, and inquiry are evaluated according to their pragmatic utility: the important question is not "How good is it?" but, instead. "To what extent and how effectively does it contribute to and further the investigation?" The inquiry is made manageable in the same way all such inquiries are made manageable, not by "choosing" and "focusing" a topic, but by seeking answers to the questions which impel the investigation.

Out of this immersion in academic inquiry and out of the ways they see themselves and others (both their immediate peers and those who have authored the literature of the field) using reading and writing to conduct the inquiry, students can construct appropriate models. That is, they can see effective and ineffective writing, reading, and inquiry conventions, strategies, and behaviors at work—not just as those conventions and behaviors can be inferred by reading in the literature, but also as they are evolved and used by their teachers and *each other*. Student and teacher roles in the workshop evolve out of their own participation in the investigation: reading and writing; exchanging and using each others' information, ideas, notes, annotations, sources; defining goals and making plans; applying "truth-seeking procedures" (Bach and Harnish 43); bringing to bear topic and world knowledge to conduct what Bereiter and Scardamalia call "reflective inquiry" (5-6).

At the core of composition studies is the virtually unchallenged conviction that what we have to study and what we have to teach is "process not product." By process, however, we presently mean something that encourages in our students the notion that through writing they can, like Plato's Gorgias "answer any question that is put to [them]" (20). Because we routinely put our students in arhetorical situations in which they can only write out of ignorance, they have little choice but to "hunt more after words than matter" (Bacon 29), and we stand open to the charge that we advocate "mere rhetoric" over writing informed by a profound relationship between writers and their worlds. It is time to redefine the writing process so that substantive social knowing is given due prominence in both our thinking and our teaching.

Works Cited

Bach, K., and R. M. Harnish, *Linguistic Communication and Speech Acts*. Cambridge: MIT P, 1979.
Bacon, Francis. *The Advancement of Learning*. Oxford: Oxford UP, 1951.
Bazerman, Charles. "A Relationship between Reading and Writing: The Conversational Model." *College English* 41 (1980): 656–661.
-----. "What Written Knowledge Does: Three Examples of Academic Discourse." *Philosophy of the Social Sciences* 11 (1981): 361–387.
Bereiter, Carl, and Marlene Scardamalia. "Levels of Inquiry in Writing Research." *Research on Writing: Principles and Methods*. Eds. Peter Mosenthal, Lynne Tamor, and Sean A. Walmsley. New York: Longman, 1983. 3–25.
Bizzell, Patricia. "Cognition, Convention, and Certainty: What We Need to Know about Writing." *PRE/TEXT* 3 (1982): 213–243.
Bruffee, Kenneth A. "Collaborative Writing and the 'Conversation of Mankind.'" *College English* 46 (1984): 635–652.
-----. "Peer Tutoring and the 'Conversation of Mankind.'" *Writing Centers: Theory and Administration*. Ed. Gary A. Olson. Urbana: NCTE, 1984. 3–15.
Cooper, Marilyn M. "Context as Vehicle: Implicatures in Writing." *What Writers Know: The Language, Process, and Structure of Written Discourse*. Ed. Martin Nystrand. New York: Academic, 1982. 105–128.

Cowan, Gregory, and Elizabeth Cowan. *Writing*. New York: Wiley, 1980.

Emig, Janet. *The Composing Processes of Twelfth Graders*. Urbana: NCTE, 1971.

Fish, Stanley. *Is There a Text in This Class?: The Authority of Interpretive Communities*. Cambridge: Harvard UP, 1980.

Fleck, Ludwik. *Genesis and Development of a Scientific Fact*. 1935. Chicago: U of Chicago P, 1979.

Flower, Linda and John R. Hayes. "A Cognitive Process Theory of Writing." *College Composition and Communication* 32 (1981): 365–387.

Gage, John. "Towards an Epistemology of Composition." *Journal of Advanced Composition* 2 (1981): 1–9.

Knolblauch, C. H., and Lil Brannon. "Modern Rhetoric in the Classroom: Making Meaning Matter." *Rhetorical Traditions and the Teaching of Writing*. Upper Montclair, NJ: Boynton/Cook, 1984. 98–117.

Kuhn, Thomas. *The Structure of Scientific Revolutions*. 2nd ed., enlarged. Chicago: U of Chicago P, 1970.

Larson, Richard L. "The Writer's Mind: Recent Research and Unanswered Questions." *The Writer's Mind: Writing as a Mode of Thinking*. Ed. Janice M. Hays, et al. Urbana: NCTE, 1983. 239–251.

Maimon, Elaine P. "Maps and Genres: Exploring Connections in the Arts and Sciences." *Composition and Literature: Bridging the Gap*. Ed. Winifred Bryan Horner. Chicago U of Chicago P, 1983. 110–125.

Maimon, Elaine P., et al. *Readings in the Arts and Sciences*. Boston: Little, 1984.

-----. *Writing in the Arts and Sciences*. Cambridge, MA: Winthrop, 1981.

Matsuhashi, Ann. "Pausing and Planning: The Tempo of Written Discourse Production." *Research in the Teaching of English* 15 (1981): 113–134.

Murray, Donald M. "Write Before Writing." *College Composition and Communication* 29 (1978): 375–381.

-----. "Writing as Process: How Writing Finds Its Own Meaning." *Eight Approaches to Teaching Composition*. Ed. Timothy R. Donovan and Ben W. McClelland, Urbana: NCTE, 1980. 3–20.

Myers, Greg. "Texts and Knowledge Claims: The Social Construction of Two Biology Articles." *Social Studies of Science*. Forthcoming.

Odell, Lee. "Reading and Writing in the Workplace." Conference on College Composition and Communication. New York City, 31 March 1984.

Odell, Lee, and Dixie Goswami. "Writing in a Nonacademic Setting." *New Directions in Composition Research*. Ed. Richard Beach and Lillian S. Bridwell. New York: Guilford, 1984. 233–258.

Perl, Sondra. "Understanding Composing." *College Composition and Communication* 31 (1980): 363–369.

Plato. *Gorgias*. Trans. Walter Hamilton. Harmondsworth: Penguin, 1971.

Polanyi, Michael. *Personal Knowledge: Towards a Post-Critical Philosophy*. Chicago: U of Chicago P, 1962.

Rohman, D. Gordon. "Pre-writing: The Stage of Discovery in the Writing Process." *College Composition and Communication* 16 (1965): 106–112.

Rorty, Richard. *Philosophy and the Mirror of Nature*. Princeton: Princeton UP, 1979.

Schor, Sandra. "Style Through Control: The Pleasures of the Beginning Writer." *Linguistics, Stylistics and the Teaching of Composition*. Ed. Donald McQuade. Akron, OH: L and S, 1979. 72–80.

Sommers, Nancy. "Revision Strategies of Student Writers and Experienced Adult Writers," *College Composition and Communication* 31 (1980): 378–388.

Notes

1. Some well-known examples: Emig combined composing-aloud sessions, observation, and interviews to examine the composing processes of twelfth-grade writers. Perl used thinking-aloud protocols to uncover patterns or subroutines that occur and recur during composing. Flower and Hayes also tape and analyze thinking-aloud protocols, created by skilled and unskilled writers; their special concern has been to construct an accurate model of what happens as writers manage such subprocesses as planning, translating, and reviewing. Matsuhashi videotaped writers in the act of writing, paying special attention to planning and decision-making processes during pauses in composing. Sommers interviewed skilled and unskilled writers after they had revised pieces of writing, and then analyzed the pieces to determine the kinds of writer-concerns that motivated changes made from draft to draft. And, just as important, Murray has written to watch himself writing to learn what was happening as he wrote.

2. I owe the metaphor to my colleague Alan W. Mason (personal communication).

3. This reductive method of writing allows one widely-adopted composition textbook. Cowan and Cowan's *Writing*, to advise students that in writing a research paper "you have to have a large number of skills—some writing skills, some nonwriting" (428). Students learning the shape and scope of the writing process from this textbook are advised that using the library, taking notes, incorporating notes into an essay, documenting sources and

using appropriate research paper forms are "nonwriting skills" (428). Inquiry outside the mind and memory of the writer, and the knowing required for conducting such inquiry, are not necessarily related and therefore readily separable from "writing."

4. In this regard, see Bazerman, "What Written Knowledge Does." See also, on a different level, the two textbooks that have come out of the Beaver College writing-across-the-curriculum program: Maimon et al. *Writing in the Arts and Sciences* and *Readings in the Arts and Sciences.*

5. Russell A. Hunt, my colleague at St. Thomas University, phrased it this way in a course description.

6. Bizzell's article and Bruffee's "Peer Tutoring" (or his recontextualization of that article, "Collaborative Writing and the 'Conversation of Mankind,' ") are important here, not only for their discussions of the social grounding of writing, but also for their references to much of the important literature in this particular scholarly field. See (for example) the following theoretical works: Fleck, *Genesis and Development of a Scientific Fact;* Rorty, *Philosophy and the Mirror of Nature,* esp. Part III; Fish, *Is There a Text in This Class?;* and, most important, Kuhn, *The Structure of Scientific Revolutions.* Finally, for a sampling of various kinds of research in this area, see Bazerman's "What Written Knowledge Does"; the work of Odell and Goswami—for example, "Writing in a Nonacademic Setting"; and Myers, "Texts as Knowledge Claims."

7. For a model of the kind of workshop this might be, see Knoblauch and Brannon. A major difference between their ideal workshop and mine is that I would embed the discourse community of the workshop in the socially-constructed knowing available in the record of the larger conversation going on in the literature of the scholarly field being investigated.

Teaching as a Rhetorical Art

Erika Lindemann

As the director of a large writing program, I have frequent opportunities to discuss teaching problems with faculty members and teaching assistants. Many of these teachers enjoy their students and discuss their writing courses enthusiastically. Others consider teaching composition a duty; they fight the assignment or believe that their efforts are wasted. Some of the time, then, I feel as if I'm sharing a conversion experience with another kindred soul. We agree on the importance of what we're doing; we willingly share teaching strategies; we solve problems by mutual consent. At other times, I encounter unhappiness, a kind of resistance which may express itself as hostility toward students or toward other teachers, as criticism of the textbooks, the syllabus, the teaching schedule, and the size of the class, or as statements about the hopelessness of teaching anyone anything about writing. Over the years, I've observed that those who most detest the teaching of writing feel least confident about what they are doing. Their complaints seem to stem mostly from insecurity, from sometimes totally subconscious feelings of inadequacy. They believe that they know how to teach writing, but at the same time they doubt that they're making much of a difference. Those who enjoy teaching composition—and they may be young or old, experienced or first-semester teachers— have confidence. They know what works, and if it doesn't, why. They aren't afraid to work through difficult teaching and writing problems with students. They risk. They stretch themselves.

What is it that separates the secure from the insecure? The confident from the reluctant writing teacher? What does one group know, or do, or believe that the other group doesn't?

Fortunately, confidence isn't a matter of age. We don't have to be near retirement to teach writing well. To be sure, I've learned much from those who have taught composition for years, who've seen fads come and go, who are experienced writers and know firsthand what wars with words are all about. But first-year teachers have also taught me much: a respect for freshmen, the value of listening instead of talking all the time, an ability to appreciate the power of language without overwhelming students with the latinate terminology of formal grammar. Becoming a confident teacher, then, isn't just a matter of age.

Nor is it the result of book learning. I know many fine writing teachers who've never read Aristotle, Quintilian, Cicero, Chomsky, Moffett, Piaget, Kinneavy, Macrorie, or Cooper and Odell. Conversely, I know some teachers thoroughly familiar with rhetorical theories but unable to translate them into practical help for students. I don't mean to underestimate book learning. We can learn much from the disciplines that explain how people use language. Literary critcism, linguistics, psychology, philosophy, education,

148

rhetoric—all of these fields and their subspecialties can prevent us from repeating mistakes or teaching by trial-and-error. More important, book learning gives us a coherent framework for our teaching. Book learning equips us with what-knowledge; it helps us know what we're doing and why. It tells us, for example, that writing teaches writing, that the best way to teach writing is to let students write and to give them constructive responses to their performances. Why? Because writing is not a subject to be talked about, but an activity to practice.

But most book learning stops there. What we learn from reading is essentially theoretical, historical, or empirical. Books too infrequently concern themselves with the practice of teaching. Effective teachers, however, have the skill, the happy ability to translate theory into practice. They manage the leap from what-knowledge to how-knowledge, transforming what they want to teach into a successful interaction with students. They have this ability, I believe, because they are effective rhetoricians. They can communicate a course outline, an assignment, a lesson plan, a set of comments on a student's paper to an audience they appreciate and know reasonably well. They may not know consciously that they are behaving rhetorically, but most of the time, effective teachers control well the balancing act Wayne Booth describes in "The Rhetorical Stance" [*CCC,* 14 (October 1963), 139–45].

The "common ingredient" Booth finds in all of the writing he admires is something he calls "the rhetorical stance, a stance which depends on discovering and maintaining in any writing situation a proper balance among the three elements that are at work in any communicative effort: the available arguments about the subject itself, the interests and peculiarities of the audience and the voice, the implied character, of the speaker." Just as effective writers find a balance between subject, audience and their voice, so do effective teachers. Teaching, like writing, occurs in a rhetorical context. Someone says something to someone else for a purpose. We need to remember, of course, that in a writing class, students are often teachers, teaching each other or themselves. The paid professional responsible for the class may also be a student, learning about composing from members of the class. Nevertheless, teaching, like writing, brings these elements—teacher, student, subject—together in proportions that vary from one teacher and class meeting to the next. Like writing, teaching expresses itself in several forms of discourse—lectures, class discussion, conference, writing workshops, assignments, comments on papers. All of these forms of discourse exhibit special rhetorical strategies and aims. How we teach depends on what we teach, who our students are, and what persona we adopt. As we plan, execute, and revise our teaching performance, we continually realign our relationship to our students and subject, eventually developing a style which best expresses our teaching self.

But teachers, like writers, sometimes fail to maintain "a proper balance among the three elements that are at work in any communicative effort." They overplay or underplay some elements, creating "unbalanced stances" which promote ineffective teaching. When the subject—a model essay, grammar, paragraph unity, a textbook, a work of literature—

becomes the primary focus of a writing class, the teacher has adopted "the pedant's stance," which Booth defines as "ignoring or underplaying the personal relationship of speaker and audience and depending entirely on statements about a subject." Such a teacher forgets that courses **about** writing give students too little practice **doing** writing. Similarly, we may know teachers who assume what Booth calls "the entertainer's stance." Such teachers need to be the center of attention, need to cultivate the persona of a comedian, an expert, a good ole boy or girl. They sacrifice substance and students to their own personalities, charms, or needs. Their students either respond by becoming embarrassed or by showing compassionate tolerance as they help the teacher affirm his or her self-esteem. Teachers can also adopt Booth's "advertiser's stance" which undervalues the subject and the teacher's voice and overvalues the audience. When this happens, students take control of the class, usually because the teacher is afraid of students or wants to give them more responsibility for their own learning than they may be able to handle. All of these unbalanced stances result from a teacher's failure to make effective rhetorical choices. They can characterize not only the classroom but also writing assignments and responses to student papers, two other contexts in which teaching-as-rhetoric occurs. Let's examine the balanced stance in each of these three contexts.

In a writing class, the confident teacher knows her material, her students, and herself well enough to act as a guide for less experienced writers. The classroom becomes a place where students practice writing. What she has to *say* matters less than what her students *do*. She spends significantly less time talking *about* writing than other teachers might but plans many more activities that encourage students to plan, draft, and rewrite progressively more complicated pieces. She replaces lectures with discussion and individual conferences as students work alone or in groups. She encourages peer-teaching so that students become better able to evaluate their own work. She tends to avoid formal rhetorical or grammatical terminology and workbook-ish exercises because they can become ends in themselves, not means to helping students develop confidence in and control over their composing habits. Students write frequently in class; they discuss student papers; they work out alternative ways to approach assignments and writing problems; they exchange drafts of work-in-progress. If something called "paragraph unity" needs attention, the effective writing teacher isn't likely to lecture on it or run the class through a series of lockstep exercises in a textbook. Instead, the class is more likely to examine several student paragraphs from previous papers, discussing what strategies the writers used to hold paragraphs together. Then, the class is likely to create several paragraphs, practicing the techniques and responding to their work. Students learn by doing. Their activity, not textbooks or lectures, defines the course. I once asked a teacher who conducts his class this way how he managed to pack so much activity into one hour. He told me that he prepares class by answering three questions:

1. What do my students need to practice?

2. What will show them how to do that? What student writing can we discuss to let them know they're halfway there?

3. What can they do in class to gain confidence with the technique?

"What can *they* do?" is a very different question, of course, from "What can *I* do in class today?"

A second context in which the writing teacher makes rhetorical choices is in drafting assignments. Traditional assignments are generally inadequate because they omit, distort, or leave to guesswork too much necessary information. They tend to ignore students' needs and overplay the topic of the assignments, the number of words required, or the widths of margins. Often, assignments are composed orally in class or slapped on the board as the bell rings. Consequently, students are likely to produce vague, general compositions addressed to no one in particular about a subject they may be only mildly interested in. Writing assignments ought to be a teaching tool. They hold a course together; they determine the kinds of practice students have with writing; they serve as the basis for much class discussion. So, we need to compose each assignment carefully, assessing its relationship to other assignments, anticipating problems students might have, planning class discussions, groupwork, or other instruction to supplement the assignment. If the assignment is to teach composing and not simply how high students can jump hurdles for a grade, we need to write them out—and rethink them and revise them—until they reflect appropriate decisions about the abilities of our students and the task we are asking them to do. We need to ask ourselves questions. What do I want my students to do? Why? Is it worth doing? How do I want them to do the assignment? In what ways am I giving them practice planning, drafting, and rewriting their work? Have I given them enough information to make effective decisions about their subject, purpose, form, mode, and audience? How does this assignment build on the practice they've had so far and prepare for more complicated tasks later on? How much time in and out of class will students need for prewriting, writing, and rewriting? How will I evaluate their work? What defines a "successful" response to this assignment? One way to answer these questions is to write with our students, responding to our own assignments. If students improve their writing through guided practice, then writing assignments represent the major means of practicing the decisions writers make. Effective assignments must be longer than one sentence and give more information than a title. They need to incorporate as many of the factors as possible which, in real life, help us define and solve rhetorical problems. When they don't, we invite students to perform poorly and miss an opportunity to help them become fluent in composing.

When we respond to the writing our students submit, we also need to remember rhetorical priniciples that govern how we express messages and how our audience is likely to respond. The only appropriate purpose for comments on student papers is to offer feedback and guide learning—to teach. Some comments, however, seem to be written for other reasons: to damn the ideas with faint praise or snide remarks, to justify a letter grade, to prove that a teacher can always find more errors than the student, to confuse the writer with cryptic correction symbols, contradictory advice, or mysterious circles and lines. Marginal comments and endnotes must do more than label strengths and weaknesses. They represent an on-going written dialogue with the student about his or her writing, a private tutorial which explains not just what to do but how.

First, comments should encourage students to review their work so that they may apply what they've learned in writing this paper or draft to the next. That means noting strengths as well as weaknesses, pointing out how something done well in paragraph three could also improve paragraph seven. Second, marginal comments should address a range of discourse features, not just spelling, punctuation, and word choice. We need to respond to or ask questions about sentence and paragraph structure, organization, supporting evidence, the writer's purpose and point of view, and so on. Third, marginal comments should avoid correction symbols, technical terminology, and the private code English teachers and editors know so well. The languages of copyediting and teaching are different. Our comments are intended for students, not other teachers, not grammarians, not typesetters. We can also monitor students' planning and rewriting strategies if we ask them to submit scratchwork, freewritings, and drafts. If scratchwork is skimpy, we can suggest additional prewriting strategies to rid future papers of unsupported generalizations. If drafts aren't messy enough or reveal that "rewriting" seems to mean "substituting a word here and there," our comments can help students change what they do when they revise.

Finally, the endnote can help us teach writing if we use it for more than justifying a grade on a paper the student has already forgotten about. That paper is finished, as far as the student is concerned, and unless it requires substantial revision, the endnote must serve a different purpose. Its purpose can be to set goals for the next writing project. We can summarize the marginal comments, applaud progress, and suggest specific ways to build on that progress next time. Most of my endnotes follow a similar formula, which nevertheless varies a little depending on the student and the kinds of problems he or she needs to work on. I compose endnotes by answering the following three questions (usually in this order):

1. What has this writer done well?

2. What are one or two major problems and why do they create difficulty for a reader? Here, I usually select one or two problems to work on in the next paper—only one or two—and explain why they make the message less effective than it could be. Sometimes the problems are ones the student wants to work on, information I learn from notes students attach to their papers when they turn them in.

3. Specifically, how can the writer solve the problem? What can he or she do to reach the goal I'm setting? Most teachers' endnotes answer the first two questions but often neglect the third. It's not enough to say "Your sentences are choppy" or "Vary sentence structure more." Those words define a problem, to be sure, but they don't offer much help to the student who wants to know how to solve it. They don't teach. Rather, they force the student to experiment by trial-and-error until perhaps three papers and four weeks later sentences stop being choppy. To reach the goal more efficiently, the end-

note could suggest how to vary sentences, could prescribe some explicit behavior the writer can practice next time. I'd want to add something like this: "After you get your ideas down in a rough draft, combine and tighten some of your sentences. Try introductory clauses, series, and some of the other constructions you've been practicing in the sentence-combining exercises in class. If I see you taking some risks with your sentences, don't worry about comma problems; we'll tackle them later."

Good writing teachers enjoy their work with students because they are confident of what they're doing. Their confidence may result from experience or from knowledge, from years of teaching or abundant reading. But the skills they have, the sorts of things they do, are not the exclusive property of the well-read and the experienced. Although writing teachers work with students in many contexts, the three settings I have discussed are perhaps the most significant. Regardless of differences among institutions, students, and teaching styles, all of us writing teachers conduct classes, make assignments, and comment on student writing. Good writing teachers approach this work in ways that seem to some to depart from traditional methods of teaching. The skill a good writing teacher possesses is the ability to question those methods, to keep asking "*How* should I do this?" Many traditional teaching practices we inherited were meant to help students learn grammar or literature or other academic subjects. As we've revised our understanding of what people do when they write, we've also had to review how we teach writing. We've had to redefine what teaching and learning mean in a writing class, where what we teach and what students learn is not a body of facts but a process, an activity which requires practice. It's appropriate, then, to rethink what goes on in a writing class, what makes a good writing assignment, and what our comments say to students about their writing. All three questions address the relationships among students, teachers, and a subject called "the composing process." Because these questions require us to know who says what to whom for what purpose, because they are questions rhetoric has always concerned itself with, the answers, I think, will come from viewing teaching as a rhetorical art.

Analyzing Audiences

Douglas B. Park

What do we expect analysis of audience to do for writers? What form should analysis of audience take, or, more precisely, what makes certain kinds of analysis more or less appropriate in given situations?

The centrality of audience in the rhetorical tradition and the detail with which current writing texts provide advice on analyzing an audience might suggest that the answers to such questions are well established. But they clearly are not. Side by side with the growing awareness in recent discussions that audience is a rich and complex concept exists a growing dissatisfaction with traditonal audience analysis—those familiar questions about an audience's age, sex, education, and social background that form the core of most proposed heuristics. (See, for instance, Barry Kroll, "Writing for Readers: Three Perspectives on Audience," *CCC*, 35 [May, 1984], 172–75; Russell Long, "Writer-Audience Relationships," *CCC*, 31 [May, 1980], 221–26; Arthur Walzer, "Articles from the 'California Divorce Project': A Case Study of the Concept of Audience," *CCC*, 36 [May, 1985], 155–58.)

The general import of the explicit criticism is that traditional audience analysis is too limited a tool: it works only for persuasive discourse; it seems inapplicable to discourse situations with general audiences about whom specific questions cannot be arrived at. But underneath these criticisms lies a greater uncertainty about the whole subject, characterized on the one hand by a sense that traditional analysis somehow fails together to provide what we now expect from audience analysis and on the other by the lack of any other widely-shared way to thinking about the subject.

To address this uncertainty, we need to return to first principles and examine just what it is that we do expect audience analysis to accomplish and just how the assumptions behind traditional analysis relate to those expectations. This examination will show why traditional analysis, for all the apparent sanction of tradition, has so little practical rhetorical value for us. More important, it will provide a backdrop for a broader and, I hope, more useful view of what can go into analyzing audiences.

In a broad sense, the purpose of audience analysis is obvious enough: to aid the writer or speaker in understanding a social situation. The advice to "know your audience" carries much of the social meaning of "know" as in knowing who another person is or what that person is like. The advice to "consider your audience" suggests a deliberate weighing of the characteristics of the audience with a view to an appropriate shaping of the discourse. If we look at a set of hypothetical discourses chosen to illustrate a range of different audiences, we can describe more precisely these undifferentiated purposes for analysis. Consider

a legal argument on behalf of an accused embezzler;
a local businessman's letter to City Council protesting a zoning decision;
a grant proposal to develop computer instruction;
a memo from a provost to his university faculty arguing for annual evaluations;
a panel presentation on invention at CCCC;
an article on food in the Pacific Northwest contemplated by a freelance journalist;
an essay on rock and roll contemplated by an English 101 student.

In all but the last two cases, the most obvious specific purpose for analysis will be to understand where a given audience stands in relation to the particular aim and issues at hand. The goal is the immediately strategic one of adapting argument to audience: What are the criteria on which the grant review board makes its decisions? Why are most of the faculty so hostile to annual evaluations? What are the current issues in the discipline's discussions of invention?

In the last two cases above, however, the writers are not yet ready for this sort of strategic analysis. The freelance writer must first choose an audience—a journal such as *Sunset Magazine*—in order to be able to think about rhetorical strategy. The student, in a yet more difficult position, must somehow imagine or invent an audience in a situation where no audience naturally exists. Here the primary purpose of audience analysis becomes not the usual one of providing information about an existing audience but rather a means of actually helping students to discover an audience. And this raises the question of just how they are to do that. What must they think about to imagine their papers as having or being capable of having an audience?

The special context of the classroom creates a peculiar purpose for audience analysis, one for which it was never intended. It does, however, usefully focus the essential question of what we mean by "having an audience." What is an audience, anyway?—as our baffled students often seem to ask. And this is just a generalized form of a need that all writers experience to understand the identity of the audience that they know they have. What does it mean to be in the situation of addresssing a CCCC audience or a grant review board or a City Council? Questions of this sort are, I think, another important part of the meaning of "know your audience." They point to a purpose for analysis which lies underneath the more obvious strategic purpose of determining the audience's responses to particular issues.

Both these purposes for analysis—the fundamental identifying and defining of an audience and the strategic analysis of particular attitudes—involve describing situations, because audience is an inherently situational concept (Lisa Ede, "On Audience and Composition," *CCC*, 30 [October, 1979], 294 ff.). The notion of accommodating discourse to an audience is one of participating in a dynamic social relationship. And "audience" itself refers to the idea of a collective entity that can exist only in relation to a discourse; it means a group of people engaged in a rhetorical situation. Therefore if we are to identify an audience and say anything useful about it, we will have to speak in terms of the situation that brings it into being and gives it identity.

From this perspective, it becomes easy to see why traditional audience analysis so often seems unsatisfactory. What it does is to take literally the idea of "knowing" an audience as examining a group already assembled and describing any or all of the characteristics that those assembled may happen to have. In so doing it directly addresses neither the situation that has brought the audience into being as an audience nor the particular states of mind that the audience may possess in relation to the issues at hand. It tries rather to describe general traits from which rhetorically useful inferences may be drawn.

> [The elderly] are positive about nothing; in all things they err by an extreme moderation. . . . The rich are insolent and superior. . . . Now the hearer is always receptive when a speech is adapted to his own character and reflects it.
> *The Rhetoric of Aristotle,* trans. Lane Cooper (Englewood Cliffs, NJ: Prentice-Hall, 1932), pp. 134–38

> Different habits . . . and different occupations in life . . . make one incline more to one passion, another to another. . . . With men of genius the most successful topic will be fame; with men of industry, riches; with men of fortune, pleasure.
> George Campbell, *The Philosophy of Rhetoric,* 2 vols. (Edinburgh, 1776, 1, 241–242

> It is . . . to begin by recording certain information about an audience and then, on the basis of experience and research, to infer about the audience such matters as knowledge, temperament, attitudes, habits of thought, language preferences or other matters that will enter into their responses to communication.
> Theodore Clevenger, Jr., *Audience Analysis* (Indianapolis, IN: Bobbs-Merrill, 1966), p. 43

Clearly, both Campbell and Aristotle envision the possibility of topoi appropriate for various ages and conditions of men. If an assembled audience in a particular situation can be seen to have a salient trait or quality—what classical rhetoric calls the "character" of the audience—then various lines of argument will fit that charcter more or less effectively. Perhaps most of the City Council are like our letter-writer businessman "men of industry," practical men who will respond best to arguments from "riches." As a general idea—which is how audience analysis usually appears in classical rhetoric (e.g. Quintilian, *Institutio Oratoria,* III, viii, 38)—the notion seems plausible. Certainly in situations involving small, immediate audiences, most of us have had the experience of sensing the overall personality of an audience, or of dominant members in it, and the need to adjust to those qualities in a general and impressionistic way. But inflated to a social-science method of the sort that the modern description suggests, traditional analysis almost completely loses touch with rhetorical usefulness. Aside from the fact that large generalizations about the psychology of age or sex are suspect in any particular application, the accumulation of demographic facts about an audience has no clear goal or limit (Clevenger, pp. 45 ff.). All it can do is amass information unlikely to add up to any sort of "character." "The characters of men," admits George Campbell, beating a retreat from the subject, "may be infinitely diversified" (243). One of our industrious business executives may also be a man of genius and education who might therefore be motivated by arguments from fame. Another is perhaps rich and therefore "insolent." Two might be in their 30's, one in his 50's, two in their 60's. Two might have high-school educations, and so on ad infinitum, the writer having no clear way to determine the relevance or weight of any of this information to the task at hand.

Of course the general assumption informing traditional audience analysis as we find it in modern speech communication texts is that it aims at the social traits held in common that shape the responses of the audience as a whole. (See, for instance, Paul Holtzman's *The Psychology of Speakers' Audiences* [Glenview, IL: Scott Foresman, 1970], pp. 73–79.) So we can observe that a CCCC audience will share many social traits: most will have advanced degrees in English; most will be between 25 and 65; probably at least half will be women; most will be politically liberal. Certainly all will have modest incomes. But although such facts might well interest a social scientist, they are merely symptoms of the situation that actually gives the audience its identity. If we were to send a speaker to the podium, shanghaied, blindfolded, armed only with the subject and the results of a demographic analysis, our victim would angrily or plaintively want to know, "But who is my audience?" The answer of course is "conferees attending a CCCC panel," a simple identification that compresses for someone in the know a wealth of necessary knowledge about the identity of the audience as an entity assembled for a collective purpose.

Bizarre as the case of the blindfolded speaker may be, it describes exactly the mistaken way in which traditional analysis is used to help students discover audiences by amassing detailed information about people, real or imaginary. "They [students] must construct in imagination an audience that is as nearly a replica as is possible of those many readers who actually exist in the world of reality and who are reading the writer's words" (Fred R. Pfister and Joanne F. Petrick, "A Heuristic Model for Creating a Writer's Audience," *CCC*, 30 [May, 1980], 213). Following this principle, discussions commonly suggest as audiences groups with analyzable traits. "Thus a reader might be delineated as being a university adminstrator, over 40, male, white, etc., or a group of readers might be defined as businessmen in a small [midwestern] community" (Winifred B. Horner, "Speech-Act and Text-Act Theory: 'Theme-ing in Freshman Composition," *CCC*, 30 [May, 1979], 168). But obviously the problem that students face is not one of just visualizing hypothetical real people; it is one of grasping a situation in which real readers could constitute an "audience." In what conceivable situations, for instance, could our student writing about rock and roll be addressing a group of midwestern businessmen?

How then do we go about describing the situations that bring audiences into being and give them their identities? Or to put the question in a more basic way, how is it that discourses of any sort can have audiences? If we look at the most concrete possible image of an audience assembled to hear a speech and ask how they come to be there, the immediate answer will be that a particular occasion has brought them together. This, indeed, is the most common way we tend to think about and characterize audiences, as a particular group assembled to hear a particular speech. But a moment's reflection shows that while an audience assembles only for a particular disourse, the discourse alone cannot bring the audience into being. Lawyers do not defend their clients on street corners; passers-by do not wander into Holiday Inns to hear lectures on teaching composition; freelance journalists do not mimeograph their articles and leave them in mailboxes—unless they have become really desperate.

In brief, an audience can assemble on a particular occasion only because a social setting already exists in which a certain kind of discourse performs a recognized function. Note that the ancient classification of judicial, deliberative, and epideictic discourse follows this principle and amounts, as Chaim Perelman points out, to the identification of three basic audiences (*The New Rhetoric: A Treatise on Argumentation*, trans. John Wilkinson and Purcell Weaver [Norte Dame, IN: University of Notre Dame Press, 1969], p. 21). To define other audiences we need simply to amplify the principle to its broadest extent, as follows.

An audience can exist when there is 1) an established social institution or social relationship, a judicial system, a legislative process, an institutional hierarchy, a charitable foundation, a social compact of any sort, a club, a nation, even a friendship between two people; 2) and an evolved and understood function that discourse performs within and for that social relationship. Speech-act theory—and sociolinguisitcs in general—has taught us to see all discourse as representing action performed within and conditioned by a social situation. We can name these actions in very general terms—making statements, contracts, promises, implications, requests. But it is also important to see that all discourse, especially of the more public or formalized kind, functions in and can be described as part of a social transaction that has defined roles for both writers and readers. If I write a grant proposal, I am making a request, but I am also participating in a highly conventionalized activity evolved to enable the distribution of resources, the manipulation of tax laws, the satisfaction of political and public relations imperatives. I write as the representative of one institution. My audience exists in terms of and reads as representatives of the granting agency.

3) Finally, for an audience to "assemble," there must be a physical setting. For written discourse, the exact analog to the place of assembly is the means of publication or distribution. Much has been made of the distance between writers and readers as opposed to the closeness of speakers and audience. Walter Ong argues that the readers of written discourse do not form an audience, a "collectivity," as do the listeners to a speech ("The Writer's Audience Is Always a Fiction," *PMLA*, 90 [January, 1975], 11). In some senses this must of course be true, but because a written discourse always exists within some larger social setting and reaches its dispersed readers through a given physical means of distribution for an accepted social function, readers of prose are very much part of a collectivity. When I read a memo from the Provost in my office

mail or a copy of *Sunset Magazine* in the public mail, I understand that I am participating in a social activity together with others. The major difference between speech and writing in their roles in social settings is that writing has been able to develop a wider range of functions. In the instance of popular journalism, the means of publication has been able to become a social institution in its own right. The reader of a newspaper or a magazine participates in a social relationship that has been largely created by the development of newspapers and magazines themselves.

All these intertwined elements of the social context for discourse define the terms in which the identity of an audience is best understood. This is why when we respond most directly and effectively to the question, "Who is the audience," we always respond in terms of the social institution and function that the discourse serves—a court, members of City Council, a grant review board, the college faculty, CCCC conferees, readers of *Sunset Magazine*. Unspoken but always present in any such simple identification of an audience is the whole complex of the social situation that has brought that audience into being. This unspoken presence is so compressed into the identification that it is easy to take for granted. But a writer who understands the identity of the audience grasps a wealth of tacit and explicit knowledge about the form of the discourse and the way the subject can be treated.

This knowledge informs the obvious rhetorical choices about appropriate formats, matters of tone, diction, stance toward the reader, kinds of allowable openings, structure, evidence, and argument. It also includes more subtle, crucial presuppositions about such things as how much the purpose of the discourse or the writer's own authority can be presumed or needs to be explained and justified. In many cases where the setting is subject specific—e.g. periodical journalism or scholarship—knowledge of the audience's identity also includes a great deal that the audience can be taken to know about the subject at hand. Awareness of the audience's identity provides, in short, all the sense of situation that makes it possible for a writer or speaker to proceed with a sense of being engaged in purposeful communication.

The identity of the audience, as I have described it above, constitutes, therefore, the necessary foundation for audience analysis. It constitutes as well the setting that shapes further considerations of strategy about the specific subject. For example, the lawyer pleading the case before the court will be concerned with the attitudes of the jurors toward the client and the issues of the case. But strategies to play on those attitudes will have to acknowledge the decorum of the courtroom and the jurors' own awareness of their special role as jurors. As Chaim Perelman points out, "it is quite common for members of an audience to adopt attitudes connected with the role they play in certain social insititutions" (p. 21). In the case of an audience for the CCCC presentation, almost everything that one can say about their attitudes toward the subject at hand will, as Arthur Walzer suggests, have to be defined in terms of that particular "rhetorical or interpretive community" and in terms of the role that academic audiences are expected to play (p. 157).

To summarize the above discussion, I would suggest that what a writer needs to understand about an audience, what we mean by "knowing" an audience, can be adequately described by two interrelated levels of questions:

I. What is the identity of the audience?
   A. What is the institution or social relationship of writer(s) and audience that the discourse serves (or creates)?
   B. How does the discourse function in the relationship?
   C. What is the physical setting or means of distribution that brings the discourse to the audience and what are the conventions and formats associated with it?
II. How does the audience view the specific subject matter and how may it view the intentions of the discourse?
   A. What is known or can be projected about specific attitudes and knowledge in the audience that affect what the discourse will have to do in order to accomplish its purpose?
   B. To what extent are the audience's attitudes toward subject and purpose affected by or describable by reference to its collective identity as audience?

Although this outline has the appearance of a heuristic, I propose it more as a general framework for thinking about what writers may actually do when they attend to audience. How much, and at what points in the process of composing, such attention may profitably take the form of deliberate analysis of the audience are questions that I hope the above framework may help others to explore further. In particular, I think this framework helps to open a more adequate view of how different kinds of writing situations may require very different kinds of attention to audience. The elements of audience that I have described above seem in different situations to take on different forms, to claim varying degrees of precedence and to interact in different ways.

For instance, our businessman writing to City Council probably knows the members of the Council well and has several social relationships to them—friend, enemy, fellow member of the Chamber of Commerce, and so on—any of which might be involved explicitly or implicitly in the letter. He has, therefore, an number of ways to conceive of and address his audience. But his attention seems most likely to be concentrated on their individual attitudes and predispositions toward the zoning issues. In the case of the grant proposal, by contrast, the writer's conception of the audience will be necessarily defined by their role as agents of the institution and by the conventions of grant proposals. The means of distribution for the discourse maintains distance, even anonymity, between the writer and the audience. Here, everything that can be said about the audience's attitudes will concern the kinds of arguments that this particular granting agency is most responsive to. Yet again, in other kinds of institutional prose, like the provost's memo to the faculty, a piece of discourse may serve more than one function and audience—e.g. the President as well as the faculty. Much of the initial attention to audience will have to fall on actually identifying and defining these multiple audiences and then on juggling issues in recognition of all of them, while perhaps explicitly addressing only one audience. (See C. H. Knoblauch, "Intentionality in the Writing Process: A Case Study," *CCC*, 31 [May, 1980], 153-59. See also Mathes and Stevenson, *Designing Technical Reports* [Indianapolis, IN: Bobbs Merrill, 1976] pp. 9–23.)

In spite of the differences in the attention to audience in the above examples, all are alike in that they aim toward the second level of the audience's specific attitudes and knowledge, and the appropriate strategies to accommodate them. This is so because the general function of the writings is transactional, by which I mean that they work to produce specific actions or responses from an audience who, as members of the institution involved, have an active part to play.

The kinds of attention a writer pays to audience seem likely to alter significantly, in ways that we do not understand at all well, when the function of discourse moves away from the transactional, as it does in the typical periodical essay and in much of what we call discourse written for a general audience. The audience for such discourse is not part of an institution—members of a jury, faculty at University X—within which the discourse performs some function. The audience comes rather to the discourse to participate in the social relationship—a sort of one-sided conversation—that is offered there. Here, understanding the identity of the audience means understanding what readers expect, the nature of the "conversation," the conventions which govern that kind of prose. In particular, it usually means understanding the setting of publication, e.g. *Sunset Magazine*, that ties those conventions to a specific format or to a set of assumed interests and attitudes in readers.

In such discourse, second-level analysis of the audience in relation to the specific subject and purpose often seems almost irrelevant, or so different from the analysis in transactional discourse that we need to find other ways of talking about it. The traditional model sees the writer as assessing and accommodating specific attitudes. The discourse is an instrument of negotiation. But here the writer is in the position of offering readers a social relationship—for entertainment, for intellectual stimulation, for general information—which they may or may not choose to enter.

One familar way to talk about this very different relationship between discourse and audience is to draw on Walter Ong's idea of the audience as a fiction evoked by the text, a series of roles that the text offers to readers, or a series of presuppositions it makes about readers that the readers can accept or not ("The Writer's Audience Is Always a Fiction," *PMLA*, 90 [January, 1975], 9–21; see also Douglas Park, "The Meanings of 'Audience,' " *College English, 44 [March, 1982], 247*–57). Accordingly, Russell Long suggests that young writers should not try to analyze their audiences but to ask rather "Who do I want my audience to be" (Writer-Audience Relationships: Analysis or Invention," *CCC*, 31 [May, 1980], 225).

Although this idea has force, it has remained too undeveloped. Further, it seems clear that all discourse must in some fashion attend to the constraints imposed by the requirements of real audiences. (See Lisa Ede and Andrea Lunsford, "Audience Addressed/Audience Invoked: The Role of Audience in Composition Theory and Pedagogy," *CCC*, 35 [May, 1984], 155–71.) Writers, that is to say, can set out to engage readers in conversation only by some appropriate estimate of what they are actually likely to find intelligible, credible, or interesting. In practice, the setting for publication usually yields such information. But it seems probable that what writers work with here is not precise formulations of particular attitudes or states of knowledge but rather an awareness of a range of possible viewpoints. Robert Roth, for example, describes successful student revisions that evolve by appealing to a variety of possible responses from readers, by casting a wider rather than a narrower net ("The Evolving Audience: Alternatives to Audience Accommodation," forthcoming in *CCC* during 1987). The general aim of such attention to audience might perhaps be described not as fitting discourse to audience but as making it possible for a variety of readers to become an audience.

This survey is too brief to give more than an idea of the range of considerations that can go into audience analysis. But it will do to indicate how the framework I have laid out might be used, and to indicate as well some areas that need more investigation. For teachers of writing, I hope this discussion demonstrates that analysis of audience cannot profitably be seen as a set of all-purpose questions to be tacked on to an assignment to help students invent or identify an audience. To identify an audience means identifying a situation. So the primary issue that our current concern with audience analysis poses for teachers of writing is not how we can help students analyze their audiences but, first, how and to what extent we can help them define situations for their writing. And to this question there are no simple answers.

The most obvious way to define a situation for writing is to pose hypothetical cases— Imagine you are a resident assistant writing a report for the Dean of Students; write an article for *Sports Illustrated*—or to use the composition class for "real" writing such as a letter to the hometown paper. In fact the only way to have an audience analyzable in the detail we usually envision when we speak of audience analysis is to have a situation for writing that includes a concrete setting for "publication." For such assignments, I hope this discussion will facilitate more useful analyses of audience than those evoked by traditional advice.

Most teachers, however, will resist turning their composition courses entirely over to the writing of letters for various occasions. They feel, with good reason, that too much emphasis upon specific and often imaginary situations can lead to crude pretense and mechanical emphasis on format that robs student writing of all genuineness. They want students' writing to be in some elusive but important sense real and self-generated. Unfortunately, this ideal is difficult to reconcile with the obvious need many students have for a clearer sense of audience. Well meaning advice like, "Be your own audience," while it seems to get at a truth, can leave many students with no way to understand their writing as being for anyone or any purpose at all.

The student who escapes this limbo—perhaps our hypothetical student writing about rock and roll—will do so partly by using various conventions of a written prose to evoke the shadow of a situation, by writing like a freelance journalist or a musicologist, or an encyclopedist, or a columnist, or some creative pastiche of these. The very use of a certain recognizable "register" (M. A. K. Halliday and R. Hasan, *Language as Social Semiotic* [London: Longmans, 1976], pp. 65–73)—a way of addressing the readers, of opening the subject, of organizing material, and so on—even though it is accompanied by no identifiable setting for publication, will evoke a sense of the paper's possessing an audience. If the student's paper is sufficiently like other discourse that exists in real settings for publication, then it too will be felt to some extent to have an audience. But such a sense of audience will, I would suggest, always be informed by a grasp of the social function of the prose—that is to say how it works as public discourse, what general kind of thing it offers to readers.

If we are to help students who do not have this grasp on audience, we need to learn more about it ourselves. We need, first of all, to give more attention to defining the social functions of various kinds of public discourse. It is easy enough to see that different composition courses and different teachers have preferences—too often barely conscious or impressionistically defined—for different kinds of audiences. Students in one course may be expected to writer like popular journalists about their personal knowledge, in another like apprentice philosophers, in another like informal essayists in the grand tradition. The current trend to center composition courses on the varieties of academic discourse seems especially constructive because it is accompanied by an attempt to understand and make more explicit the nature of such discourse (Walzer, p. 157).

Second, we need to learn more about how different kinds of discourse written for public or "general" audiences actually work rhetorically. Recognizing that the model of audience accommodation which works for transactional prose does not apply well to all discourse situations is a starting point. Doing more to describe the conventions of such prose would also be useful, as for instance in George Dillon's *Constructing Texts* (Bloomington, IN: Indiana University Press, 1981). His description of how students fail to understand some of the basic conventions of expository prose gets at a fundamental part of what we mean by a sense of audience. Although it is difficult to say how far such material should be taught directly, my own experience is that students are more receptive to descriptions and discussions of writing conventions as matters of social form and function than they are to descriptions of absolute criteria for good writing.

Finally, we need to keep in mind that the culture of the classroom can be a pervasive influence on a student's ability to understand an audience. In "Collaborative Learning and the 'Conversation of Mankind,'" (*College English,* 46 [November, 1984], 635–52), Kenneth Bruffee provides a fine account of the way that students can learn through social interaction to internalize and then re-externalize the kind of "conversation" that defines "a community of knowledgeable peers" (p. 642). At this point the discussion may appear to have moved far from analysis of audience, but as its most basic the issue of audience in writing instruction is one of social development and maturation—of student writers learning to see themselves as social beings in a social situation. Only in such a context can the art of rhetoric and of audience analysis have any real meaning or force in our teaching of writing.

Minimal Marking

Richard H. Haswell

It is a disturbing fact of the profession that many teachers still look toward the marking of a set of compositions with distaste and discouragement. Reasons are obvious, not the least being the intuition that hours must be put in with little return in terms of effect on the students or on their writing. C. H. Knoblauch and Lil Brannon's recent survey of the research on the effect of marking unfortunately supports this intuition. Positive results of teacher intervention through written commentary simply have not yet been found ("Teacher Commentary on Student Writing," *Freshman English News*, 10 [1981], 1–4). The problem is analogous to that of the teaching of grammar in composition courses—hundreds of thousands of hours spent, and being spent right now, on a task of little proven benefit. Fortunately, however, Knoblauch and Brannon balance their description of unfruitful paths with a model of paths still promising. Otherwise, an essentially useful method that is easily discredited because easily disliked might seem finally unprofitable.

Whether Knoblauch and Brannon's model of beneficial written commentary can be verified by research remains to be seen, but I would like to provide evidence here that suggests it will be. In essence they propose commentary that 1) facilitates rather than judges, 2) emphasizes performance rather than finished product, 3) provides double feedback, before and after revision, and 4) helps bridge successive drafts by requiring immediate revision. All these requirements are met by a method of marking surface errors in writing that I have been using for several years and recommending for use by teaching assistants. Admittedly errors of this sort—misspelling, mispunctuation, etc.— constitute a nonessential element of writing, or at least one I do not wish to spend much time on at any level of instruction. But the method by which I comment on these errors, besides conforming to Knoblauch and Brannon's criteria, brings measurable improvements and serves as a paradigm for a scheme of written commentary that may be transferable to more central aspects of writing, especially aspects not amenable to peer evaluation.

The method itself is by no means solely my own, no doubt having undergone autogenesis time and again. I developed it for my own use six or seven years ago; a retired colleague of mine said he knew of a teacher at Vassar who used it in the early 1940s; recently Sheila Ann Lisman has described it as her "X system" ("The Best of All Possible Worlds: Where X Replaces AWK," in Gene Stanford, et al., eds., *Classroom Practices in Teaching English 1979-1980: How to Handle the Paper Load* [Urbana, Ill.: National Council of Teachers of English, 1979], pp. 103-105). My own application is as follows. All surface mistakes in a student's paper are left totally unmarked within the text. These are unquestionable errors in spelling, punctuation, capitalization, and grammar (including pronoun antecedence.) Each of these mistakes is indicated only with a check in the margin by the line in which it occurs. A line with two checks by it, for instance, means the presence of two errors, no more, within the boundary of that line. The sum of checks is recorded at the end of the paper and in the gradebook. Papers, with checks and other commentary, are then returned fifteen minutes before the end of class. Students have time to search for, circle, and correct the errors. As papers are returned to me I review the corrections, mending those errors left undiscovered, miscorrected, or newly generated. Where I feel it is useful, mistakes are explained or handbooks cited. Within those fifteen minutes I can return about one third of the papers in a class of twenty-five, and the rest I return the next session. Until a student attempts to correct checked errors, the grade on the essay remains unrecorded.

The simplicity of this method belies it benefit. First, it shortens, gladdens, and improves the act of marking papers. Because the teacher responds to a surface mistake only with a check in the margin, attention can be maintained on more substantial problems. The method perhaps goes a long way toward dimming the halo effect of surface mistakes on evaluation, since much of this negative influence may arise from the irritation that comes from correcting and explaining common errors (*its* and *it's!*) over and over. On the second reading the teacher does not lose the time gained initially, for according to my count students will correct on their own sixty to seventy percent of their errors. (Lisman reports her "least capable students" are able to find sixty percent of their errors.) Conservatively, I would say the method saves me about four minutes a paper. That is nearly two hours saved with a set of twenty-five essays.

Second, the method forces students to act in a number of ways that have current pedagogic sanction. In reducing the amount of teacher comment on the page, it helps to avoid the mental dazzle of information overload. It shows the student that the teacher initially assumed that carelessness and not stupidity was the source of error. It forces the student, not the teacher, to answer the question. It challenges students with a puzzle (where is the mistake in this line?) and reinforces learning with a high rate of successful solutions. It engages students in an activity that comes much nearer to the very activity they need to learn, namely editing—not the abstract understanding of a mistake someone else has discovered, but the detection and correction of errors on one's own. Finally, improvement is self-motivated. The fewer mistakes students submit originally, the sooner they leave other students still struggling in the classroom with checks by every third line. Progress during the semester is also easily seen, if not by checks on individual papers at least by totals in the gradebook shared with a student during conference.

Third, this method will help teachers analyze the nature and sources of error in ways that lately have proved so insightful among composition specialists.[1] Consider the following breakdown of the corrections that twenty-four freshmen in one of my recent classes made on their first inclass essay (without recourse to a dictionary).

Category of Error	Number of Errors Checked in Margin by Teacher	Number of Errors Correctly Emended by Students	Percent Corrected by Students
Semantic Signalling (capitalization, underlining, quotation marks, apostrophes)	97	74	76.3%
Syntactic Punctuation	142	81	57.0%
Spelling (including hyphenation)	132	74	56.1%
Grammar (including tense change, omission of word, pronoun disagreement)	30	16	53.3%
All Errors	401	245	61.1%

Crude as this breakdown is, a useful fact immediately emerges. Students are able to find and correct different kinds of errors at about the same rate. In short, more than half of the surface errors students make, *regardless of type*, occupy a kind of halfway house between purely conceptual and purely performance-based (only a few seem truly slips of the pen). They are threshold errors, standing on the edge of competence in an unstable posture of disjunction ("I know it is either *conceive* or *concieve*") or of half-discarded fossilization ("I don't know why I capitalized 'Fraternities.' I *know* that's wrong."). It is good for the teacher to be reminded that, after all, the majority of errors—all kinds of errors, and differently for different students—"mark stages," in David Batholomae's words, "on route to mastery" ("The Study of Error," p. 257). Further, the method isolates, for each individual student, those errors of deeper etiology. It is remarkable how often the method winnows away a heterogeneous clutter of threshold errors to leave just a few conceptual errors—errors, though again idiosyncratic and multiplied by repetition, now accessible for focused treatment. So the method is an ideal first step in the pedagogical attack on error recommended by Paul B. Diederich, Beth Newman, Ellen W. Nold, and others: keep records, isolate a few serious errors, individualize instruction.[2]

Even for teachers who have less time than they would like for individual instruction, there will be progress if this method of marginal checking is maintained during the entire course. At least there has been in my classes. Using inclass, fifty-minute, impromptu essays written the first and last week of the semester, with two switched topics to eliminate influence of topic, I have calculated change in error rate in three regular freshman composition sections. Overall, the drop was from 4.6 errors per 100 words to 2.2 (52%). This rate of decline was consistent despite different semesters and different topics and considerably different course plans (52%, 53%, 50%). Further, nearly all students participated in the improvement; only four of the sixty-nine did not register a decline in rate. This improvement in error rate, it should be noted, was not acquired at the expense of fluency, for final essays were 23% longer than first essays. Pearson product-moment correlation between initial and final error rates is high (.79), suggesting little connection between initial verbal skill and subsequent gain. Even though, given the above figures, it was nearly superfluous, I calculated a correlated t-test for significance of pre/post change in rate, largely to relish (at least once in my life) a truly giant t-value ($t = 25.43$, $p < .001$). Of course what other factors influenced this gain must remain conjectural. I devoted a small amount of class time to three or four common errors of punctuation, worked occasionally in conference with individual problems, and reminded students to save five minutes at the end of an inclass essay to proofread. I have not had the heart to set up a control group to isolate this marking technique; it has been valuable enough for me that I prefer to sell it rather than to deprive any students of it deliberately.

The ultimate value of this method for me is that it relegates what I consider a minor aspect of the course to a minor role in time spent on marking and in class, while at least maintaining and probably increasing the rate of improvement in that aspect. Crudely put, less work for the teacher, more gain for the student. But the gain may be compounded in ways more complex than this suggests. Knoblauch and Brannon rightly point out that commenting must be evaluated in terms of the "full teacher-student dialogue." Now too much commenting can harm this dialogue in at least two ways. It will embitter the teacher with the knowledge that the time and energy spent on it is incommensurate with the subject and the results. And it will frustrate both teacher and student because judgmental commentary unbalances the teacher-student equilibrium in an authentic learning situation, that is, where the student is doing most of the work. Long ago Comenius put it best: the more the teacher teaches, the less the student learns. (The more you teach, one of our older teaching assistants said to me mournfully, the more you quote that maxim.) In terms of Elaine O. Lee's useful scale ("Evaluating Student Writing," *CCC*, 30 [1979], 370-374), this marking technique postpones correcting, emoting, and describing—where the teacher does all of the work—and instead suggests, questions, reminds, and assigns. Because students do most of the work, the discouragement of which I first spoke subsides, and a certain freshness and candor return to the dialogue. (Lisman's article describes this renewed energy well.)

Can this method be transferred to other aspects of writing? I think so, although right now I must speculate. Certainly problems of writing that lend themselves to spot im provement could well be marked with marginal checks: injudicious diction, needed transitions, unsupported generalities. Larger, structural problems such as stumbling introductions and disordered paragraphs might be signalled with marginal lines. More interestingly, so might fallacies and other lapses in thinking. In each case the effort would be to find the minimal functional mark. The best mark is that which allows students to correct the most on their own with the least help. An obvious pedagogical truth—but one that runs counter to the still established tradition of full correction.

Notes

1. See especially Mina P. Shaughnessey, *Errors and Expectations: A Guide for the Teacher of Basic Writing* (New York: Oxford, 1977); Barry M. Kroll and John C. Schafer, "Error-Analysis and the Teaching of Composition," *College Composition and Communication,* 29 (1978), 242–248; and David Bartholomae, "The Study of Error," *CCC,* 31 (1980), 253–269.

2. Diederich, *Measuring Growth in English* (Urbana, Ill.: National Council of Teachers of English, 1974), pp. 21–22; Newman, *Teaching Students to Write* (Columbus, Ohio: Merrill, 1980). pp. 292–297, 398; Nold, "Alternatives to Mad-Hatterism," in Donald McQuade, ed., *Linguistics, Stylisitics, and the Teaching of Composition* (Conway, AK: L&S Books, 1980), pp. 103–117. See also Shaughessy, Kroll and Schafer, and Bartholomae above. Marginal checking isolates deep errors in a way parallel, but not identical, to Bartholomae's method of "oral reconstruction" ("Study of Error,"pp. 259–268). The two methods may prove to have different, though overlapping, diagnostic values.

Responding to Student Writing

Nancy Sommers

More than any other enterprise in the teaching of writing, responding to and commenting on student writing consumes the largest proportion of our time. Most teachers estimate that it takes them at least 20 to 40 minutes to comment on an individual student paper, and those 20 to 40 minutes times 20 students per class, times 8 papers, more or less, during the course of a semester add up to an enormous amount of time. With so much time and energy directed to a single activity, it is important for us to understand the nature of the enterprise. For it seems, paradoxically enough, that although commenting on student writing is the most widely used method for responding to student writing, it is the least understood. We do not know in any definitive way what constitutes thoughtful commentary or what effect, if any, our comments have on helping our students become more effective writers.

Theoretically, at least, we know that we comment on our students' writing for the same reasons professional editors comment on the work of professional writers or for the same reasons we ask our colleagues to read and respond to our own writing. As writers we need and want thoughtful commentary to show us when we have communicated our ideas and when not, raising questions from a reader's point of view that may not have occured to us as writers. We want to know if our writing has communicated our intended meaning and, if not, what questions or discrepancies our reader sees that we, as writers, are blind to.

In commenting on our students' writing, however, we have an additional pedagogical purpose. As teachers, we know that most students find it difficult to imagine a reader's response in advance, and to use such responses as a guide in composing. Thus, we comment on student writing to dramatize the presence of a reader, to help our students to become that questioning reader themselves, because, ultimately, we believe that becoming such a reader will help them to evaluate what they have written and develop control over their writing.[1]

Even more specifically, however, we comment on student writing because we believe that it is necessary for us to offer assistance to student writers when they are in the process of composing a text, rather than after the text has been completed. Comments create the motive for doing something different in the next draft; thoughtful comments create the motive for revising. Without comments from their teachers or from their peers, student writers will revise in a consistently narrow and predictable way. Without comments from readers, students assume that their writing has communicated their meaning and perceive no need for revising the substance of their text.[2]

Yet as much as we as informed professionals believe in the soundness of this approach to responding to student writing, we also realize that we don't know how our

170

theory squares with teachers' actual practice—do teachers comment and students revise as the theory predicts they should? For the past year my colleagues, Lil Brannon, Cyril Knoblach, and I have been researching this problem, attempting to discover not only what messages teachers give their students through their comments, but also what determines which of these comments the students choose to use or to ignore when revising. Our research has been entirely focused on comments teachers write to motivate revisions. We have studied the commenting styles of thirty-five teachers at New York University and the University of Oklahoma, studying the comments these teachers wrote on first and second drafts, and interviewing a representative number of these teachers and their students. All teachers also commented on the same set of three student essays. As an additional reference point, one of the student essays was typed into the computer that had been programed with the "Writer's Workbench," a package of twenty-three programs developed by Bell Laboratories to help computers and writers work together to improve a text rapidly. Within a few minutes, the computer delivered editorial comments on the student's text, identifying all spelling and punctuation errors, isolating problems with wordy or misued phrases, and suggesting alternatives, offering a stylistic analysis of sentence types, sentence beginnings, and sentence lengths, and finally, giving our freshman essay a Kincaid readability score of 8th grade which, as the computer program informed us, "is a low score for this type of document." The sharp contrast between the teachers' comments and those of the computer highlighted how arbitrary and idiosyncratic most of our teachers' comments are. Besides, the calm, reasonable language of the computer provided quite a contrast to the hostility and mean-spiritedness of most of the teachers' comments.

The first finding from our research on styles of commenting is that *teachers' comments can take students' attention away from their own purposes in writing a particular text and focus that attention on the teachers' purpose in commenting.* The teacher appropriates the text from the student by confusing the student's purpose in writing the text with her own purpose in commenting. Students make the changes the teacher wants rather than those that the student perceives are necessary, since the teachers' concerns imposed on the text create the reasons for the subsequent changes. We have all heard our perplexed students say to us when confused by our comments: "I don't understand how you want me to change this" or "Tell me what **you** want me to do." In the beginning of the process there was the writer, her words, and her desire to communicate her ideas. But after the comments of the teacher are imposed on the first or second draft, the student's attention dramatically shifts from "This is what I want to say," to "This is what **you** the teacher are asking me to do."

This appropriation of the text by the teacher happens particularly when teachers identify errors in usage, diction, and style in a first draft and ask students to correct these errors when they revise; such comments give the student an impression of the importance of these errors that is all out of proportion to how they should view these errors at this point in the process. The comments create the concern that these "accidents of discourse" need to be attended to before the meaning of the text is attended to.

It would not be so bad if students were only commanded to correct errors, but, more often than not, students are given contradictory messages; they are commanded to edit a sentence to avoid an error or to condense a sentence to achieve greater brevity of style, and then told in the margins that the particular paragraph needs to be more specific or to be developed more. An example of this problem can be seen in the following student paragraph:

> *wordy - be precise   which   /comma needed*
> Every year[on one Sunday in the middle of January]tens of millions of
>
> *word choice*
> people cancel all events, plans or work to watch the Super Bowl. This au-
>
> *wordy*
> dience includes[little boys and girls, old people, and housewives and men.]
>
> *Be specific - what reasons?*
> Many reasons have been given to explain why the Super Bowl has become
>
> *and why   what spots?)   awkward*
> so popular that commercial spots cost up to $100,000.00. One explanation
>
> *Another what?*
> is that people like to take sides and root for a team. Another is that some
>
> *+spelling*
> people like the pageantry and excitement of the event. These reasons alone,
>
> *too colloquial*
> however, do not explain a happening as big as the Super Bowl.

You need to do more research

This paragraph needs to be expanded in order to be more interesting to a reader.

In commenting on this draft, the teacher has shown the student how to edit the sentences, but then commands the student to expand the paragraph in order to make it more interesting to a reader. The interlinear comments and the marginal comments represent two separate tasks for this student; the interlinear comments encourage the student to see the text as a fixed piece, frozen in time, that just needs some editing. The marginal comments, however, suggest that the meaning of the text is not fixed, but rather that the student still needs to develop the meaning by doing some more research. Students are commanded to edit and develop at the same time; the remarkable contradiction of developing a paragraph after editing the sentences in it represents the confusion we encountered in our teachers' commenting styles. These different signals given to students, to edit and develop, to condense and elaborate, represent also the failure of teachers' comments to direct genuine revision of the text as a whole.

Moreover, the comments are worded in such a way that it is difficult for students to know what is the most important problem in the text and what problems are of lesser importance. No scale of concerns is offered to a student, with the result that a comment about spelling or a comment about an awkward sentence is given weight equal to a comment about organization or logic. The comment that seemed to represent this problem best was one teacher's command to his student: "Check your commas and semicolons and think more about what you are thinking about." The language of the comments makes it difficult for a student to sort out and decide what is most important and what is least important.

When the teacher appropriates the text for the student in this way, students are encouraged to see their writing as a series of parts—words, sentences, paragraphs—and not as a whole discourse. The comments encourage students to believe that their first drafts are finished drafts, not invention drafts, and that all they need to do is patch and polish their writing. That is, teachers' comments do not provide their students with an inherent reason for revising the structure and meaning of their texts, since the comments suggest to students that the meaning of their text is already there, finished, produced, and all that is necessary is a better word or phrase. The processes of revising, editing, and proofreading are collapsed and reduced to a single trivial activity, and the students' misunderstanding of the revision process as a rewording activity is reinforced by their teachers' comments.

It is possible, and it quite often happens, that students follow every comment and fix their texts appropriately as requested, but their texts are not improved substantially, or, even worse, their revised drafts are inferior to their previous drafts. Since the teachers' comments take the students' attention away from their own original purposes, students concentrate more, as I have noted, on what the teachers commanded them to do than on what they are trying to say. Sometimes students do not understand the purpose behind their teachers' comments and take those comments very literally. At other times students understand the comments, but the teacher has misread the text and the comments, unfortunately, are not applicable. For instance, we repeatedly saw comments in which teachers commanded students to reduce and condense what was written, when in fact what the text really needed at this stage was to be expanded in conception and scope.

The process of revising always involves a risk. But, too often revision becomes a balancing act for students in which they make the changes that are requested but do not take the risk of changing anything that was not commented on, even if the students sense that other changes are needed. A more effective text does not often evolve from such changes alone, yet the student does not want to take the chance of reducing a finished, albeit inadequate, paragraph to chaos—to fragments—in order to rebuild it, if such changes have not been requested by the teacher.

The second finding from our study is that *most teachers' comments are not text-specific and could be interchanged, rubber-stamped, from text to text.* The comments are not anchored in the particulars of the students' texts, but rather are a series of vague directives that are not text-specific. Students are commanded to "Think more about [their] audience, avoid colloquial language, avoid the passive, avoid prepositions at the end of sentences or conjunctions at the beginning of sentences, be clear, be specific, be precise, but above all, think more about what [they] are thinking about." The comments on the following student paragraph illustrate this problem:

Begin by telling your reader what you are going to write about.

In the sixties it was drugs, in the seventies it was rock and roll. Now in

avoid "one of the"

the eighties, one of the most controversial subjects is nuclear power. The

elaborate

United States is in great need of its own source of power. Because of en-

vironmentalists, coal is not an acceptable source of energy. [Solar and wind

be specific   *Avoid "it seems"*

power have not yet received the technology necessary to use them.] It seems

that nuclear power is the only feasible means right now for obtaining self-

sufficient power. However, too large a percentage of the population are

be precise

against nuclear power claiming it is unsafe. With as many problems as the

Think about your reader

United States is having concerning energy, it seems a shame that the public

is so quick to "can" a very feasible means of power. Nuclear energy should

not be given up on, but rather, more nuclear plants should be built.

These sentences needed

One could easily remove all the comments from this paragraph and rubber-stamp them on another student text, and they would make as much or as little sense on the second text as they do here.

We have observed an overwhelming similarity in the generalities and abstract commands given to students. There seems to be among teachers an accepted, albeit unwritten canon for commenting on student texts. This uniform code of commands, requests, and pleadings demonstrates that the teacher holds a license for vagueness while the student is commanded to be specific. The students we interviewed admitted to having great difficulty with these vague directives. The students stated that when a teacher writes in the margins or as an end comment, "choose precise language," or "think more about your audience," revising becomes a guessing game. In effect, the teacher is saying to the student, "Somewhere in this paper is imprecise language or lack of awareness of an audience and you must find it." The problem presented by these vague commands is compounded for the students when they are not offered any strategies for carrying out these commands. Students are told that they have done something wrong and that there is something in their text that needs to be fixed before the text is acceptable. But to tell students that they have done something wrong is not to tell them what to do about it. In order to offer a useful revision strategy to a student, the teacher must anchor that strategy in the specifics of the student's text. For instance, to tell our student, the author of the above paragraph, "to be specific," or "to elaborate," does not show our student what questions the reader has about the meaning of the text, or what breaks in logic exist, that could be resolved if the writer supplied specific information; nor is the student shown how to achieve the desired specificity.

Instead of offering strategies, the teachers offer what is interpreted by students as rules for composing; the comments suggest to students that writing is just a matter of following the rules. Indeed, the teachers seem to impose a series of abstract rules about written products even when some of them are not appropriate for the specific text the student is creating.[3] For instance, the student author of our sample paragraph presented above is commanded to follow the conventional rules for writing a five paragraph essay— to begin the introductory paragraph by telling his reader what he is going to say and to end the paragraph with a thesis sentence. Somehow these abstract rules about what five-paragraph products should look like do not seem applicable to the problems this student must confront when revising, nor are the rules specific strategies he could use when revising. There are many inchoate ideas ready to be exploited in this paragraph, but the rules do not help the student to take stock of his (or her) ideas and use the opportunity he has, during revision, to develop those ideas.

The problem here is a confusion of process and product; what one has to say about the process is different from what one has to say about the product. Teachers who use this method of commenting are formulating their comments as if these drafts were finished drafts and were not going to be revised. Their commenting vocabularies have not been adapted to revision and they comment on first drafts if they were justifying a grade or as if the first draft were the final draft.

Our summary finding, therefore, from this research on styles of commenting is that the news from the classroom is not good. For the most part, teachers do not respond to student writing with the kind of thoughtful commentary which will help them think about their purposes and goals in writing a specific text. In defense of our teachers, however, they told us that responding to student writing was rarely stressed in their teacher-training or in writing workshops; they had been trained in various prewriting techniques, in constructing assignments, and in evaluating papers for grades, but rarely in the process of reading a student text for meaning or in offering commentary to motivate revision. The problem is that most of us as teachers of writing have been trained to read and interpret literary texts for meaning, but, unfortunately, we have not been trained to act upon the same set of assumptions in reading student texts as we follow in reading literary texts.[4] Thus, we read student texts with biases about what the writer should have said or about what he or she should have written, and our biases determine how we will comprehend the text. We read with our preconceptions and preoccupations, expecting to find errors, and the result is that we find errors and misread our students' texts.[5] We find what we look for; instead of reading and responding to the meaning of a text, we correct our students' writing. We need to reverse this approach. Instead of finding errors or showing students how to patch up parts of their texts, we need to sabotage our students' conviction that the drafts thay have written are complete and coherent. Our comments need to offer students revision tasks of a different order of complexity and sophistication from the ones that they themselves identify, by forcing students back into the chaos, back to the point where they are shaping and restructuring their meaning.[6]

For if the content of a student text is lacking in substance and meaning, if the order of the parts must be rearranged significantly in the next draft, if paragraphs must be restructured for logic and clarity, then many sentences are likely to be changed or deleted anyway. There seems to be no point in having students correct usage errors or condense sentences that are likely to disappear before the next draft is completed. In fact, to identify such problems in a text at this early first draft stage, when such problems are likely to abound, can give a student a disproportionate sense of their importance at this stage in the writing process.[7] In responding to our students' writing, we should be guided by the recognition that it is not spelling or usage problems that we as writers first worry about when drafting and revising our texts.

We need to develop an appropriate level of response for commenting on a first draft, and to differentiate that from the level suitable to a second or third draft. Our comments need to be suited to the draft we are reading. In a first or second draft, we need to respond as any reader would, registering questions, reflecting befuddlement, and noting places where we are puzzled about the meaning of the text. Comments should point to breaks in logic, disruptions in meaning, or missing information. Our goal in commenting on early drafts should be to engage students with the issues they are considering and help them clarify their purposes and reasons in writing their specific text.

For instance, the major rhetorical problem of the essay written by the student who wrote the first paragraph (the paragraph on nuclear power) quoted above was that the student had two principal arguments running through his text, each of which brought the other into question. On the one hand, he argued that we must use nuclear power, unpleasant as it is, because we have nothing else to use; though nuclear energy is a problematic source of energy, it is the best of a bad lot. On the other hand, he also argued that nuclear energy is really quite safe and therefore should be our primary resource. Comments on this student's first draft need to point out this break in logic and show the student that if we accept his first argument, then his second argument sounds fishy. But if we accept his second argument, his first argument sounds contradictory.

The teacher's comments need to engage this student writer with this basic rhetorical and conceptual problem in his first draft rather than impose a series of abstract commands and rules upon his text.

Written comments need to be viewed not as an end in themselves—a way for teachers to satisfy themselves that they have done their jobs—but rather as a means for helping students to become more effective writers. As a means for helping students, they have limitations; they are, in fact, disembodied remarks—one absent writer responding to another absent writer. The key to successful commenting is to have what is said in the comments and what is done in the classroom mutually reinforce and enrich each other. Commenting on papers assists the writing course in achieving its purpose; classroom activities and the comments we write to our students need to be connected. Written comments need to be an extension of the teacher's voice—an extension of the teacher as reader. Exercises in such activities as revising a whole text or individual paragraphs together in class, noting how the sense of the whole dictates the smaller changes, looking at options, evaluating actual choices, and then discussing the effect of these changes on revised drafts—such exercises need to be designed to take students through the cycles of revising and to help them overcome their anxiety about revising: that anxiety we all feel at reducing what looks like a finished draft into fragments and chaos.

The challenge we face as teachers is to develop comments which will provide an inherent reason for students to revise; it is a sense of revision as discovery, as a repeated process of beginning again, as starting out new, that our students have not learned. We need to show our students how to seek, in the possibility of revision, the dissonances of discovery—to show them through our comments why new choices would positively change their texts, and thus to show them the potential for development implicit in their own writing.

Notes

1. C. H. Knoblach and Lil Brannon, "Teacher Commentary on Student Writing: The State of the Art," *Freshman English News,* 10 (Fall, 1981), 1–3.

2. For an extended discussion of revision strategies of student writers see Nancy Sommers, "Revision Strategies of Student Writers and Experienced Adult Writers," *College Composition and Communication,* 31 (December, 1980), 378–388.

3. Nancy Sommers and Ronald Schleifer, "Means and Ends: Some Assumptions of Student Writers," *Composition and Teaching,* 2 (December, 1980), 69–76.

4. Janet Emig and Robert P. Parker, Jr., "Responding to Student Writing: Building a Theory of the Evaluating Process," unpublished papers, Rutgers University.

5. For an extended discussion of this problem see Joseph Williams, "The Phenomenology of Error," *College Composition and Communication,* 32 (May, 1981), 152–168.

6. Ann Berthoff, *The Making of Meaning* (Montclair, NJ: Boynton/Cook Publishers, 1981).

7. W. U. McDonald, "The Revising Process and the Marking of Student Papers," *College Composition and Communication,* 24 (May, 1978), 167–170.

The Winds of Change:
Thomas Kuhn and the Revolution
in the Teaching of Writing

Maxine Hairston

In 1963, the University of Chicago Press published a book titled *The Structure of Scientific Revolutions*, written by Thomas Kuhn, a University of California professor of the history of science. In the book Kuhn hypothesizes about the process by which major changes come about in scientific fields, and conjectures that they probably do not evolve gradually from patient and orderly inquiry by established investigators in the field. Rather, he suggests, revolutions in science come about as the result of breakdowns in intellectual systems, breakdowns that occur when old methods won't solve new problems. He calls the change in theory that underlies this kind of revolution a *paradigm shift.* I believe we are currently at the point of such a paradigm shift in the teaching of writing, and that it has been brought about by a variety of developments that have taken place in the last 25 years.

Briefly, Kuhn's thesis in *The Structure of Scientific Revolutions* is this.

When a scientific field is going through a stable period, most of the practitioners in the discipline hold a common body of beliefs and assumptions; they agree on the problems that need to be solved, the rules that govern research, and on the standards by which performance is to be measured. They share a conceptual model that Kuhn calls a paradigm, and that paradigm governs activity in their profession. Students who enter the discipline prepare for membership in its intellectual community by studying that paradigm.

But paradigms are not necessarily immutable. When several people working in a field begin to encounter anomalies or phenomena that cannot be explained by the established model, the paradigm begins to show signs of instability. For a while, those who subscribe to the paradigm try to ignore the contradictions and inconsistencies that they find, or they make improvised, *ad hoc* changes to cope with immediate crises. Eventually, however, when enough anomalies accumulate to make a substantial number of scientists in the field question whether the traditional paradigm can solve many of the serious problems that face them, a few innovative thinkers will devise a new model. And if enough scientists become convinced that the new paradigm works better than the old one, they will accept it as the new norm.

This replacement of one conceptual model by another one is Kuhn's *paradigm shift.* He cites as classic examples the astronomers' substitution of the Copernican model of the solar system for the Ptolemaic model and the development of Newtonian physics.

Such shifts are usually disorderly and often controversial, and the period in which they occur is apt to be marked by insecurity and conflict within the discipline.

Kuhn believes that because these shifts are so disruptive, they will occur only when the number of unsolved problems in a discipline reaches crisis proportions and some major figures in the field begin to focus on those unsolved problems. But even with mounting evidence that their conceptual model doesn't work, supporters of the traditional paradigm resist change because they have an intellectual and sometimes emotional investment in the accepted view. They particularly resist abandoning the conventional textbooks that set forth the precepts of their discipline in clear and unqualified terms. Those texts, as Richard Young points out in his essay, "Paradigms and Problems: Needed Research in Rhetorical Theory," are usually so similar that one way to discover the traditional paradigm of a field is to examine its textbooks.[1]

Finally, however, most of the resistance to the new paradigm will dissipate when its advocates can demonstrate that it will solve problems that the traditional paradigm could not solve. Most of the new generation of scholars working in the field will adopt the new model, and the older practitioners will gradually come around to it. Those who cling to the old paradigm lose their influence in the field because the leaders in the profession simply ignore their work. When that happens, the paradigm shift is complete, and the theory that was revolutionary becomes conventional.

This summary of Kuhn's book is sketchy and too simple, but I think it accurately reflects the key points in his theory. When he developed the theory, he considered only the so-called hard sciences, particularly chemistry, astronomy, and physics. He did not claim or even suggest that his model for scientific revolution could or should apply to social sciences or the humanities, where research is not done in laboratories and usually does not involve measurements or formulas. Nevertheless, I believe that composition theorists and writing teachers can learn from Thomas Kuhn if they see his theory of scientific revolutions as an analogy that can illuminate developments that are taking place in our profession. Those developments, the most prominent of which is the move to a process-centered theory of teaching writing, indicates that our profession is probably in the first stages of a paradigm shift.

THE CURRENT-TRADITIONAL PARADIGM AND ITS PROPONENTS

In order to understand the nature of that shift, we need to look at the principal features of the paradigm that has been the basis of composition teaching for several decades. In "Paradigms and Patterns" Richard Young describes it this way:

> The overt features . . . are obvious enough: the emphasis on the composed product rather than the composing process; the analysis of discourse into description, narration, exposition, and argument; the strong concern with usage . . . and with style; the preoccupation with the informal essay and research paper; and so on.[2]

Young adds that underlying the traditional paradigm is what he calls the "vitalist" attitude toward composing: that is, the assumption that no one can really teach anyone else how to write because writing is a mysterious creative activity that cannot be categorized or analyzed.

In an article in the Winter, 1980, *Freshman English News* James Berlin and Robert Inkster ascribe other features to the conventional paradigm. Basing their conclusions on an analysis of repeated patterns in four well-known and commercially successful rhetoric texts, they add that the traditional paradigm stresses expository writing to the virtual exclusion of all other forms, that it posits an unchanging reality which is independent of the writer and which all writers are expected to describe in the same way regardless of the rhetorical situation, that it neglects invention almost entirely, and that it makes style the most important element in writing.[3]

I would make three other points about the traditional paradigm. First, its adherents believe that competent writers know what they are going to say before they begin to write; thus their most important task when they are preparing to write is finding a form into which to organize their content. They also believe that the composing process is linear, that it proceeds systematically from prewriting to writing to rewriting. Finally, they believe that teaching editing is teaching writing.

It is important to note that the traditional paradigm did not grow out of research or experimentation. It derives partly from the classical rhetorical model that organizes the production of discourse into invention, arrangement, and style, but mostly it seems to be based on some idealized and orderly vision of what literature scholars, whose professional focus is on the written product, seem to imagine is an efficient method of writing. It is a prescriptive and orderly view of the creative act, a view that defines the successful writer as one who can systematically produce a 500-word theme of five paragraphs, each with a topic sentence. Its proponents hold it *a priori;* they have not tested it against the composing processes of actual writers.

At this point, some of my readers may want to protest that I am belaboring a dead issue—that the admonition to "teach process, not product" is now conventional wisdom. I disagree. Although those in the vanguard of the profession have by and large adopted the process model for teaching composition and are now attentively watching the research on the composing process in order to extract some pedagogical principles from it, the overwhelming majority of college writing teachers in the United States are not professional writing teachers. They do not do research or publish on rhetoric or composition, and they do not know the scholarship in the field; they do not read the professional journals and they do not attend professional meetings such as the annual Conference on College Communication and Composition; they do not participate in faculty development workshops for writing teachers. They are trained as literary critics first and as teachers of literature second, yet out of necessity most of them are doing half or more of their teaching in composition. And they teach it by the traditional paradigm, just as they did when they were untrained teaching assistants ten or twenty or forty years ago. Often they use a newer edition of the same book they used as teaching assistants.

Out of necessity, apathy, and what I see as a benighted and patronizing view of the essential nature of composition courses, English department administrators encourage this unprofessional approach to the teaching of writing. In the first place, they may believe that they have so many writing classes to staff that they could not possibly hire well-qualified professionals to teach them; only a comparatively few such specialists exist. Second, most departmental chairpersons don't believe that an English instructor needs special qualifications to teach writing. As one of my colleagues says, our department wouldn't think of letting her teach Chaucer courses because she is not qualified; yet the chairman is delighted for her to teach advanced composition, for which she is far more unqualified. The assumption is that anyone with a Ph.D. in English is an expert writing teacher.

I think, however, that the people who do most to promote a static and unexamined approach to teaching writing are those who define writing courses as service courses and skills courses; that group probably includes most administrators and teachers of writing. Such a view, which denies that writing requires intellectual activity and ignores the importance of writing as a basic method of learning, takes away any incentive for the writing teacher to grow professionally. People who teach skills and provide services are traditionally less respected and rewarded than those who teach theory, and hiring hordes of adjuncts and temporary instructors and assigning them to composition courses reinforces this value system. Consequently there is no external pressure to find a better way to teach writing.

In spite of this often discouraging situation, many teachers who cling to the traditional paradigm work very hard at teaching writing. They devote far more time than they can professionally afford to working with their students, but because they haven't read Elbow or Bruffee they have no way of knowing that their students might benefit far more from small group meetings with each other than from the exhausting one-to-one conferences that the teachers hold. They both complain and brag about how much time they spend meticulously marking each paper, but because they haven't read Diederich or Irmscher they don't know that an hour spent meticulously marking every error in a paper is probably doing more harm than good. They are exhausting themselves trying to teach writing from an outmoded model, and they come to despise the job more and more because many of their students improve so little despite their time and effort.

But the writing teacher's frustration and disenchantment may be less important than the fact that if they teach from the traditional paradigm, they are frequently emphasizing techniques that the research has largely discredited. As Kuhn points out, the paradigm that a group of professionals accepts will govern the kinds of problems they decide to work on, and that very paradigm keeps them from recognizing important problems that cannot be discussed in the terminology of their model. Thus teachers who concentrate their efforts on teaching style, organization, and correctness are not likely to recognize that their students need work in invention. And if they stress that proofreading and editing are the chief skills one uses to revise a paper, they won't realize that their students have no concept of what it means to make substantive revisions in a paper. The traditional paradigm hides these problems.

Textbooks complicate the problem further. As Kuhn repeatedly points out, the standard texts in any discipline constitute a major block to a paradigm shift because they represent accepted authority. Many, though certainly not all, of the standard textbooks in rhetoric and composition for the past two decades have been product-centered books that focus on style, usage, and argumentation; Sheridan Baker's *The Practical Stylist* and Brooks and Warren's *Modern Rhetoric* are typical examples. When Donald Stewart made an analysis of rhetoric texts three years ago, he found that only seven out of the thirty-four he examined showed any awareness of current research in rhetoric. The others were, as he put it, "strictly current-traditional in their discussions of invention, arrangement, and style."[4] And textbooks change slowly. Publishers want to keep what sells, and they tend to direct the appeals of their book to what they believe the average composition teacher wants, not to what those in the vanguard of the profession would like to have.

SIGNS OF CHANGE

Nevertheless, changes are under way, and I see in the current state of our profession enough evidence of insecurity and instability to suggest that the traditional prescriptive and product-centered paradigm that underlies writing instruction is beginning to crumble. I think that the forces contributing to its demise are both theoretical and concrete and come from both inside and outside of the profession. Changes in theory probably started, in the middle 1950's from intellectual inquiry and speculation about language and language learning that was going on in several fields, notably linguistics, anthropology, and clinical and cognitive psychology. To identify and trace all these complex developments would go far beyond the scope of this article and beyond my current state of enlightenment. I can only touch on some of them here.

Probably one of the most important developments to affect writing theory was the publication of Noam Chomsky's *Syntactic Structures* in 1957. His theory of transformational grammar, with its insistent look at the rules by which language is generated, caused a new focus on the process by which language comes into being.* The publication of Francis Christensen's essays on the generative rhetoric of the sentence and the paragraph in the early 1960's also stimulated new interest in the processes by which writers produce texts. Certainly the tagmemicists also provoked a fresh look at the act of writing when they urged writers to generate ideas by thinking about subjects from a dynamic,

---

*I am indebted to my colleague Stephen Witte for bringing this development to my attention.

three-faceted perspective. And when the humanistic psychologist Carl Rogers began to criticize behaviorist psychology just as Chomsky had criticized behaviorist theories of language, he probably hastened the shift away from product-response evaluation of writing.

A major event that encouraged the shift of attention to the process of writing was the famous Anglo-American Seminar on the Teaching of English, held at Dartmouth College in the summer of 1966. In the final report of this gathering of eminent educators from Britain and the United States, the participants deemphasized the formal teaching of grammar and usage in the classroom and emphasized having children engage directly in the writing process in a non-prescriptive atmosphere.

So the intellectual climate conducive to this change has been developing for more than two decades. Of course, if these shifts in theory and attitudes were the only forces that were putting pressure on the traditional approach to teaching writing, revolution in the profession would probably be long in coming. But other concrete and external forces have also been putting pressure on writing teachers. These teachers are plagued by embarrassing stories about college graduates who can't pass teacher competency tests, and by angry complaints about employees who can't write reports. And the professors agree. Their students come to them writing badly and they leave writing badly. Handbooks won't solve their problems, and having them revise papers does no good.

Worse, just at this time when they are most disheartened about teaching writing, large numbers of English professors are beginning to realize that most of them are going to be teaching a lot of writing to a lot of students from now on. The prospect is grim, so grim that the English departments at Harvard and the University of Michigan have given up and turned the bulk of their composition teaching over to specialists outside the departments. But most professors can't do that, and instead they feel insecure and angry because they know they are teaching badly. In Kuhn's terminology, their methods have become anomalous; the system that they have always depended on no longer seems to work.

But why should the paradigm begin to break down just now? After all, as Richard Young points out, thousand of people have learned to write by the trial-and-error method of producing a text and having it criticized. Why shouldn't that slow, but often effective, method continue to work most of the time? Once more, I think, Kuhn has the answer. He says, "One need look no further than Copernicus and the calendar to discover that external conditions may help to transform a mere anomaly into a source of acute crisis."[5] I believe that the external conditions which have hastened the crisis in the teaching of writing are open admissions policies, the return to school of veterans and other groups of older students who are less docile and rule-bound than traditional freshmen; the national decline in conventional verbal skills, and the ever larger number of high school graduates going on to college as our society demands more and more credentials for economic citzenship. Any instructional system would come close to collapse under such a strain, and our system for teaching writing has been particularly vulnerable because it has been staffed largely by untrained teachers who have had little scholarly interest in this kind of teaching.

Following the pattern that Kuhn describes in his book, our first response to crisis has been to improvise *ad hoc* measures to try to patch the cracks and keep the system running. Among the first responses were the writing labs that sprang up about ten years ago to give first aid to students who seemed unable to function within the traditional paradigm. Those labs are still with us, but they're still giving only first aid and treating symptoms. They have not solved the problem. Another *ad hoc* remedy took the form of individualized instruction, but it has faded from the scene along with computer-assisted instruction. The first was too costly and too isolated, the second one proved too limited and impersonal. And the experiments with expressive writing also turned out be *ad hoc* measures, although for a while they seemed to have enough strength to foreshadow a paradigm shift. Sentence combining, I predict, will prove to be another *ad hoc* measure that serves as only a temporary palliative for serious writing problems.

All these remedies have proved temporarily or partially useful; none, however, has answered the crucial question: what is the basic flaw in the traditional paradigm for teaching writing? Why doesn't it work?

THE TRANSITION PERIOD

Someone who cares has to ask that question before the revolution can start because, as Kuhn points out, "novelty ordinarily emerges only for the man who, knowing *with precision* what he should expect, is able to recognize that something has gone wrong."[6] In the teaching of composition, the essential person who asked that question may not have been a man, but a woman, Mina Shaughnessy. In her book *Errors and Expectations,* Shaughnessy describes the educational experience that made her, a professor at a prestigious university, stop to ask, "What went wrong?"

> In the spring of 1970, the City University of New York adopted an admissions policy that guaranteed to every city resident with a high school diploma a place in one of its eighteen tuition-free colleges, thereby opening its doors not only to a larger population of students than it had ever had before . . . but to a wider range of students than any college had probably ever admitted or thought of admitting to its campus. . . .
> One of the first tasks these students faced when they arrived at college was to write a placement essay. . . . Judged by the results of these tests, the young men and women who were to be known as open admissions students fell into one of three groups: 1. Those who met the traditional requirements for college work, who appeared from their tests . . . to be able to begin at the traditional starting points; 2. those who had survived their secondary schooling . . . and whose writing reflected a flat competence; 3. [those] who had been left so far behind the others

in their formal education that they appeared to have little chance of catching up, students whose difficulties with the written language seemed of a different order from those of other groups, as if they had come, you might say, from a different country.

. . . The third group contained true outsiders, . . . strangers in academia, unacquainted with the rules and rituals of college life, unprepared for the sorts of tasks their teachers were about to assign them. . . .

Not surprisingly, the essays these students wrote during their first weeks of class stunned the teachers who read them. Nothing, it seemed, short of a miracle was going to turn such students into writers. . . . To make matters worse, there were no studies nor guides, nor even suitable textbooks to turn to. Here were teachers trained to analyze the belletristic achievements of the ages marooned in basic writing classrooms with adult student writers who appeared by college standards to be illiterate.[7]

Relying on their previous experience with selectively-admitted students at the City University, Shaughnessy and her colleagues thought they knew what to expect from "college writers." The shock of facing a kind of writing that fit no familiar category, that met no traditional standards, forced Shaughnessy, at least, to recognize an anomaly. If these students had come through schools in which writing had been taught with standard textbooks and standard methods, then one had to conclude that the method and the textbooks did not work, at least not for a substantial and important group of students. The question was, "Why?"

To find the answer, Shaughnessy analyzed the placement essays of 4000 students and over a period of five years worked at trying to get at the roots of their problems and devise a way to overcome them. Eventually she became persuaded

. . . that basic writers write the way they do, not because they are slow or nonverbal, indifferent to or incapable of academic excellence, but because they are beginners and must, like all beginners, learn by making mistakes. . . . And the keys to their development as writers often lie in the very features of their writing that English teachers have been trained to brush aside with a marginal code letter or a scribbled injunction to "Proofread!" Such strategies ram at the doors of their incompetence while the keys that would open them lie in view. . . . The work [of teaching these students to write] must be informed by an understanding not only of what is missing or awry, but of *why this is so.*[8] (italics added)

Shaughnessy's insight is utterly simple and vitally important: we cannot teach students to write by looking at what they have written. We must also understand *how* that product came into being, and *why* it assumed the form that it did. We have to try to understand what goes on during the internal act of writing and we have to intervene during the act of writing if we want to affect its outcome. We have to do the hard thing, examine the intangible process, rather than the easy thing, evaluate the tangible product.

Although Shaughnessy was not the first investigator to try to move behind students' written products and find out how those products came into being—Janet Emig and Charles Stallard had both done limited studies at about the same time as Shaughnessy, and James Britton and his colleagues in Great Britian were working on a very ambitious study of the development of writing abilities—she was the first to undertake a large-scale research project whose goal was to find practical ways to teach the new students of the seventies to write. Her example, her book, and her repeated calls for new research in composition have undoubtedly been important stimuli in spurring the profession's search for a new paradigm.

Others in the profession have also given impetus to the search. In 1968 a journalist and professor named Donald Murray published a book called *A Writer Teaches Writing*, in which he suggests that if we want to teach students to write, we have to initiate them into the process that writers go through, not give them a set of rules. He insists that writers find their real topics only through the act of writing. In fact, Murray may have originated the admonition, "Teach Writing as Process, Not Product" in a 1972 article by that title.[9] A resurgence of interest in classical rhetoric in the seventies also sparked interest in a new approach to the teaching of writing. The books by rhetoricians Richard Weaver and Edward P. J. Corbett provided the theoretical foundations for the view that writing can not be separated from its context, that audience and intention should affect every stage of the creative process. When this premise became widely accepted at major universities—for example, the University of Iowa and the University of Texas—it inevitably put strains on the old product-centered paradigm.

Another major influence on the teaching of writing across the nation has come from California's Bay Area Writing Project, initiated in 1975. A cardinal principle of that project has been the revolutionary thesis that all writing teachers should write in order to understand the writing process first-hand. When teachers began to do so, the traditional textbook model for writing inevitably came into question. And as spin-offs of the Bay Area Writing Project have proliferated across the country, largely funded by grant money donated by agencies and foundations alarmed about the writing crisis, a growing number of teachers are changing to process-centered writing instruction.

THE EMERGING PARADIGM

But the most promising indication that we are poised for a paradigm shift is that for the first time in the history of teaching writing we have specialists who are doing controlled and directed research on writers' composing processes. Sondra Perl of Herbert Lehman College of the City University of New York and Linda Flower and John Hayes of Carnegie-Mellon University are tape recording students' oral reports of the thoughts that come to them as they write and of the choices they make. The call their investigative strategy "protocol analysis," and they supplement it with interviews and questionnaires to put together composite pictures of the processes followed by working writers. Sharon

Pianko of Rutgers University has done a study in which she matched groups of traditional and remedial writers, men and women writers, and 18-year-old and adult writers and compared their composing habits. Nancy Sommers of New York University has done a study comparing the revising practices of college freshmen and experienced professional writers, and Lester Faigley and Stephen Witte of the University of Texas now have a federal grant to do a more comprehensive study on revising. (An article based on this study appeared in the December, 1981, issue of *CCC*.) Lee Odell of Rensselaer Polytechnic Institute and Dixie Goswami are currently involved in a federally-funded study of the practices of writers in business.

From these and other studies we are beginning to find out something about how people's minds work as they write, to chart the rhythm of their writing, to find out what constraints they are aware of as they write, and to see what physical behaviors are involved in writing and how they vary among different groups of writers. So far only a small amount of data have been collected, and the inferences we can draw from the studies are necessarily tentative. As Linda Flower puts it, because we are trying to chart and analyze an activity that goes on largely out of sight, the process is rather like trying to trace the path of a dolphin by catching glimpses of it when it leaps out of the water. We are seeing only a tiny part of the whole process, but from it we can infer much about what is going on beneath the surface.[10]

What are we finding out? One point that is becoming clear is that writing is an act of discovery for both skilled and unskilled writers; most writers have only a partial notion of what they want to say when they begin to write, and their ideas develop in the process of writing. They develop their topics intuitively, not methodically. Another truth is that usually the writing process is not linear, moving smoothly in one direction from start to finish. It is messy, recursive, convoluted, and uneven. Writers write, plan, revise, anticipate, and review throughout the writing process, moving back and forth among the different operations involved in writing without any apparent plan. No practicing writer will be surprised at these findings: nevertheless, they seriously contradict the traditional paradigm that has dominated writing textbooks for years.

But for me the most interesting data emerging from these studies are those that show us profound differences between the writing behaviors of skilled and unskilled writers and the behaviors of student and professional writers. Those differences involve the amount of time spent on writing, the amount of time preparing to write, the number of drafts written, the concern for audience, the number of changes made and the stages at which they are made, the frequency and length of pauses during writing, the way in which those pauses are used, the amount of time spent rereading and reformulating, and the kind and number of constraints that the writers are aware of as they work. This kind of information enables us to construct a tentative profile of the writing behaviors of effective writers; I have sketched such a profile in another paper, not yet published.

From all this activity in the field, the new paradigm for teaching writing is emerging. Its principal features are these:

1. It focuses on the writing process; instructors intervene in students' writing during the process.
2. It teaches strategies for invention and discovery; instructors help students to generate content and discover purpose.
3. It is rhetorically based; audience, purpose, and occasion figure prominently in the assignment of writing tasks.
4. Instructors evaluate the written product by how well it fulfills the writer's intention and meets the audience's needs.
5. It views writing as a recursive rather than a linear process; pre-writing, writing, and revision are activities that overlap and intertwine.
6. It is holistic, viewing writing as an activity that involves the intuitive and non-rational as well as the rational faculties.
7. It emphasizes that writing is a way of learning and developing as well as a communication skill.
8. It includes a variety of writing modes, expressive as well as expository.
9. It is informed by other disciplines, especially cognitive psychology and linguistics.
10. It views writing as a disciplined creative activity that can be analyzed and described; its practitioners believe that writing can be taught.
11. It is based on linguistic research and research into the composing process.
12. It stresses the principle that writing teachers should be people who write.

PORTENTS FOR THE FUTURE

I believe that important events of the recent past are going to speed the revolution and help to establish this new paradigm in the nation's classrooms.

First, the University of Iowa's Writing Institute, which received a $680,000 grant from the National Endowment for the Humanities to train freshman composition directors, has this year completed its work and sent out forty administrators for writing programs who will almost certainly base those programs on the new model. They are bound to have a profound influence on their institutions.

Second, graduate programs in rhetoric are rapidly increasing across the country. The last count in the Spring, 1980, *Freshman English News* showed that fifty-three institutions have added graduate rhetoric courses since 1974, and that was not a complete list. Enrollment in these programs is climbing because students realize that English departments now offer more jobs in rhetoric and composition than in any other specialization. Most of these programs are going to produce young professionals who have been taught by scholars who know recent research and are committed to the new paradigm: Richard Young, Ross Winterowd, Joseph Comprone, James Kinneavy, Andrea Lunsford, Elizabeth Cowan, Linda Flower, to name just a few. When these new graduates go into English departments where the traditional paradigm prevails, they are certain to start working for change.

Third, in many schools, even graduate assistants who are in traditional literary programs rather than rhetoric programs are getting their in-service training from the rhetoric and composition specialists in their departments. They are being trained in process-centered approaches to the teaching of composition, and when they enter the profession and begin teaching lower-division writing courses along with their literary specialties, they are most likely to follow the new paradigm. And, more and more, the methods courses for high-school teachers are also being taught by the rhetoric specialists; that change will have a profound effect on secondary school teaching.

Fourth, we now have process-based texts on the teaching of writing. Shaughnessy's *Errors and Expectations* is well known and widely used. It has been joined by Irmscher's *Teaching Expository Writing* and Neman's *Teaching Students to Write.* The authors of both these latter books incorporate research findings and recent developments in the profession into their philosophies of and methodologies for teaching writing.

Fifth, college composition textbooks are changing. Along with their traditional books, most publishers are now publishing at least one process-oriented, rhetorically-based writing text. Several are now on the market and more are forthcoming, most of them written by scholars and teachers who are leaders in the profession. Moreover, many major publishing houses now retain well-known composition specialists to advise them on manuscripts. The publishers sense change in the wind and realize that the new crop of well-informed and committed writing program directors who will be taking over are going to insist on up-to-date textbooks. The change will even reach into some high schools because one large company has hired one of the country's leading rheticians to supervise and edit their high school composition series. Many others will probably follow their example.

But no revolution brings the millenium nor a guarantee of salvation, and we must remember that the new paradigm is sketchy and leaves many problems about the teaching or writing unresolved. As Kuhn points out, new paradigms are apt to be crude, and they seldom possess all the capabilities of their predecessors. So it is important for us to preserve the best parts of earlier methods for teaching writing: the concern for style and the preservation of high standards for the written product. I believe we also need to continue giving students models of excellence to imitate.

Kuhn contends that "the transition between competing paradigms cannot be made a step at a time, forced by logic. . . . Like the gestalt switch, it must occur all at once (though not necessarily in an instant) or not at all."[11] He says, however, that, "if its supporters are competent, they will improve it [the paradigm], explore its possibilities, and show what it would be like to belong to the community guided by it."[12] I see this last opportunity as the challenge to today's community of composition and rhetoric scholars: to refine the new paradigm for teaching composition so that it provides a rewarding, productive, and feasible way of teaching writing for the non-specialists who do most of the composition teaching in our colleges and universities.

Notes

1. Richard Young, "Paradigms and Problems: Needed Research in Rhetorical Invention," *Research in Composing,* ed. Charles Cooper and Lee Odell (Urbana, Illinois: National Council of Teachers of English, 1978), p. 31.

2. Young, p. 31.

3. James A. Berlin and Robert P. Inkster, "Current-Traditional Rhetoric: Paradigm and Practice," *Freshman English News,* 8 (Winter, 1980), 1–4, 13–14.

4. Donald Stewart, "Composition Textbooks and the Assault on Tradition," *College Composition and Communication*, 29 (May, 1978), 174.

5. Thomas Kuhn, *The Structure of Scientific Revolutions*, Second Edition (Chicago: University of Chicago Press, 1970), p. x.

6. Kuhn, p. 65.

7. Mina Shaughnessy, *Errors and Expectations* (New York and London: Oxford University Press, 1977), pp. 1–3.

8. Shaughnessy, p. 5.

9. Donald Murray, "Teach Writing As Process, Not Product," in *Rhetoric and Composition*, ed., Richard L. Graves (Rochelle Park, New Jersey: Hayden Book Company, 1976), pp. 79–82.

10. Linda Flower and John Hayes, "Identifying the Organization of the Writing Processes," *Cognitive Processes in Writing*, ed., Lee W. Gregg and Erwin R. Steinberg (Hillsdale, NJ: Lawrence Erlbaum Associates, 1980), pp. 9–10.

11. Kuhn, p. 150.

12. Kuhn, p. 159.

Literacy in the Department of English

Jay L. Robinson

Over the past ten years or so, I have had the mixed pleasures of being rather deeply involved in academic administration, at a low enough level to be able to look at the landscape close hand. From 1974 to 1981, I was chairman of Michigan's Department of English Language and Literature; since January of 1983, I have been chairman of Michigan's English Composition Board—the unit charged in our institution with administering and conducting some parts of a college-wide writing program—a program, by the way, *not* housed in an English department. In these ten years, I have had a chance to stand at each side of the great divide that separates the home of literature from the home of composition, and I have gazed into the space between them, wondering not so much about ways to get home as about where home is or should be.

In the quieter moments of my two chairmanships, I have explored some other territory. I have looked at linguistics at Michigan from the perspective of a chairman of a review committee. And I have looked at an Education School—Michigan's—as a member of a transition team charged with reorganizing Michigan's School after another review committee (on which somehow I did not serve) imposed upon it a 40 percent budget cut.

That sounds like my own biographical headnote, but that is not why I begin with personal history. Rather, it is to say that quite by chance I have had an unusual opportunity to think about some of the issues now being actively discussed in the profession, an unusual opportunity to view from several perspectives what might be involved in trying to bridge the gap between literature and composition as some of my colleagues now want to do. From my various perspectives, I see at least these questions as necessary ones for bridge builders:

(1) Is the gap between literature and composition bridgeable?
(2) Should the gap be bridged, and if so, for whose benefit? Who should bridge to whom? and why? and from which side?
(3) Is it probable or possible that the gap will be bridged, and if so, who will be the engineers?

The questions suggest at least three avenues of approach to the bridge site:

(1) One is through theory, with students of literature and students of composition leaving their separate homes to find a place for candid, critical discussion of whether synthesis of their now separate theories is possible;
(2) The second is through careful consideration of what we do in our separate classrooms, and whether what we do meets the needs of our students and the legitimate expectations of society;

(3) The third is through sober reflection upon the performance and potential of various institutions, such as academic departments, with special attention to their histories, to what in other contexts is sometimes called a "track record."

Thinking about these questions and about possibly useful approaches to them led me to my own topic: *"Literacy* in the Department of English."

Literacy is a wonderfully ambivalent term, its meaning dependent upon the contexts in which it is used. Thinking about how the term is typically used in English departments led me to another question: Will instructional programs in reading and writing—the two main activities most often associated with the term literacy—continue to be housed in English departments as they have been in the past? Or will such programs find another home—one less subject to domestic strife, one not divided into separate spaces with no sure and safe passage between them? The question, I would suggest, is not an empty or academic one. You as well as I can read statements like this:

> Writing instruction was for years a stepchild of English departments, who have always dominated it. As recently as fifteen years ago many colleges dropped composition altogether—partly on the basis that the high schools were handling the job, and mainly to give still greater emphasis to literary study. That development should make us hesitate about trusting that English departments, as they are presently constituted, will solve the problem [of ineffective instruction in composition].
>
> Now there has been a resurgence of active involvement by English faculty along with others. Writing instruction could be a boon for underemployed humanists, a large and influential group. But teachers trained in literature may not necessarily be well situated to work with beginning students, nor to prepare students for the kinds of writing tasks they will likely face after school. English professors are not even necessarily good writers themselves, and their commitment to specialization has been at least as strong as any other discipline's. (1:56)

The author of these paragraphs is Richard Hendrix, who at the time he composed them was associated with the Fund for the Improvement of Postsecondary Education (our beloved and now endangered FIPSE); his paper was prepared for a conference sponsored by the National Institute of Education. Among the thirteen papers published in the proceedings, only two were by members of English departments (one a rhetorician, the other a linguist); the remaining eleven were by education professors, anthropologists, sociologists, and linguists from linguistics departments.

There are, my point is, competitors to English departments for the tasks and rewards of teaching literacy. Funding agencies, my other point is, are not unaware of track records. Do English departments have the horses for what could become a very tough race? Do they really want to run in it?

I think we all recognize that there are both powerful and quite diverse social needs for the competencies referred to by the term literacy: reading, writing, comprehending, and communicating. There is need for programs that enable students to acquire these competencies—and especially for programs that make it possible for *all* students to acquire them, not just white middle and upper class students whose native language is English. There is need as well for research that will enable us to understand these competencies better, and thus make possible the construction of better programs. Need there is, and needs there are, but I do not see in our colleges and universities, certainly not in mine, despite our success with a good writing program, units deliberately designed or adequately institutionalized to meet present needs: neither needs for research nor needs for adequate instructional programs.

"Literacy in the English Department"? Maybe. But I doubt it.

I know of few English departments, and none in major research-oriented universities, that have deliberately made a comfortable home for those teacher-scholars who wish and are adequately prepared to teach composition and reading and do research in the various domains of literacy and its uses. English departments mean by the term literacy one particular and quite specialized thing: an easy familiarity with a certain body of texts, a particular attitude toward them, and special practices for reading texts so that they will yield the appropriate attitudes—attitudes that might lead a professor to call one student "cultured," another "urbane," and still another a "candidate for graduate school." It is literacy thus defined that English departments strive most energetically to institutionalize: through allocation of budget resources, through vigilant protection of the tenure-track and of tenure itself, through always watchful graduate admissions, through exclusive course offerings, through careful limits placed upon what counts as serious discourse in the discipline—upon what one may say and where one may safely publish.

It is with help from this system of discourse that we in English departments find means to ignore the needs of our students, especially those of our most needy students, and yet feel good about it. Except when we are talking about our "introductions to literature," we characterize our students' difficulties with reading and writing as "deficiencies" needful of "remediation"; we characterize what students in composition courses do as a practice in basic skills. We do so comfortably, because we do not teach the courses or the students. We do so the more comfortably because we tell ourselves that this is how composition specialists and reading specialists define literacy—even though we could find out, if we wished to read, that no knowledgeable and self-respecting composition or reading specialist would use the term skill, or more surely the modifier basic, to characterize the activities of writing and reading. Not in our time.

What I have learned from talking with my colleagues who teach and think about reading and writing are these lessons: reading and writing are complexly constituted and potentially enabling competencies that develop only when they are practiced; literacy that is worthy of the name, these practitioners tell me, develops only through the productive exercise of available and developing competencies with language—through the use of such competencies in composing and comprehending texts, through the use of language to make meanings that count for something in contexts where learning and sharing what is learned counts for something. Literacy is an outcome, not a skill, and not (even) a competency. It is something that is achieved when competencies are enabled through exercise of the human capacity to make meaning.

Exercise of that kind is a serious business, and should count for more than it does in English departments, or in the academy.

To think of literacy as a set of skills and to think of these skills as basic, as mere rudiments, is to misconceive it badly, perhaps maliciously. The misconception of the real competencies involved in achieving literacy has harmed all students much, but most of all those students whom we characterize as most needful of special help. John Goodlad, in his recent study of schools and schooling, found in the majority of language arts classrooms in elementary and secondary schools a "dominant emphasis [upon] teaching basic language use skills and mastering mechanics. . . . " The emphasis, he found, intensifies the farther down the ladder of tracks one looks:

> . . . lower track classes tended to emphasize the mechanics of English usage, whereas high track classes were likely to stress the intellectual skills of analysis, evaluation, and judgment especially through literature. The low track classes were unlikely to encounter the high status knowledge dealt with in the upper tracks and normally considered essential for college admission. (205)

The myth of basic skills, when applied in classrooms, deprives students of what they most need. Those most frequently deprived, of course, are members of racial, social, and linguistic minorities, for their children most numerously populate our lower-track and remedial classes. And the myth operates another way: it allows those of us who teach advanced courses to look down our noses upon those who teach lower-track and basic ones—allows us to say, because we view such courses as basic, that those who teach them need little knowledge, no special preparation, no particular expertise, and exactly such recognition as accrues to these absences. Tasks that are basic can safely be assigned to lesser mortals than those riding high on the tenure-track: to graduate students, no matter what their preparation, or to part-time lecturers, no matter what their past or future.

Recent arguments for bridging the gap between composition and literature like those in a recent collection of essays sanctioned by MLA (Horner) can be seen, if one wishes so to see them, as attempts to enrich the intellectual content of composition courses, thus raising their status in the English profession—something that could benefit teachers of composition, though not so much as English departments themselves. But will such bridge building benefit students?

I do not think so. We will not meet the needs of our students, neither our current ones nor those who may come to us in the future; nor will we meet the expectations and requirements of our academies or of our society, unless we in English departments are willing to change—to challenge inertia, to alter the nature of English studies, to redefine what we think of as centers and peripheries, to reshape our departments and alter their priorities.

To change effectively we must begin with theory, thinking of the task of theory-building in new ways. We will not prevail with quasi-theories that are mere apologetics for the teaching of literature as we have come to know and love it; nor will we prevail by trying to smuggle poems and novels into composition classrooms, by trying to impose our own preferences and our own wishes upon a clientele with other needs and other interests. As we build theories, we must also try to build new departmental structures, structures designed as deliberately as our theories to rectify past inequities and inequalities. What we will need in effect is an affirmative action program for at least three oppressed minorities: those many who have been excluded for reasons of color, linguistic background, or poverty from the attainment of literacy; those few who are seriously interested in theories of composing and comprehending; and those more numerous yet still far too few who do not suffer shock or burnout when they are asked to teach those many who would compose and comprehend, write and read, but don't know how to begin, or haven't yet found that they can.

When we look only at the surface of things, as some now do, it would seem that the time is ripe for at least a detente between the two hostile camps—the literati and the rhetoricians. I read, for example, in Winifred Horner's "Introduction" to the volume *Composition and Literature* a report of change in the profession that begins with the imperative of social change:

> In the 1970s the situation in the English discipline changed drastically, again for a number of pragmatic reasons. As the post-World War II baby-boom babies grew up and graduated from colleges across the nation, enrollments at large universities dropped or leveled off, and, worse still for the humanities, students turned to more practical degrees that would ensure them a share of the dollar pie.

> At the same time that literature enrollments dropped, enrollments in writing courses increased. In many cases administrators withdrew funds from literature programs and added them to writing projects.

Affected were, she writes, those

> senior scholars who had not taught writing since their graduate-school days [and who now] were forced to teach composition when their seminars failed to "make."

Also affected were

junior members of English departments. In most cases their entire Ph.D. training had been in literary studies, but, if . . . fortunate enough to obtain university positions, [they would find] all or a large portion of their teaching . . . in composition. (7)

Familiar facts, though one might ask a stranger's question: Why were even these fortunate few hired if they didn't offer appropriate qualifications for the primary teaching task? But we know the answers to that question already, though it is rarely asked openly.

Horner finds, in what might seem to the stranger a rather bizarre and dismal situation, reason for hope:

Since the inception of the Teaching of Writing Division [in MLA], I have attended most of the sessions. In talking with the members of the division, the second largest of the association, I discovered that most were persons whose first interests were in literature and critical theory, but they had chosen the Teaching of Writing Division because they were, in fact, now seriously engaged in teaching composition. Most readily admitted that all their training had been in literature and that they attended sessions to learn about research in the teaching of writing. (1)

Once more, a reflex of the pragmatics of history. But Horner wishes to claim more in the way of change than a shift of budget priorities, a matter of making a living, a matter of making the best of what has happened by undesign. "The size of the division," she writes, "reflects dramatically the changing nature of our discipline. . . . " But not only that, it is occasion for opportunity of another sort, for

In reality, literature and composition cannot be separated either in theory or in teaching practice. Composition theory and critical theory are indeed opposite sides of the same coin, and the 'teaching' of writing and the 'teaching' of literature are applications of theories that are closely connected, often inseparable, and always fundamental to the study of language. (1–2)

Now in reality, or at least in the one I occupy, literature and composition *are* separated, certainly in anything that can be called practice, and certainly in the way they are regarded and supported as practices. As I read the history of critical theory in my working lifetime, critical theory and composition theory have indeed not been "opposite sides of the same coin" but currencies as different as the pound and the yen. And as I read the institutional history of the thing called *English studies*, with special attention to its dominant and dominating concepts, I see nothing that suggests complementary bonding, nothing to suggest more than a rather tenuous linking, like a plank thrown across a steep-sided deep creek. Those of us who would build bridges between composition and literature had better be good historians, and better theorists, or risk getting very wet indeed.

Raymond Williams writes instructively about the institutionalization of certain conceptions of literature in our immediate past and our inertial present in two works that I would recommend to all bridge builders: *Marxism and Literature* and *Writing in Society*.

It is common in our time, Williams writes, to "see 'literature' defined as 'full, central, immediate human experience,' " and as such to find it privileged as an essential and unique way of knowing or coming to know (*Marxism* 45). To have students study literature, we sometimes argue, is not merely to provide materials from which a past can be constructed, an identity found—something that historians, sociologists, anthropologists, psychologists do; rather it is to provide immediate experience of the past or of the present—"full, central, immediate human experience." Thus literary experience is conceived as unique; and as such, given its essence, it is thought essentially fundamental to the activity of being human. From this perspective, literature becomes its own epistemology: it is not a subject among many, not an alternative perspective on reality, but the preeminent way to apprehend it. There is literature, and through it, because it is experience, we apprehend the world as humans do; and then there is science, or worse yet social science, whose practitioners glimpse only partially, and then never centrally, either the world or the experience of humans in it. From this set of notions, it is so easy to make an argument for literature in the composition classroom: for just as writing is a means of coming to terms with experience, a means of coming to know, so literature *is* experience and a unique way of knowing what it is valuable to know. In literature is embodied all we need to know about composition, about language as it apprehends reality. "Shakespeare and Composition"—the perfect composer, the perfect composition. The bridge is built.

But Williams complains that this definition, or concept, of literature is

> a powerful and often forbidding system of abstraction, in which the concept of 'literature' becomes actively ideological. Theory can do something against it, in the necessary recognition . . . that whatever else 'it' may be, literature is the process and the result of formal composition within the social and formal properties of a language. (*Marxism* 45–46)

The conception of literature as "immediate living experience," says Williams, suppresses "the very process that *is* specific, that of actual composition." From the privileged perspective, literature is a thing in and of itself, not a thing made through writing or remade through reading. Literature becomes, in this way of conceiving it, a self-justifying body of texts that in themselves constitute the literary experience and authenticate it as finer even than human experience itself, for real experience is embarrassingly rough and diverse. Through literature, a reader may refine and cultivate his own experience, remove himself from conflict and accident, and achieve a tranquil and civil sanity.[1] To read literature is to refine one's sense and sensibility; no further justification is either needed or warranted.

To conclude his argument about the ideological privileging of "literature" as a concept, Williams turns to semantic history, tracing development of the term from its early usages, in which its reference was often close to what we now mean by *literacy* ("a condition of reading: of being able to read and of having read") to its now more specialized one: a body of texts of a particular kind and quality. In tracing the history, Williams reminds us that the term "literature" once referred to more than imaginative works: histories, biographies, works of philosophy, political and scientific treatises, were all works of literature and thus grist for the mill of literary study; literature was a condition of reading, of having read, not a set of special procedures for interpreting a body of specially privileged texts. Williams traces the specialization of the concept of "reading" to the narrower professional activity of criticism, a shift from reading as learning to reading as the exercise of taste and sensibility. To read is human; to criticize, professional (*Marxism* 46–54).

We could retain our notion of literature as a particular body of imaginative works, and our special definition of reading and writing as criticism, if we were content merely to add writing assignments to our syllabi for literature courses, merely to smuggle composition into them just as some of our colleagues have smuggled it into history, political science classes, or even into biology classes. But we seem to want more than that: English departments still seem to want to teach *all* students, not just those interested or dabbling in literature; they seem to want to teach introductory composition courses; and they seem to want to keep hold of college writing programs. And they want to keep "literature" in introductory courses, and professors of literature in control of writing programs.

If we want such things, then I think we had better be ready to rethink what we mean by the term "literature." And we had better be ready to rethink what we mean by reading and by writing. As things are now in our intellectual world, literature (in its generally accepted meanings) and composition (in certain of its currently framed ones) *are* separated. Composition theory and critical theory can perhaps be *made* to be opposite sides of the same coin, but only if the coin is deliberately minted.

When literature was at the core of humane learning, which was some time ago, the very term meant something quite different from what it means today—it applied to a different range of texts and to texts of different kinds, to reading and to writing, not to specialized kinds and uses of these activities. University teachers of literature thought of themselves as teachers of reading and writing. When, in more recent times, literature—in its specialized senses—could still be taken as the core of humane learning, institutions were different. They were attended by a smaller and more homogeneous percentage of the population, biased in favor of the white and well-to-do. Sometimes these institutions were even headed and administered by professors of literature, for scientists and economists have come even more recently than we humanists to the halls of power and influence. But our academic world is at present a diverse one, and its diversity exists along at least two dimensions: the clientele to be educated and the intellectual world into which they are to be led. In our present world, privileged definitions of literature, of reading and of writing, will serve neither students nor the world of ideas. Such definitions cannot compatibly be wedded to emerging definitions and descriptions of composing and comprehending, or to emergent definitions and descriptions of literacy and its uses in the world. What one fears, of course, is that a shotgun marriage will take place, because it is clear in present circumstances who owns the key to the armory.

Richard Lanham, in an important contribution to the volume *Composition and Literature,* takes up some of the same history Williams does in tracing the development of English studies from the foundation of the Oxford English School in 1894 to what he calls its "maturation"—the achievement of "departmental and disciplinary status." Lanham traces the development toward maturity from its origins in an argument "that literature constitutes a reality apart from ordinary reality, [thus] deserving of study in and of itself"; he sees this argument coming into its own with New Criticism, and later "with the work of Northrop Frye and others"; then, Lanham writes:

> The maturation was accelerated by the two go-go decades of academic prosperity from 1955 to 1975, [when] a flood of students and money . . . released English studies not only from composition instruction, until then its historic base in America, but also from routine instruction in the lower division. The discipline was thus freed to draw in upon itself, become graduate- and professional-centered, and sponsor metalevel reflections upon literary texts and inquiry—upon, that is, itself.

The consequences of this? Two for Lanham: impressive achievement in the discipline—in philology, in criticism, but at considerable cost. "No knowledgeable person," Lanham writes, "would want to belittle, or to damage, this powerful maturity in the discipline. But, as we are now finding out, such maturity assumed a specific social base—the reigning society, in fact, when the Oxford English School was founded in 1894: white, literate, and at least middle class." "English studies," he concludes, "now provides a superb instrument to educate such a society. That society, alas, no longer exists" (15–16).

If our students are no longer similar in color, background, language, aims, or aspirations, the world of ideas they will encounter in the academy is no less diverse. "The felt center for studying man," says Lanham, the renegade Renaissance scholar, "is shifting from the traditional humanities to other disciplines in much the same way that the traditional European focus for Western thought has now diffused throughout the globe." He speaks of a "new humanist curriculum" constructed from sources of literature so wide as to include evolutionary biology (22). Clifford Geertz, an anthropologist who offers his own view of intellectual diversity, glimpses a similar redrawing of boundaries by calling our attention to what he calls "blurred genres"—works of scholarship and literature that drive typologists and librarians berserk by refusing to be either history or philosophy, linguistics or criticism, fact or fiction. Works of this kind now appear frequently, Geertz argues, and their appearance is more than accidental:

> . . . it is more than a matter of odd sports and occasional curiosities, or of the admitted fact that the innovative is, by definition, hard to categorize. It is a phenomenon general enough and distinctive enough to suggest that what we are seeing is not just another redrawing of the cultural map—the moving of a few

disputed borders, the marking of some more picturesque mountain lakes—but an alteration of the principles of mapping. Something is happening to the way we think about the way we think. ("Blurred Genres" 20)

To write his own brand of cultural anthropology, Geertz creates his own blurred genres, adopting perspectives alien to the specialized social scientist, plundering the methods, concepts, and vocabularies of textual and literary critics to describe and interpret not texts themselves but cultural events, actions in the world.

And yet when Geertz looks to the academic disciplines, to discourse in the modern academy, to codes our young students must somehow crack and then learn to use, he is struck mainly by difference, by multiplicity:

> . . . the various disciplines . . . , humanistic, natural scientific, social scientific alike, that make up the scattered discourse of modern scholarship are more than just intellectual coigns of vantage but are ways of being in the world, to invoke a Heideggerian formula, forms of life, to use a Wittgensteinian, or varieties of noetic experience, to adapt a Jamesian. In the same way that Papuans or Amazonians inhabit the world they imagine, so do high energy physicists or historians of the Mediterranean in the age of Phillip II—or so, at least, an anthropologist imagines. It is when we begin to see this, to see that to set out to deconstruct Yeats' imagery, absorb oneself in black holes, or measure the effect of schooling on economic achievement is not just to take up a technical task but to take on a cultural frame that defines a great part of one's life, that an ethnography of modern thought begins to seem an imperative project. Those roles we think to occupy turn out to be minds we find ourselves to have. ("The Way We Think Now" 155)

So how do we use discourse to lead our students from their diverse homes and minds to where they may want to go, through an academic world that we inhabit and they must somehow enter, a world that is itself composed of diverse homes and minds? How do we make our world, our discourse, meaningful to them, as they pass from there to here and beyond? These are questions bridge builders *must* ask, especially those who ask for the task, those who want to teach all students.

I would suggest that a proper aim for *introductory* composition courses in the modern academy is to help students learn to play the various roles that will lead to development of their minds, in so far as minds can usefully be shaped by the discourse and noetic systems of modern scholarship. Such is the aim and argument of the better informed of those who would spread writing across the curriculum, but still find place and purpose for a generally required introductory composition course. This aim and argument is better than that which argues for an introductory composition course based in "literature" that serves only as introduction to discourse about "literary" texts, and is better by far than introductory literature-composition courses that make no argument for themselves but nearly presume a privileged place in the academy.

Yet even the better arguments do not go far enough. What we should aim for in college and university *writing programs* is not only capacity and competence in specialized discourse systems, but also capacity and competence in a common language, a generally available educated discourse: one that enables our students to move from mutually unintelligible or difficult academic jargons to talk and writing that they can share with other specialists and non-specialists, and to talk and writing that puts our students, and us, in contact with others who are differently educated and with our various selves, our mutually separated selves. What we really need is a discourse that puts us in contact with the resonances and echoes of the experiences that constitute our own separately-lived lives and our all-too-often separated social identities, our ways of being in a world that we did not necessarily choose.

A proper aim for writing programs in colleges and universities, maybe even in schools, might well be to invite and help students to develop as ethnographers of thought—as careful and reflective participant-observers, critical thinkers of their own thoughts, able to reach beyond the constraints of discourse, able to escape from narrow perspectives, able to move from restricted and restricting ways of being and behaving in the world, able to assert and make a place for themselves as makers of meanings that are personally satisfying, no matter how constrained by the language they must use.

To reach toward aims like these will of course require much more than a bridge between literature and composition, much more than current talk even suggests about bridge building, much more thought and talk than the current uses of terms "literature" or even "composition" begin to imply. What is needed is not talk about bridging from literature to composition or from composition to literature, but more serious talk about the human uses of language—the uses diverse humans make of language. We need talk not about "composition" and "literature," but about talking and listening and reading and writing as centrally human and humanizing activities.

Rudiments of theory that might make possible such serious thought about talk and writing and listening and reading are readily available for our use, if we have energy and will and opportunity to avail ourselves of them. Theories linking reading and writing are becoming the dominant ones among those who study either reading or composition— theories that reconceive reading as the active construction of texts and their meanings; theories that reconceive writing as an act of perpetual making, perpetual revision, with publication or submission for a grade an arbitrary stopping point. As readers of Cassirer, Langer, and Burke know, theories defining reading and writing as symbolic action, linking the written to the spoken word, have been with us from some time; and, as readers of Austin, Searle, Pratt, and Goffman know, theories defining talk and listening as intentional yet ordered actions in a social world, linking the spoken to the written word, have been with us for almost as long. Theories that re-place reading, as process and procedure, at the heart of literacy criticism—as central to interpretation— are readily adaptable to the classroom from the work of semioticians like Johnathan Culler and Umberto Eco, and from the work of reader-response theorists like Louise Rosenblatt and Stanley Fish. Those who have read Michel Foucault know how discourse can constrain as well as liberate; those who have read Paolo Friere and other theoretical Marxists know why it does, and what its potential is and isn't.

If the activity of reading and writing were defined as it is by modern workers in the field, who have knowledge not only of where they come from, but also of the consequences and constraints that attend upon their engagements with students, then we could worry less about the inclusion of "literature" in the composition classroom, inhabited as it is by those diverse students. When reading and writing are defined as activities then we come closer to something we can do for all students, with all students, for mutual benefit and enlightenment. We reach, I think, toward a common language when we put in practice what Raymond Williams tells us can come from a proper engagement with texts:

> A newly active social sense of writing and reading, through the social and material historical realities of language, in a world in which it is closely and precisely known, in every act of writing and reading, that these practices connect with, are inseparable from, the whole set of social practices and relationships which define writers and readers as active human beings, as distinct from the idealized and projected 'authors' and 'trained readers' who are assumed to float, on a guarded privilege, above the rough, divisive and diverse world of which yet, by some alchemy, they possess the essential secret. ("Cambridge English Past and Present," *Writing* 189)

Student writers, of course, are authors too, and inhabitants of their own particular worlds; and their own works should be read in the same spirit and with the same rigor that we would have our students read the texts we assign them. What others have written, and what they write, are equally constructed as are their very selves from a "whole set of social practices and relationships which define writers and readers as active human beings." Our own teaching practices come out of a similar matrix, and we are disingenuous when we do not recognize and act upon that fact.

It will, in short, finally matter which texts we include in our composition courses—even in our literature courses—introductory or more advanced. For we have our students and the responsibility to prepare them for productive intellectual life.

In thinking about the texts I will choose for the next composition course I will teach, I will not forget Geertz's notion of blurred genres, his fascination with those works that refuse easy classification, those that fall in the empty spaces between the lines of disciplinary division, those that require some uneasy accommodation to what is comfortably categorized. At the same time, I will be plagued by his insistence that "the hallmark of modern consciousness . . . is its enormous multiplicity," a result of sharp divisions among ways of knowing, ways of acting in the world. Geertz, like many in the world we now inhabit, worries about "where the 'general' went in 'general education,' " about the need for integration of cultural life, a concern of humanists as well; and with me, Geertz worries about the very possibility of reaching toward a common language. With him, I see no possibility for integration in "some kind of diffuse humanism," no possibility for integration in easy attempts to build bridges:

> The problem of the integration of cultural life [he argues] becomes one of making it possible for people inhabiting different worlds to have a genuine, and reciprocal, impact upon one another. If it is true that insofar as there is a general conscious-ness it consists of the interplay of a disorderly crowd of not wholly commensurable visions, then the vitality of that consciousness depends upon creating the condi-tions under which such interplay will occur. And for that, the first step is surely to accept the depth of the differences; the second to understand what these dif-ferences are; and the third to construct some sort of vocabulary in which they can be publicly formulated—one in which econometricians, epigraphers, cytochemists, and iconologists can give a credible account of themselves to each other. ("The Way We Think Now" 160-61)

To accept a depth of difference, to understand what the differences are, and then deliberately to construct a vocabulary in which they can be formulated so that we may talk intelligibly to one another, write what another can read, to "begin to find something circumstantial to say to one another again"—that, says Geertz, "would be that rarest of phenomena, a *useful* miracle" (160). That is the miracle we should seek in building bridges. It is, in my view, no unwarranted leap to see in composition programs the op-portunity to try to find a common vocabulary, to establish a common means of discourse, to try to call into being and use a genuinely public language. But we must not be led to think of this task as easy, its achievement as anything less than miraculous, should we somehow achieve it. In the academy, we inhabit a complex world, and our separate languages create a multiplicity of thoughts and forms, of words and actions, and with them, worlds we cause ourselves to inhabit. And because, as composition teachers, we somehow inherit the responsibility to bring our students into the academy without insisting that they leave their own lives and worlds behind—for we *are* both humane and humanists—our task is more difficult than even Geertz imagines.

Yet were I to teach a composition course in which the founding of a public language was the aim—were I to teach a course including works of imagination, I would still take Geertz as my model and two works of his as my teacher's manual: "Blurred Genres: The Refiguration of Social Thought," and "Deep Play: Notes on a Balinese Cockfight." In these two essays, Geertz offers a meeting ground for humanists like me and social scientists like him, a meeting ground he and I can stand on to talk about our convergent preoccupation with interpretation, with using language to make sense of human actions, either in their forms as written texts or in their forms as cultural events. In "Deep Play," Geertz bridges the gap between writing and event by deliberately treating an action in the world, a cockfight, as if it were a text, written by actors, read by spectators, serving in its meanings as a tale the Balinese tell themselves to make meaning in their lives. I would begin with Geertz in my search for a public discourse because he gives me a place to stand in my attempt to understand his vocation as an anthropologist, because he has borrowed my vocabulary to talk about his subject. And he builds a bridge for my students because he gives them a vocabulary that is useful to them and to me for talking together about events in the world as well as events in the worlds made by texts, and about texts as events. And in building bridges like these, maybe I can find, or maybe my students can if I can't, ways to bridge toward other ways of seeing and saying that are less accessible to me or to them: how econometricians, epigraphers, cytochemists, see and say. In building bridges, I want to begin first with something relatively easy—something with pontoons perhaps, certainly something with easy instructions.

If I can meet Geertz on his ground, and he me on mine, I will have something to offer my students, living as I do in an academy that they are venturing their young energies to enter. In trying to write about the meaning of actions in the world, and being willing to use a vocabulary that is familiar to me, yet wishing to be critical in his use of it, Geertz has reached out to me, opened the door from his department to mine. And I remember, as I think about the gesture, these words of his:

> It is when we begin to see this, to see that to set out to deconstruct Yeats' imagery, absorb oneself in black holes, or measure the effect of schooling on economic achievement is not just to take up a technical task but to take on a cultural frame that defines a great part of one's life. . . .

I do not want my students, especially those who write for and to me, to think of what they do as a technical task, to make of what they are learning and know some kind of meaningless exercise. When I teach a composition class, I must remember that my cultural frames are not my students' or theirs mine. I must remember that their experiences are neither mine, nor something I want to appropriate by investing them with my meanings. And yet, I want them to learn; and yes, I want to work with them toward common meanings, meanings that we can share, meanings that will make possible the possibility of a common language, a public discourse made of and constitutive both of self and community.

In a language that allows me, as a member of the academy and a user of its discourse and them as newcomers and learners, to talk in the same terms both about events and texts, I find a bridge: from their experiences to a way we can talk about them; and from there, with luck and patience, a way to say that all texts work like that—even works of "literature." Even great works of literature, after all, like experiences we comfortably or uncomfortably participate in and remember, are stories that people tell themselves to make sense of their lives. To engage in this kind of meaning-making excludes no one, no matter what their experiences, no matter what kinds of cultural frames they have constructed. A common language, a public discourse, must bridge not only from discipline to discipline, from the jargon of anthropology to the jargon of literary criticism, but from each equally to the discourse systems constructed for our students by their ways of being in the world, the discourse systems of self, family, and neighborhood. Community is made possible only when diversity and its expression are made equally possible.

And that is why it seems to me far too easy to talk in our time about building bridges between what we customarily call "literature" and what we have more recently learned to call "composition."

In his essay "Beyond Cambridge English," Williams writes of another gap, that between literature and literacy. It is this gap, or to use his metaphor this "unevenness" that poses the real challenge to the future of English studies:

> It is often said that there are more than six centuries of English literature. It is not often said that there are less than two centuries of English literacy. Of course 'English,' in those two statements, has different meanings. The first refers primarily to the language, the second to the people. But then it is the ordinarily unexamined relationship between these meanings that can reveal a central problem in English studies. The idea of literature, throughout, has been so closely connected with the condition of literacy that it can hardly be said that this deeper relationship needs to be forced. Powerful social and cultural conventions control or displace what is otherwise an obvious connection. What then is 'English literacy,' for professional students and teachers of English? Is it their own condition and that of people much like them currently and retrospectively applied? Or is it the diverse and changing conditions of their whole nominal people? To approach two centuries of English literacy means restricting our count to a bare majority. General literacy has a bare century, and within that many are still disadvantaged. In relation to what is seen as 'our' literature, where then do students and teachers of English stand?
>
> I have made my own awkward stand. By my educational history I belong with the literate and the literary. But by inheritance and still by affiliation I belong with an illiterate and relatively illiterate majority. It is said that as the whole society develops, and has for the past century been developing, these inherited problems and contradictions resolve themselves. I do not think so. Beyond our local and diverse histories there are major intellectual issues, of a fully objective kind, which need to be traced to this radical unevenness between literature and general literacy. Underlying them, always, are the complex general problems of language, and it is how these problems are dealt with, in the coming years, that the success or failure of English studies will, in my view, be decided. (*Writing* 212–13)

As members of English departments, where will we make our stand? Will we continue to confuse literacy with literature, remaining insensitive to the needs of those who would move from the ranks of the relatively illiterate? Will we continue to believe that literature and literacy are synonymous terms? Will we refuse to see that literacy and literature are social constructions, the products of social and historical forces? Will we be open to new theories that offer new concepts and suggest new relations, and recognize that there are other gaps to be bridged, new techniques for building bridges?

When I think about my life in an English department, I have to shift to the cruder metaphors I have played with. What is our track record? A few questions, merely:

1. Have English departments been hospitable to interdisciplinary work, or competent in it?
2. How many critical theorists find colleagues to talk to? (Linguists don't count, because they're so lonely they will listen to anyone).
3. When was the last time that an English professor thought of himself or herself as teaching reading?
4. How many English departments try to steal remedial reading and writing courses from support units?
5. Who gets to direct freshman composition? How much competition is there for the job?
6. Who gets to teach freshman composition? If the job market were good, how much competition would there be for that job?
7. Who plans freshman comp courses? The best and most experienced literary critics?
8. Who gets tenure, and how many composition and reading specialists are there nationally among the tenured ranks? Outside of Education schools, that is?
9. Who kids whom, and for how long?

The needs are there, the theories are emerging, and some few are seeing the question of bridge building as crucial to the development of the profession. Richard Lanham does, for example, as well as in his own way, does Raymond Williams: "The relation with composition," says Lanham, "stands at the center of the basic decisions for English studies" (25).

So what does the future hold?

Composition in the English department? Maybe—but what will it mean, and whose needs will it meet, and whose will it ignore.

Literacy in the English department? Maybe. It could be, but I doubt it.

And where will literature go, should we once again begin to think seriously about its uses for all students?

Works Cited

Geertz, Clifford. "Blurred Genres: The Refiguration of Social Thought." *Local Knowledge: Further Essays in Interpretive Anthropology.* New York: Basic, 1983. 19–35.
-----. "Deep Play: Notes on the Balinese Cockfight." *Daedalus* 101 (1972): 1–37.

-----. "The Way We Think Now: Toward an Ethnography of Modern Thought." *Local Knowledge*. 147–163.

Goodlad, John I. *A Place Called School: Prospects for the Future*. New York: McGraw, 1984.

Hendrix, Richard. "The Status and Politics of Writing Instruction." *Variation in Writing: Functional and Linguistic-Cultural Differences*. Ed. Marcia Farr Whiteman. Vol. 1 of *Writing: The Nature, Development, and Teaching of Written Communication*. 2 Vols. Hillsdale, NJ: Lawrence Erlbaum, 1981. 53–70.

Horner, Winifred Bryan, ed. *Composition and Literature: Bridging the Gap*. Chicago: U of Chicago P, 1983.

Lanham, Richard. "One, Two Three." Horner, 14–29.

Williams, Raymond. *Marxism and Literature*. Oxford: Oxford UP, 1977.

-----. *Writing in Society*. Thetford, Norfolk: Thetford-Verso, 1983.

A BASIC REFERENCE LIBRARY FOR TEACHERS OF WRITING

As the field of rhetoric and composition studies expands, so does the number of excellent books and articles that a writing teacher could acquire. Below you'll find a very
brief list of works the beginning writing teacher might wish to own. As you continue
in the field, you'll want to add your own favorites to this list.

Bartholmae, David, and Anthony Petrosky. *Facts, Counterfacts, Artifacts: Theory and
Method for a Reading and Writing Course.* Upper Montclair, NJ: Boynton/Cook,
1986. An essay on reading and writing as tools for understanding academic
discourse; a description of a course embodying the principles described in the
essay; and five essays commenting on aspects of the course by instructors who
have taught it. A provoking combination of theory and practice.

Berthoff, Ann. *The Making of Meaning: Metaphors, Models, and Maxims for Writing
Teachers.* Upper Montclair, NJ: Boynton/Cook, 1981. Twelve essays explore
the role of imagination in the use of reading and writing as meaning-making processes. Both theoretical and practical concerns are treated.

Cooper, Charles R., and Lee Odell, eds. *Evaluating Writing: Describing, Measuring,
Judging.* Urbana, IL: NCTE, 1977. Six essays discuss various techniques for
assessing student progress. The essays on primary trait scoring and holistic evaluation are essential for anyone dealing with standardized test scores.

Elbow, Peter. *Writing Without Teachers.* NY: Oxford, 1973. Students can use writing
as a means to create meaning by freewriting (sustained written association of ideas),
which leads to multiple drafts as the writer shapes and defines content. The response of readers also can help the writer improve drafts. A very influential book
in the study of invention.

Emig, Janet. *The Web of Meaning.* Upper Montclair, NJ: Boynton/Cook, 1983. Eleven
selections (including two chapters from her ground-breaking *The Composing Process of Twelfth Graders*) reflect the development of Emig's understanding of the
relationship between reading and writing. Particularly strong on the uses of writing
to create meaning and on writing as a mode of inquiry and learning.

Foster, David. *A Primer for Writing Teachers: Theories, Theorists, Issues, Problems.*
Upper Montclair, NJ: Boynton/Cook, 1983. A discussion and clarification of the
traditions in teaching writing, recent discourse systems, points of disagreement
in teaching, and the design of courses. More theoretical than practical, but concise and lucid.

Graves, Richard L., ed. *Rhetoric and Composition: A Sourcebook for Teachers and
Writers.* 1976; 2nd ed. Upper Montclair, NJ: Boynton/Cook, 1983. Both editions are well worth owning; of the 38 essays in the second edition, only eight

are repeated from the first. Reprints major articles in all aspects of scholarship; if you own these two books, you'll save yourself countless trips to the library.

Hartwell, Patrick. "Grammar, Grammars, and the Teaching of Grammar." *CE*, 47.2 (1985): 105–127. Reviews almost every empirical study of the effect of grammar instruction (complete with invaluable bibliography) and concludes that there are five major meanings of grammar and that actively working with language is more effective in improving student writing than drills in any or all of the five areas.

Lindemann, Erika. *A Rhetoric for Writing Teachers,* 2nd ed. NY: Oxford, 1987. Covers the supporting fields (rhetoric, cognition, linguistics) needed to understand composition theory and provides a wealth of practical advice on designing courses and writing assignments, teaching all segments of the writing process, and surviving as a writing teacher. The practical complement to Foster's survey of theory; extraordinarily reassuring for neophyte teachers.

Murray, Donald M. *A Writer Teaches Writing.* 2nd ed. Boston: Houghton Mifflin, 1985. Cogent, humane, practical advice for conducting writing classes as inquiries after surprise and truth. Excellent materials on working in groups and a marvelous bibliography of sources where writers describe their own writing processes.

Perelman, Les. "The Context of Classroom Writing." *CE*, 48.5 (1986): 471–479. Discusses the expansion of the writing process to include its institutional constraints, with provoking suggestions of how this expansion might take place in the classroom. Doubly valuable for its summary and critique of other theories of the writing process (especially as represented by Murray, Flower, and the traditional composition textbook).

Scholes, Robert. *Textual Power: Literary Theory and the Teaching of English.* New Haven: Yale, 1985. Nine essays constitute "a dialogue between teaching and theory," with emphasis on intertextuality, the role of the reader, and the ways in which texts may be used in the classroom. Also includes critiques of structuralism, reader-response theory as practiced by Stanley Fish, and some versions of deconstruction.

Shaughnessy, Mina. *Errors and Expectations: A Guide for the Teacher of Basic Writing.* NY: Oxford, 1977. Arguably the most influential book on the teaching of writing produced in the last decade, not only for its suggestions for classroom practice and teaching basic writers, but also for its suggestions for understanding the kinds of writing students not familiar with academic conventions produce. It reminded us of what we had forgotten—that students don't make errors deliberately—and suggested ways in which we could help students diagnose and adjust their hypotheses about language to meet the standards of the academy.

Sommers, Nancy. "Revision Strategies of Student Writers and Experienced Writers." *CCC*, 31.4 (1980): 378–388. Students understand revision as a process of fixing and correcting mistakes; experienced adult writers understand it as the process of adjusting and shaping ideas for an audience. Students must learn that revision is a recursive process occuring in all drafts, not a task performed on the final copy.

Stanford, Gene, ed. *Classroom Practices in Teaching English 1979–1980: How to Handle the Paper Load.* Urbana: NCTE, 1979. Twenty-seven suggestion-laden essays for coping with student papers; includes strategies for focused commenting, peer evaluation, ungraded writing, and teacher involvement.

Tate, Gary, ed. *Teaching Composition: 10 Bibliographic Essays.* Fort Worth: Texas Christian U.P., 1976 (2nd edition announced for late 1987). Although somewhat dated, the ten bibliographic essays provide an excellent starting point for study of composition theory. The lack of an index is, however, a bit of a drawback; not all works are covered in the sections where you'd expect to find them.

Weaver, Constance. *Grammar for Teachers: Perspectives and Definitions.* Urbana: NCTE, 1979. A brief primer of transformational-generative grammar and discussions of the relationships of grammar to psycholinguistics, reading, and writing. The chapter "What to Do With Grammar" provides model exercises for integrating the study of grammar into students' reading and writing. A brief but truly useful book.

BIBLIOGRAPHY

Abbreviations used are *College Composition and Communication; CE, College English; RTE, Research in the Teaching of English.*

Anson, Chris M. "A Computerized List of Journals Publishing Articles in Composition," *CCC* 37.2 (1986): 154–166.

Atkins, G. Douglas. *Reading Deconstruction/Deconstructive Reading.* Lexington: UP of Kentucky, 1983.

Bain, Alexander. *English Composition and Rhetoric: A Manual.* American Edition (revised) 1866; rpt. NY: Appleton, 1980.

Bain, Robert. "A Framework for Judging." *CCC* 25.3 (1974): 307–309.

Bartholmae, David. "Inventing the University." In *When a Writer Can't Write,* ed. Mike Rose. NY: Guilford, 1985: 134–165.

-----. "The Study of Error." *CCC* 31 (1980): 253–69.

Bator, Paul. "Aristotelian and Rogerian Rhetoric." *CCC* 31 (1980): 427–32.

Beard, Ruth M. *An Outline of Piaget's Developmental Psychology for Students and Teachers.* NY: New American Library, 1969.

Berthoff, Ann E. "Is Teaching Still Possible? Writing, Meaning, and Higher Order Reasoning," *CE* 46.8 (1984): 743–55.

-----. *Reclaiming the Imagination.* Upper Montclair, NJ: Boynton/Cook, 1984.

Bitzer, Lloyd F. "The Rhetorical Situation," *Philosophy and Rhetoric* 1.1 (1968): 1–14.

Bizzell, Patricia. "College Composition: Initiation into the Academic Discourse Community," *Curriculum Inquiry* 12.2 (1982): 191–207.

Bloom, Allan. *The Closing of the American Mind.* NY: Simon & Schuster, 1987.

Boley, Thomas J. "A Heuristic for Persuasion." *CCC* 30.2 (1979): 187–191.

Booth, Wayne. "The Rhetorical Stance." *CCC* 14.3 (1963): 139–145.

Braddock, Richard. "The Frequency and Placement of Topic Sentences in Expository Prose." *RTE* 8 (1974): 287–302.

Bridges, Charles W., ed. *Training the New Teacher of College Composition.* Urbana, IL: NCTE, 1986.

Britton, James, et al. *The Development of Writing Abilities (11–18).* London: Macmillan, 1975.

Burke, Kenneth. *A Grammar of Motives.* Englewood Cliffs, NJ: Prentice-Hall, 1945.

Christensen, Francis. "A Generative Rhetoric of the Sentence." *CCC* 14.3 (1963): 155–61.

-----. *Notes Toward a New Rhetoric.* NY: Harper & Row, 1967.

Cliflord, John, and John Schilb. "Composition Theory and Literary Theory." In *Perspectives on Research and Scholarship in Composition,* ed. Ben W. McClelland and Timothy R. Donovan. NY: MLA, 1985: 45–67.

Coles, William E., Jr. *Composing: Writing as a Self-Creating Process.* Rochelle Park, NJ: Hayden, 1974.

-----. *The Plural I: The Teaching of Writing.* NY: Holt, 1978.

Comprone, Joseph. "Kenneth Burke and the Teaching of Writing." *CCC* 29 (Dec. 1978): 336–40.

Connors, Patricia. "Some Attitudes of Returning or Older Students of Composition," *CCC* 33.3 (1982): 263–66.

Cooper, Charles R., and Lee Odell, eds. *Research on Composing: Points of Departure.* Urbana, IL: NCTE, 1978.

Corbett, Edward P. J. *Classical Rhetoric for the Modern Student*, 2nd ed. NY: Oxford, 1971.

-----. *The Little English Handbook,* 5th ed. Glenview, IL: Scott, Foresman, 1986.

-----. "Literature and Composition: Allies or Rivals in the Classroom?" In *Composition and Literature: Bridging the Gap,* ed. Winifred Bryan Horner (Chicago: U Chicago P, 1983): 168–184.

Daiker, Donald, Andrew Kerek, Max Morenberg, eds. *Sentence Combining and the Teaching of Writing.* Conway, AK: L&S Books, 1979.

D'Angelo, Frank J. *A Conceptual Theory of Rhetoric.* Cambridge, MA: Winthrop, 1975.

-----. "The Search for Intelligible Structure in the Teaching of Composition," *CCC* 27.2 (1976): 142–147.

Derrida, Jacques. *Of Grammatology.* Baltimore: John Hopkins UP, 1976.

Dick, John A. R. and Robert M. Esch. "Dialogues Across Disciplines: A Plan for Faculty Discussions of Writing Across the Curriculum," *CCC* 36.2 (1985): 178–182.

Eagleton, Terry. *Literary Theory: An Introduction.* Minneapolis: U. Minnesota P, 1983.

Eco, Umberto. *The Role of the Reader.* Bloomington: Indiana UP, 1979.

Ehninger, Douglas. *Influence, Belief, and Argument: An Introduction to Responsible Persuasion.* Glenview, IL: Scott, Foresman, 1974.

Elbow, Peter. "Embracing Contraries in the Teaching Process." *CE* 45.4 (1983): 3277–39.

-----. *Writing With Power.* NY: Oxford, 1981.

Emig, Janet. *The Composing Processes of Twelfth Graders.* Urbana, IL: NCTE, 1971.

"Evaluating Instruction in Writing: Approaches and Instruments." *CCC* 33 (1982): 213–229.

Fahnestock, Jeanne, and Marie Secor. "Teaching Argument: A Theory of Types." *CCC* 34 (February 1983): 20–30.

Faigley, Lester. "Competing Theories of Process: A Critique and a Proposal," *CE* 48.6 (1986): 527–542.

Faigley, Lester, and Stephen Witte. "Analyzing Revision." *CE* 32 (Dec. 1981): 400–14.

Fish, Stanley. *Is There a Text in this Class?* Cambridge: Harvard UP, 1980.

Flower, Linda. "Writer-Based Prose: A Cognitive Basis for Problems in Writing," *CE* 41.1 (1979): 19–37.

Flower, Linda, and Hayes, John R. "A Cognitive Process Theory of Writing." *CCC* 32 (Dec. 1981): 365–87.

Flower, Linda, John R. Hayes, Linda Carey, Karen Schriver, and James Stratman. "Detection, Diagnosis, and the Strategies of Revision." *CCC* 37.1 (1986): 16–55.

Freedman, Aviva, and Ian Pringle. *Reinventing the Rhetorical Tradition.* Conway, AK: L&S Books for the Canadian Council of Teachers of English, 1980.

Freire, Paolo. *Pedagogy of the Oppressed.* Trans. M. B. Ramos. NY: Seabury, 1968.

-----. *Education for Critical Consciousness.* NY: Seabury, 1973.

Fulwiler, Toby, and Art Young, eds. *Language Connections: Writing and Reading Across the Curriculum.* Urbana, IL: NCTE, 1978.

Garrison, Roger. "One-to-One: Tutorial Instruction in Freshman Composition." *New Directions for Community Colleges* 2 (Spring 1974): 55–84.

Gebhardt, Richard C. "Unifying Diversity in the Training of Writing Teachers." In *Training the New Teacher of College Composition,* ed. Charles W. Bridges. Urbana, IL: NCTE, 1986: 1–12.

Gordon, Karen Elizabeth. *The Transitive Vampire: A Handbook of Grammar for the Innocent, the Eager, and the Doomed.* NY: Times Books, 1984.

Gorrell, Robert M., Patricia Bizzell, and Bruce Herzberg. *The Bedford Bibliography for Teachers of Writing* (Boston: Bedford Books of St. Martin's Press, 1984).

Goswami, Dixie, et al. *Writing in the Workplace.* U. Mass./Boston Dept. of English, Fall 1983.

Hairston, Maxine. "Breaking our Bonds and Reaffirming our Connections." *CCC* 36.3 (1985): 272–82.

-----. "Not All Errors Are Created Equal: Nonacademic Readers in the Professions Respond to Lapses in Usage." *CE* 41 (1981): 794–806.

-----. "On Not Being a Composition Slave." In *Training the New Teacher of College Composition,* ed. Charles W. Bridges. Urbana, IL: NCTE, 1986: 117–124.

Harned, Jon, Thomas E. Dasher, Michael R. Dressman, Robert M. Esch, and Erika Lindemann. "Should English Teachers Oppose 'Minimal Competency' Writing Tests?" *CEA Forum* 17.1 (1986/87): 10–19.

Hiatt, Mary P. "The Feminine Style: Theory and Fact." *CCC* 29 (Oct. 1978): 222–26.

Hirsch, E. D., Jr. *Cultural Literacy: What Every American Needs to Know.* Boston: Houghton Mifflin, 1987.

Hoffman, Eleanor M., and John P. Schifsky. "Designing Writing Assignments," *English Journal* 66.9 (1977): 41–45.

Horner, Winifred Bryan, ed. *Composition and Literature: Bridging the Gap.* Chicago: U. Chicago P, 1983.

Huff, Roland K. "Teaching Revision: A Model of the Drafting Process," *CE* 45.8 (1983): 800–816.

Hunt, Kellogg W. *Grammatical Structures Written at Three Grade Levels.* Urbana, IL: NCTE, 1965.

Irmscher, William. *The Holt Guide to English,* 3rd ed. NY: Holt, 1981.

-----. *Teaching Expository Writing.* NY: Holt, Rinehart, & Winston, 1979.

Jefferson, Ann, and David Robey. *Modern Literary Theory: A Comparative Introduction.* Totowa, NJ: Barnes & Noble, 1982.

Kasden, Lawrence N., and Daniel R. Hoeber, eds. *Basic Writing: Essays for Teachers, Researchers, Administrators.* Urbana, IL: NCTE, 1980.

Kennedy, George A., *Classical Rhetoric and Its Christian and Secular Tradition from Ancient to Modern Times.* Chapel Hill: UNC Press, 1980.

Kinneavy, James. "A Pluralistic Synthesis of Four Models for Teaching Composition," in *Reinventing the Rhetorical Tradition,* ed. Aviva Freedman and Ian Pringle. Conway, AK: L&S Books for the Canadian Council of Teachers of English, 37–52.

-----. *A Theory of Discourse.* 1971; rpt. NY: Norton, 1980.

Kneupper, Charles W. "Revising the Tagmemic Heuristic: Theoretical and Pedagogical Considerations." *CCC* 31 (May 1980): 160–68.

Labov, William. *The Study of Nonstandard English.* Urbana, IL: NCTE, 1970.

Lanham, Richard. *Revising Prose.* NY: Scribners, 1980.

Larson, Richard L. "Discovery Through Questioning." *CE* 30 (1968): 126–134.

-----. "Selected Bibliography of Research and Writing about the Teaching of Writing," *CCC* (May 1975–79).

Lauer, Janice M., Gene Montague, Andrea Lunsford, and Janet Emig. *Four Worlds of Writing.* NY: Harper & Row, 1981.

Lindemann, Erika, ed. *The Longman Bibliography of Composition and Rhetoric.* NY: Longman, 1987 (covering 1984–85).

Machina, Kenton. "Evaluating Student Evaluations," *Academe* (May–June 1987): 19–22.

Macrorie, Ken. *Searching Writing.* Montclair, NJ: Boynton-Cook, 1980.

-----. *Writing to be Read,* rev. 3rd. ed. Montclair, NJ: Boynton-Cook, 1984.

----- *Uptaught!* 1970; rpt, Montclair, NJ: Boynton-Cook, 19XX.

McClelland, Ben W., and Timothy R. Donovan. *Prespectives on Research and Scholarship in Composition.* NY: MLA, 1985.

Memering, Dean, and Frank O'Hare. *The Writer's Work.* Englewood Cliffs: Prentice Hall, 1980.

Moffett, James. *Teaching the Universe of Discourse.* Boston: Houghton Mifflin, 1968.

----- and Betty Jane Wagner. *Student-Centered Language Arts and Reading, K–13,* 3rd ed. Boston: Houghton Mifflin, 1983.

Moran, Michael G. and Ronald F. Lunsford, eds. *Research in Composition and Rhetoric: A Bibliographic Sourcebook.* Westport, CT: Greenwood Press, 1984.

Murphy, James J., ed. *The Rhetorical Tradition and Modern Writing.* NY: MLA, 1982.

Neeld, Elizabeth Cowan. *Writing.* 2nd ed.: Glenview, IL: Scott, Foresman, 1986.

Odell, Lee, and Dixie Goswami. "Writing in a Nonacademic Setting." In *New Directions in Composition Research,* ed. Richard Beach and Lillian S. Bridwell. NY: Guilford, 1984.

O'Hare, Frank. *Sentence Combining: Improving Student Writing Without Formal Grammar Instruction.* Urbana, IL: NCTE, 1973.

Ong, Walter S., S. J. "The Writer's Audience Is Always a Fiction," *PMLA* 90 (January 1975): 9–21.

Parker, Robert. "The 'Language Across the Curriculum' Movement: A Brief Overview and Bibliography," *CCC* 36.2 (1985): 173–178.

Passmore, John. *The Philosophy of Teaching.* Cambridge: Harvard UP, 1980.

Rohman, D. Gordon, and Albert O. Wlecke. *Pre-Writing: The Construction and Application of Models for Concept-Formation in Writing.* USOE Cooperative Research Project No. 2174. E. Lansing, MI: Michigan State University, 1964.

Rose, Mike. "Remedial Writing Courses: A Critique and a Proposal." *CE* 45 (February 1983): 109–28.

-----. ed. *When A Writer Can't Write: Studies in Writer's Block and Other Composing Process Problems.* NY: Guilford, 1985.

Rosenblatt, Louise. *Literature as Exploration.* 1938; rpt. NY: MLA, 1983.

-----. *The Reader, the Text, the Poem: The Transactional Theory of the Literary Work.* Carbondale: Southern Illinois UP, 1978.

Scott, Patrick. "Bibliographical Problems in Research on Composition," *CCC* 37.2 (1986): 167–77.

Scott, Patrick, and Bruce Castner. "Reference Sources for Composition Research: A Practical Survey," *CE* 45.8 (1983): 756–768.

Shuy, Roger. *Discovering American Dialects.* Urbana, IL: NCTE, 1967.

Simmons, Jo An McGuire. "The One-to-One Method of Teaching Composition." *CCC* 35.3 (1984): 227–29.

Slevin, James F. "Acclaiming the Imagination," *CE* 47.5 (1985): 514–520.

Smitherman, Geneva. *Talkin' and Testifyin'.* Boston: Houghton Mifflin, 1977.

Steinberg, Edwin R. "Protocols, Retrospective Reports, and the Stream of Consciousness, *CE* 48.7 (1986): 697–712.

Tibbetts, Arn, and Charlene Tibbetts, "Can Composition Textbooks Use Composition Research?" *CE* 44.8 (1982): 855–858.

Tate, Gary, and Edward P. J. Corbett, eds. *The Writing Teacher's Sourcebook.* NY: Oxford, 1981.

Toulmin, Stephen, R. Rieke, and Allen Janik. *An Introduction to Reasoning.* NY: Macmillan, 1979.

Wallace, Karl. "*Topoi* and the Problem of Invention." *Quarterly Journal of Speech* 58 (1972): 387–395.

Weiner, Harvey S. "Collaborative Learning in the Classroom: A Guide to Evaluation," *CE* 48.1 (1986): 52–61.

White, Edward M. "Post-Structural Literary Criticism and the Response to Student Writing." *CCC* 35.2 (1984): 186–95.

-----. *Teaching and Assessing Writing.* San Francisco: Jossey-Bass, 1985.

Williams, Joseph P. *Style: Ten Lessons in Clarity and Grace.* NY: Scott, Foresman, 1984.

Winterowd, W. Ross, ed. *Contemporary Rhetoric: A Conceptual Background with Readings.* NY: Harcourt, 1975.

-----. *The Contemporary Writer,* 2nd ed. NY: Harcourt, Brace, Jovanovich, 1981.

Witte, Stephen. Review of *Sentence Combining and the Teaching of Writing,* ed. Donald Daiker et al. *CCC* 31 (1980): 433–37

Witte, Stephen, and Lester Faigley. "Coherence, Cohesion and Writing Quality." *CCC* 32 (May 1981): 189–204.

-----. *Evaluating College Writing Programs.* Carbondale: Southern Illinois UP, 1983.

Young, Richard E., Alton L. Becker, and Kenneth L. Pike. *Rhetoric: Discovery and Change.* NY: Harcourt, 1970.

Zinsser, William. *On Writing Well,* 3rd ed. NY: Harper & Row, 1985.